Uncollapsable Soul

How do you endure a broken heart without crushing your spirit?

Mike Noriega

Table of Contents

Uncollapsable

un·col·laps·a·ble· / *un-kuh-lap-suh-bol* /

adjective
an unofficial word not found in the dictionary referring to that which is not able to collapse or to be caused to fall in; not capable of being compressed or destroyed.

noun
an informal expression for something incapable of being collapsed: not collapsible.

soul

soul· / *sol* /

noun
the immaterial, spiritual embodiment which causes the immortal life force of a human being's existence, both presently and eternally.

noun
all the seen and unseen parts that identify the entirety of an individual's being, including the physical, mental, emotional, relational, and spiritual components of a person's vitality.

Message From the Author + Dedication

Some of the greatest advice I've ever received is to take my calling very seriously, but not to take myself too seriously. *Uncollapsable Soul* is a heavy read with light moments because it represents 98 precious lives, lost tragically, to share the story. Despite its heavy toll, there's a deeper message of profound hope within these pages.

Although "uncollapsable" is not a word found in the dictionary, its meaning is obvious. None of us are spared from collapses around us, but we can spare a collapse within us. Everyone faces despair and grief. Not everyone finds repair and relief.

First and foremost, I'd like to express my heartfelt gratitude to my parents, Carlos and Sally Noriega, for their unwavering love and support, as well as my siblings Stephen, Danny, Michelle, and my brother-in-law Joe. My nephew, Luca, was born a year after the tragedy and brought joy from sorrow. Kima hoped to be a great-grandmother and loved you before you existed. Our family wouldn't have made it through this without each other. *Uncollapsable Soul* wouldn't exist without you. I love each of you deeply. To my best friend AJ Milam, thanks for standing by my side, closer than a brother, through my darkest of times.

Additionally, I'm deeply grateful to every first responder from every agency across the globe that put their lives on the line to save as many as possible. I extend my thanks to Leo Soto for the Wall of Hope, Michael Capponi and the Global Empowerment Mission for their incredible work, and Neil Handler for the Phoenix Life Project. The vision of each nonprofit vividly exemplifies transformation of pain into purpose. Your organizations are changing lives, including my own. You have each inspired me to form my own 501(c)(3), Light Into the Night, to bring hope and healing to crushed communities in the future.

I'd like to express my heartfelt appreciation to VOUS Church and to my pastors, Rich and DawnCheré Wilkerson, for your vision, love, and support. You've shown me the true essence of being the church rather than just attending church. The DNA of what you've poured into me is infused throughout my writing, and has equipped me for such a time as this. The unity of our VOUS community helped carry me when I couldn't carry myself, and rallied around me during my greatest time of need!

Additionally, thank you to CASA Church for being a hospital for the broken, especially during the crisis. Your church was placed 2 blocks away from the disaster site by divine orchestration. I also extend my sincerest gratitude to Jewish Community Services of South Florida for actively providing resources for support and healing. Your compassion and kindness has been second to none!

To every politician, news anchor, and media outlet that allotted me the opportunity to share my grandmother's story for God's glory, thank you.

Lastly, to all the Surfside families who lost a loved one, my prayers are with you. May these pages bring you healing and remind you that you're not alone. To the survivors and surviving family members that have suffered immensely, thank you for bravely sharing your stories. You're an inspiration to me and so many others.

But most importantly, I'm eternally grateful for the gift that was my grandmother's life. Kima was a second mother to me, and is missed beyond measure! *Uncollapsable Soul* is part of her legacy. This is for you Kima...

98 Points of Light

In honor of every distinguished soul that tragically lost their life in the condo collapse. May their legacies of love burn forever in our hearts. (in order of recovery)[122]

Day 1: June 24, 2021
Stacie Dawn Fang, 54 years old
Antonio Lozano, 83 years old

Day 2: June 25, 2021
Gladys Lozano, 79 years old
Manuel "Manny" LaFont,
54 years old

Day 3: June 26, 2021
Leon Oliwkowicz, 80 years old
Marcus Joseph Guara,
52 years old
Luis Bermudez, 26 years old
Ana Ortiz, 46 years old

Day 4: June 27, 2021
Christina Beatriz Elvira Oliwkowicz,
74 years old

Day 5: June 28, 2021
Frank Kleiman, 55 years old
Michael Altman, 50 years old

Day 6: June 29, 2021
Hilda "Kima" Noriega, 92 years old

Day 7: June 30, 2021
Lucia Guara, 11 years old
Emma Guara, 4 years old
Anaely Rodriguez, 42 years old
Andreas Giannitsopoulos,
21 years old
Magaly Elena Delgado,
80 years old
Bonnie Epstein, 56 years old

Day 9: July 2, 2021
Stella Cattarossi, 7 years old
Graciela Cattarossi, 48 years old
David Epstein, 58 years old
Maria Obias-Bonnefoy,
69 years old
Claudio Bonnefoy, 85 years old
Gonzalo Torre, 81 years old

Day 12: July 5, 2021
Jay Kleiman, 52 years old.
Andrea Cattarossi, 56 years old.
Linda March, 58 years old.
Elena Blasser, 64 years old.
Ingrid Ainsworth, 66 years old.
Tzvi Ainsworth, 68 years old.
Francis Fernandez, 67 years old.
Nancy Kress Levin, 76 years old.

Day 13: July 6, 2021
Aishani Gia Patel, 1 year old.
Bhavna Patel, 36 years old
(pregnant).
Vishai Patel, 42 years old.
Elaine Lia Sabino, 71 years old.
Richard Augustine, 77 years old.
Graciela Cattarossi, 86 years old.
Gino Cattarossi, 89 years old.
Simon Segal, 80 years old.
Elena Chavez, 87 years old.

Day 14: July 7, 2021
Luis Lopez Moreira III, 3 years old.
Anna Sophia Pettengill,
6 years old.
Alexia Maria Pettengill,
9 years old.
Deborah Berezdivin, 21 years old.
Ilan Naibryf, 21 years old.
Leidy Vanessa Luna Villalba,
23 years old.
Nicole Langesfeld, 26 years old.
Luis Sadovnic, 28 years old.
Juan Alberto Mora Jr.,
32 years old.
Luis Pettengill, 36 years old.
Ruslan Manashirov, 36 years old.
Brad Cohen, 51 years old.
Harold Rosenberg, 52 years old.
Maria Teresa Rovirosa,
58 years old.
Gary Cohen, 58 years old.
Ana Mora, 70 years old.
Gloria Machado, 71 years old.
Marina Restrepo Azen,
76 years old.
Juan Alberto Mora, 80 years old.

Day 15: July 8, 2021
Lorenzo Leone, 5 years old.
Sofia Nunez, 5 years old.
Benny Weisz, 31 years old.
Sophia Lopez Moreira,
36 years old.
Theresa Velasquez, 36 years old.
Edgar Gonzalez, 42 years old.
Andres Galfrascoli, 44 years old.
Alfredo Leone, 48 years old.
Beatriz "Betty" Rodriguez,
52 years old.
Miguel Pazos, 55 years old.
Fabián Núñez, 57 years old.
Angela Velasquez, 60 years old.
Richard Rovirosa, 60 years old.
Oresme Gil Guerra, 60 years old.
Maria Gabriela Camou,
64 years old.
Maria Torre, 76 years old.

Day 16: July 9, 2021
Michelle Anna Pazos,
23 years old.
Lisa Rosenberg (AKA) Malki Weisz,
27 years old.
Nicole Dawn Doran, 43 years old.
Judith Spiegel, 65 years old.
Miguel Leonardo Kaufman,
65 years old.
Julio Cesar Velasquez,
66 years old.
Maria Popa, 79 years old.
Maria Notkin, 81 years old.
Mihai Radulescu, 82 years old.
Arnold "Arnie" Notkin,
87 years old.

Day 17: July 10, 2021
Cassondra "Cassie" Billedeau
Stratton, 40 years old.
Catalina Gomez Ramirez,
45 years old.
Luis F. Barth Tobar, 51 years old.
Margarita "Maggie"
Vasquez Bello, 68 years old.
Rosa Saez, 70 years old.

Day 18: July 11, 2021
Valeria Barth, 14 years old.
Andres Levine, 26 years old.
Moises Rodan Brief, 28 years old.
Mercedes Fuentes Urgelles,
61 years old.
Raymond Urgelles, 61 years old.

Day 25: July 18, 2021
Anastasiya Gromova, 24 years
old. She was visiting her friend,
Michelle Pazos. Before moving to
Japan to teach English for a year.

Day 27: July 20, 2021
Estelle Hedaya, 54 years old.

Hole in Your Soul

Though we experience every kind of pressure, we're not crushed. At times we don't know what to do, but quitting is not an option. We are persecuted by others, but God has not forsaken us. We may be knocked down, but not out.

2 Corinthians 4:8-9 (TPT)

Heart Collapse

As a child, there are few things scarier than being separated from your parents in a crowded mall or theme park. The terror of being lost and alone is dreadful. Fear grips your heart, causing a surge of adrenaline that heightens your senses. Every sound becomes amplified, every movement scrutinized, scanning the crowd, for a familiar face. People rush past them like a blur of colors and shapes, as the child desperately cries out for their parents in a sea of strangers. Anxiety sets in, often manifesting as a knot in their stomach. Confusion also seeps in, making it even more difficult to make sense of the agony that comes with feeling abandoned. The only thing the lost child wants is to be reunited with his/her loved ones again, to feel that sense of safety and security. Yet, as we grow older, that fear of being disconnected from the ones we love doesn't disappear, it remains.

Instead, it may take different forms through the heart-stopping panic of receiving a phone call in the middle of the night, with terrible news that you never imagined could happen to you. It's a helpless feeling that takes your heart captive, as trauma pulses through your body, like an electric shock. Suddenly, without warning, the lights go out inside of us, and we're left stumbling in the dark, with no idea how to find our way back. It's that moment when you've hit rock bottom, when you don't know how to get back up, to look up. It's as if the world stops spinning, and everything that once made sense no longer does. Maybe you haven't experienced this personally, but you likely know someone who has.

Structural Collapse

We often think these things only happen in movies, but the reality is, life can bring unpredictable seasons of crushing. Buildings aren't supposed to collapse without warning, especially in developed countries. But that's exactly what happened in the blink of an eye on January 28, 1922. It was a seemingly normal, snowy winter in Washington D.C., until a 28-hr. long blizzard brought in heavy amounts of snowfall. The locals had been shut in for days and were anxious to get back to normal life. Some casual entertainment seemed to fit the bill. After the blizzard cleared up, the largest movie house in the area, the Knickerbocker Theatre, showed a silent comedy called *Get-Rich-Quick Wallingford*. Hundreds of patrons were enjoying the film with smiles and laughter lighting up the venue.

During a 9:00 pm intermission, those laughs quickly turned into screams and shrieks of panic. The accumulation of snow and ice put an overwhelming amount of extra weight on the flat roof, causing catastrophic structural failure. On that fateful day, the roof collapsed, killing 98 victims, and injuring 133 others. The blizzard was renamed the *Knickerbocker Storm* for having contributed to the third deadliest structural engineering failure in U.S. history.

Sydney J. Harris is credited with the quote, "History repeats itself, but in such cunning disguise that we never detect the resemblance until the damage is done." Fast forward almost a century later, history repeated itself in a different location, with a different building, yet with the same tragic outcome. On June 24, 2021, the third most fatal structural failure recorded in U.S. history was about to be matched, and my family's matriarch was right in the middle of it. The Surfside Condo collapse echoed the Knickerbocker Theatre in a hauntingly similar way, claiming the same number of lives and leaving countless others injured and traumatized. Nothing could have prepared me for the horror of showing up to the disaster scene that transformed my life.

The echoes of the Knickerbocker Theatre and the Surfside Condo collapse have reverberated across time and space. In both cases, warning signs were ignored or overlooked, and the consequences were disastrous. They're tragedies that could've been prevented, and yet they happened, leaving a trail of devastation and unnecessary heartbreak in its wake. The tragedy of the Knickerbocker Theatre and the Surfside Condo Collapse were not just random accidents, but rather a result of a system that failed to prioritize safety and accountability.

Both the tragedies of the Knickerbocker Theatre and the Surfside Condo Collapse are chilling reminders that we must never forget the lessons learned from the past. They also remind us of life's fragility and the importance of learning from history. We owe it to ourselves and to future generations to learn from these tragedies and take action to prevent them from happening again. Although preventing structural failures through stronger regulation is vital, it's only part of the intervention that must be taken.

Emotional Collapse

The emotional, psychological, and spiritual toll of senseless calamity can be devastating, both for those directly impacted, and the broader community. The trauma of losing loved ones and homes, leaves gruesome wounds in our hearts that can crush our spirits. Maybe your season of crushing had nothing to do with the collapse of a physical structure. But at some point, we all face the reality of an existential crisis that can cripple our hearts while threatening to crush each of our spirits, resulting in a collapse of the soul.

It happens when you're married to the love of your life, and divorce papers arrive, or when the faith that stitched you together begins to unravel. It happens when someone you've loved leaves you or breaks an important promise. Maybe you were given a deadly diagnosis or have suffered the unfathomable loss of a child. Whether you've endured the devastation of a death, divorce, a crisis of faith, betrayal, or a broken promise, the paradox of familiarity and pain is a profound aspect of the human experience.

We tend to take things for granted that are essential to us until they're gone. For example, have you ever slammed a door on your finger or dropped a heavy object on your toe? Our fingers and toes, at times can go unnoticed until we injure them, making us painfully aware of how important they are to daily activities. Emotional pain from relational loss is similar. We often take our closest relationships for granted, assuming they'll always be around. When we lose a loved one, we also lose the absence of their support, love, and companionship, which makes us acutely aware of the significance of their presence.

The paradox of familiarity and pain is that, while familiarity can numb us to gratitude and appreciation, pain can also bring us back to a state of awareness. It's here that we find the blessing hidden within the curse of heartbreak. Grieving can be a powerful reminder of just how much we value the people in our lives. It's only when we experience the agony of loss, that we're reminded of the magnitude of how these relationships contributed to our souls. These experiences sober us to how fleeting life can be so that we can live with purpose in the present and cherish the ones we still have.

Crushed by Heartbreak

When it's time to walk through the valley of the shadow of death, we need a strong support system that will walk with us through the darkness. We need familiar presence, comfort, and support. That may look like someone holding your hand during a diagnosis, wiping your tears while you weep, or staying by your side when a big mistake is exposed. For my family and I, the collapse of the building meant rallying around my father and offering him our support for what felt like endless hours, despite our own pain.

My heart was helpless as I watched my father break down publicly, knowing that his sweet mother was buried under tons of concrete and rubble. It was surreal and agonizing for our family, as we struggled to come to terms with the probability of losing such an important member of our family.

We were all deeply affected by the tragedy, torn between the sadness of our loss and the anguish of imagining our loved one suffer in such an unbearable way. Despite the deep sadness, we refused to give up hope. We spent countless hours huddled together in front of the concrete avalanche, praying, and waiting for any news from the rescue teams. We clung to each other for support, and our faith was a constant source of comfort and strength during those long, uncertain stretches.

As the hours turned into days, we watched as the search and rescue teams worked tirelessly to find survivors. Our hope was slowly fading, but we continued to hold onto it, praying for a miracle. Although the outcome was devastating, and we ultimately lost my grandmother in the tragedy, we held onto the love and support that we had shown each other during those long hours in the valley of the shadow of death. This tragedy marked our lives, but it also taught us the importance of cherishing every moment with our loved ones and finding strength in the support of others. The day we laid my grandmother to rest, my father began his final words to her, carrying the heavy weight of grief and gratitude from a lifetime of memories:

*The two best words that I have, to describe the type of person she was and represented to all who knew her are…**unconditional love**. It's true what is said…you don't realize just how fortunate and lucky you are until something, or someone is gone. Well, reality hit me as hard as it ever has at around 1:30 a.m. on June 24th, when I received a frantic call that my mom's building had collapsed and was gone. About an hour later, I stood in disbelief at the corner of 88th St. & Collins Ave. as I looked upon the remains of her collapsed building—a mangled pile of rubble. At that moment, I realized that the most amazing person that my family and I had ever known was, in all likelihood, lost for the remainder of our time on this planet. I can't begin to explain the infinite number of how's and why's that charged into my mind on everything I observed and could possibly think of.*

That day marked the only instance that he spoke publicly in 2021, regarding the events that took his mother's life. As the eulogy concluded, there wasn't a dry eye in the church. It was in that hushed stillness that my dad, overcome by an unbearable sense of longing, dared to break the barrier between the living and the departed. Without reservation, he threw his arms around the casket containing the Noriega family matriarch, as if his embrace were an act of defiance against the cruelty of mortality. His deep mourning reflected that of a child weeping, clinging desperately to their mother's leg, begging her not to leave. As tears cascaded down his face, floodgates of our own restrained emotions burst open.

Heart of Uncollapsable Soul

What made Hilda Noriega's legacy come to life was not how she died, but in how she lived. In her late age, she embodied the innocence of a child, the energy of a teenager, the social circle of a college student, the nurturance of a mother, the sweet tenderness of a grandmother, and the loving heart of God. My grandmother had an unconditional love for me, even before my birth. She became my second mother, and though I couldn't pronounce "grandma" as a baby, she happily accepted the name "Kima" which was my best shot. The rest of my family followed my lead, and Kima became the name of the beloved matriarch of our family. Kima embodied the definition of a grandmother, in every sense of the word. The *Oxford English Dictionary* has 4 definitions of the word "grand" as an adjective: magnificent, most important, excellent, and one generation removed in a family relationship[59].

For Kima, love was the most valuable commodity. Her love was unconditional, it wasn't performance-based or transactional. Her love was freely given and inspiring to us all. It was what made her truly magnificent. Her love unified our family, instilled a spirit of excellence in us, and created a legacy that still lives on today. Every conversation with her ended the same way—I'd tell her I love her, and she would reply, "I love you more." Despite beating Covid-19, cancer, living independently as a 92-year-old widow, and maintaining an active social life, we all thought she had many years left. We figured she'd pass away peacefully in the distant future, surrounded by family, and I'd get to cherish that last "I love you more" before she went into eternity. But that never happened.

This book is inspired by my deep desire to honor the memory of my beloved, Hilda "Kima" Noriega. Her life was a beautiful example of living in the fullness of God's love, and I've witnessed how her story has the power to inspire and encourage others. Kima lived a life overflowing with love, and her legacy is something that deserves to be shared with the world. It's part of my life's mission to share her story and ultimately, give God the glory. This is both a memorial to her and a part of her legacy that I hope will endure for generations to come. This is for you, Kima! I love and miss you so much and our family feels the same way. Oh, what I would do to turn back the hands of time to live out a memory that never happened... to look you in the eyes with tears streaming down my face before that last sweet, warm embrace goodbye to cherish in my heart forever.

In the same light, the scale of loss resulting from the Surfside Collapse was so much greater than the loss my family and I endured. Entire families were wiped out! Aside from 3 miraculous survivors that fell dangerously close to their death, everyone else perished. The lifeblood of *Uncollapsable Soul* is to honor all 98 souls who were killed in the Surfside Condo Collapse. You'll feel the heartbeat of survivors, first responders, and those who have endured immense suffering through their heartfelt stories. These stories aren't about living from your past. They're about learning from your past to live an 'uncollapsable' life today. It'll remind you to fight against familiarity so that you don't have to wait for someone's funeral to honor them. It liberates us to live in the moment, now, as if it's a gift, because that's exactly what the present is.

That's why healing from your wounds is so important. Building stronger structures is important, but healing our souls after such devastating events is paramount. No matter how many precautions are taken to prevent disasters, unwelcome tragedies will find a way. We live in a fallen world where the only collapse you can truly prevent is the one inside of yourself. What good is it to rebuild everything around you if everything within you is still collapsed? *"What do you benefit to gain from the whole world but to lose your soul?"* (Matt. 16:26) This book isn't about building stronger buildings; it's about rebuilding and restoring your soul. Only when we take both of these actions—rebuilding within us to build back better around us—can we move forward.

The pages ahead don't sugarcoat the raw, intense, and, at times, downright gruesome, details of the suffering endured by those affected. But that's precisely why you should give it a chance and read it. While this is not strictly a "Christian" book, specifically for a Christian audience, it's written from my perspective as a believer, because my faith is an integral part of my story. But I also recognize not everyone shares these beliefs, and I want this book to be accessible to anyone seeking hope and healing, amidst the suffering. But, regardless of your own beliefs or lack thereof, there's something in these pages for everyone. At the end of the day, we all face suffering in the form of loss, heartache, and pain. That's why we need hope to cling to in those moments.

Scripture doesn't shy away from the harsh realities of life. It confronts them head-on. My wish is that you approach this message with an open mind and a humble heart. It'll require a soft heart and thick skin. It was the Apostle Paul, who said in 2 Corinthians 4:8-9 (TPT), "Though we experience every kind of pressure, we're not crushed. At times we don't know what to do, but quitting is not an option. We are persecuted by others, but God has not forsaken us. We may be knocked down, but not out." His words capture the essence of suffering and pain, along with the hope of healing. It's a journey through the valley of the shadow of death, but it's a journey that leads to the other side.

God doesn't waste our wounds. If you're so shattered that you can't bear to look up at the sky and believe that God's promises are true, know that you're not alone. From the womb to the tomb, wherever a promise is placed, there is a process to face. You might not have lost someone in this tragedy specifically, but crushing seasons come in many forms. Your "Surfside Collapse" experience in the timeline of your life might be completely different from mine. Although our circumstances may be diverse, the feelings are the same, and so is the process of healing. Losing hope for an outcome doesn't equate to losing hope for your future. Your heart may have collapsed, but your spirit doesn't need to be crushed. A crushed spirit leaves a hole in your soul, but the endgame of these pages is your total healing revives your heart, rescues your spirit, and restores your soul to become whole.

Either your pain will define you, or you'll ordain it to refine you. Your soul is meant to be uncollapsable.

Unforeseen Cracks:
The Surfside Condo Collapse

CHAPTER 1

Sole Survivor

I come to you, Lord, for protection; never let me be defeated. You are a righteous God; save me, I pray!
Psalm 31:1 (GNT)

Strange Supernatural Force

In December 2020, just 6 months before tragedy struck the small town of Surfside, a 64-year-old woman by the name of Maria Iliana Monteagudo became the proud owner of Unit #611 in the South Champlain Tower. Her 6th-floor beachfront apartment faced southeast toward the pool deck, which overlooked the vast turquoise-blue open waters of the North Atlantic Ocean. She had just poured her life savings into her beachside paradise, where she looked forward to enjoying her golden years away from harsh winters. Iliana's slice of heaven immediately felt like home when a vibrant, outgoing, sweet woman went out of her way to give her a warm welcome. It turns out that woman was her neighbor across the hall, my grandmother.

In the moments leading up to the collapse, Maria Iliana was sleeping in her bed, completely unaware of the impending danger. A few hours prior, she'd decided not to take her nightly sleeping pill to avoid oversleeping, since she had an appointment the next morning. Later that night, at approximately 1:15 am, a "strange supernatural force" awoke her. Strange noises were coming from the living room. When she sprung out of bed to investigate, the balcony sliding glass door was inexplicably wide open. By her own account, she told me in somewhat broken English, "When I woke up, I heard sounds coming into my apartment. Sounds like cracking... crack, crack, crack. And I think I left my sliding door open. I tried to close it, and I can't do it because the building was moved, and the rails and door can't close. At the same moment, I felt a crack close to me!"

That's when Iliana saw a 2-inch-thick crack in her ceiling, tearing down her wall to the floor. Her survival instincts instantly kicked in as the warping wall caused all her wine and spirits to fall from her bar. "When I saw the crack on the wall and the wall was opening, that's when my mind started to speak to me and say, *RUN*, because this building will be coming down soon!"

She quickly dressed, grabbed her purse, and blew out a candle before rushing out the door. To her surprise, the quiet hallway was void of panic. No alarms, no activated emergency systems, no other residents running for their lives. Unbeknownst at the time, there were emergency stairs just a few feet to the right of her front door, but she ran left toward the farthest set of stairs. Before passing Kima's apartment, she stopped at her door briefly.

My grandmother, Hilda, would often stay long weekends at my parents' home. She was a fiercely strong, independent, widowed 92-year-old woman that had so much energy. More than anything, Kima loved using that energy to spend time with her family, especially because she lived by herself. My siblings and I would visit my parents' place to share meals, have conversations, and play her favorite games, such as 'Rummikub' or dominoes. She deeply cherished quality family time more than anything! It was very typical for my father to pick her up after finishing his workday in the neighboring city of North Bay Village so she could stay long weekends at my parents' home.

Iliana remembered how months prior, her "only friend in the building" was my grandmother. Kima's hearing wasn't the greatest, so she'd often fall asleep with the TV blaring through her front door. To warn her friend, Iliana put her ear to the door, but heard silence. The silence gave Iliana enough hope to believe she may have been staying with family, and she knew Kima probably wouldn't have heard frantic knocks on the door even if she was sleeping in her distant bedroom. Iliana later recalled this in an interview with *The Washington Post*:

> *She is thinking about an 80-year-old woman who lived across the hall, who welcomed her when she first moved in months ago. "I thought that she was with her son that day. I called her daughter-in-law. She disappeared. She hasn't been found," she said. "I feel so bad. I told them I felt so bad. I cry a lot. I feel so guilty."*

It's interesting to note my grandmother was so youthful in her elderly age that her neighbors saw her as an 80-year-old, 12 years younger than her actual age.

In a moment of unimaginable fear and desperation, Monteagudo found herself faced with a life-or-death decision. Adrenaline surged through her veins as she instinctively rushed towards the stairs, desperately seeking to escape. Each step she took was filled with uncertainty as the haunting sounds of destruction echoed in her ears. While descending the stairs, a violent and terrifying thunder rocked the building. Believing she'd be crushed in the seconds to come, she screamed to Heaven in a distraught plea for help. "God, help me, please help me. I want to see my sons, I want to see my grandsons, I want to live, please help me, God!" Iliana emerged as the sole survivor that escaped above the first floor, from within the wing that fell victim to the deadly collapse.

Coincidence or Miracle?

In an epic story of survival against all odds, God answered her cries for help. Maria Iliana Monteagudo is the only survivor above the first floor who managed to physically escape the wrath of the collapsed section of the building. She emerged in the visitor parking lot unharmed. It's hard not to wonder about the what ifs: *What if she had taken her sleeping pill? What if a "supernatural force" hadn't awoken her? What if that crack in her unit's wall never appeared? What if she had taken the emergency stairs closest to her unit? What if she had refused to evacuate until my grandmother answered the door?* It's impossible to ignore the countless factors that led to her survival! Were these mere coincidences or divine miracles? The answer is up to you.

One thing we know for sure: we're eternally grateful for her life, and we believe that if she could do it all over again, she shouldn't change a thing. Altering the circumstances would not have made things better; it would've only increased the death toll from 98 to 99. We don't want Iliana to imprison herself with guilt or shame. We know my grandmother would've wanted her to live, and we're so relieved that she escaped. Had Iliana waited for my grandmother, she wouldn't have been spared. I'm so grateful she's alive to tell her story. Despite the tragic circumstances that brought her to the brink of death, she emerged as a beacon of hope and an inspiration to us all. While we may never fully understand why certain things happen, my family and I take comfort in knowing that miracles do happen, and Iliana is one of them.

Although Iliana survived, it's not without being haunted by the atrocious mental images that have plagued her with anxiety and anguish. "Every night, I can't sleep without a pill because it's coming like a film in my mind every night," Monteagudo said. "And you know how long one year to suffer? Do you know how many months, how many hours, and how many minutes? To think about it and suffer." She continued, "Fifty years of collecting things lost it in seven minutes—in seven minutes… everything." Monteagudo said, "I don't have one picture of my parents. The last picture that I take a look at when I am leaving is my father and my mother in Las Vegas laughing, both of them." Monteagudo further said, "I try hard to find happiness, but I lost it. I can't find it."

Iliana escaped from the building, but she did not escape the suffering. Just because her life was relieved of going down in the collapse does not mean her soul was rescued from the trauma. Iliana's story is a testament to the fact that even if you escape physical harm, you can still suffer from the emotional weight of a heartbreaking event. This is a reality that many people can relate to, but you must validate your own pain.

Hope Against All Odds

That night, a story emerged that gave me a glimmer of hope. My grandmother could still be alive. Southeastern Iran is known for the Bam fault, which causes frequent seismic activity, with an average of one earthquake per day. On December 26, 2003, a devastating 6.6 magnitude earthquake destroyed the city of Bam, claiming the lives of 31,000 people and leaving another 30,000 injured. Approximately 85% of buildings were damaged beyond repair, leaving 75,000 residents homeless[8]. In contrast, a similar earthquake with the same magnitude struck California four days earlier, causing only 3 fatalities. The reason for this significant disparity was due to poor construction practices, lack of structural regulations, and minimal building codes in underdeveloped third-world countries[9]. The odds of survival in Bam were low, especially for someone who was nearing 100 years old.

Despite the bleak odds, a miraculous story emerged. A rescue team found a 97-year-old woman, Sharbanou Mazandarani, alive and unharmed after being buried under rubble for nine days. The rescue workers attributed her survival to a piece of furniture that shielded her from falling debris. When asked how she survived, Mazandarani replied, "God kept me alive"[10]. Her story gave me hope that my grandmother's survival was possible, leading me to believe that she could've survived, and long for that outcome.

Few moments in our lives are as turbulent with anxiety and fear as the space between receiving bad news and waiting for good news. It's healthy to have fear, but crippling when fear has you. Undoubtedly, there are times when a traumatic experience will understandably consume you, just as I experienced. But you must eventually evict the dominion of fear. It carries a heavy price, as it gradually erodes and weakens your spirit until it collapses entirely. A symptom of a spirit of fear is overthinking. Overthinking leads to under-living. Overthinking for too long can trick you into believing lies that control you through confusion.

Sometimes God uses what seems like an impossible circumstance to remind us of our desperate need for Him. Encountering His presence reshapes our hearts, teaches us reliance on Him which refines our character. When we ask God for help, He often responds with hope, because it's the fuel that keeps the fire burning in our hearts. It's what sustains our souls in suffering, strengthening our spirits to face another day. God uses uncertainty to remodel our hearts. While we cry out to be rescued from devastation, the truth is that it's not always within our control. We can control our choice to look for Him amidst our fear.

Hope restores the life fear tries to steal. It's the antidote to fear and the lifeline that pulls us out of the depths of despair. When the lights have gone out and you're stumbling in the darkness, remember that hope is your compass. Fear may attempt to shrivel your heart and crush your spirit, but hope expands your heart. Hope reminds us that our individual circumstances may be unique to each of us, but the pain is not unique to any one of us. Hope bridges the gap between your grief and your miracle.

But what happens when you're clinging to hope, only to be met with devastation instead of the miracle you so desperately desired? How do you bridge the gap between grief and the miracle that never came to pass? I desperately prayed and believed for the miraculous rescue of my grandmother, envisioning a moment she'd be triumphantly rescued from the rubble. It would've been a miracle of monumental proportions, a story to be told for ages. to hear her say, "God kept me alive", like Sharbanou. But the painful reality is that she didn't survive, and countless others perished alongside her.

These pages are for those who feel betrayed by hope. They serve as a guide for anyone finding themselves wandering the treacherous terrain of unbearable pain. It's a readily available emergency kit for any emotional hit. Consider this book a life vest if you're drowning in the depths of despair.

Before we delve into the stories ahead, it's essential to understand the broader scale of the Surfside collapse. The magnitude of the tragedy, the lives forever altered, and the collective mourning that enveloped a community. By comprehending the grander context that these individual stories unfold, we can begin to grasp the depth of our shared pain to reclaim our lives. While our situations may diverge us, our sufferings converge us. We each face different circumstances. But we all face the same feelings that need healing. As you read ahead, my prayer is that you make the promises of Psalms 73:25-26 your prayer. "Who do I have in heaven? There is no one on earth who I desire besides you. My flesh and my heart may fail, but God is the strength of my heart and my portion forever."[125]

CHAPTER 2

The Morning of Mourning

Hear me! Save me now! Be my refuge to protect me; my defense to save me.

Psalm 31:2 (GNT)

7 Minute Window

The nightmarish scene, in the small Miami town of Surfside, commenced when the pool deck collapsed into the parking garage at 1:15 am, which triggered a distress signal to the alarm company. It's widely reported that, although the company was successfully notified, the sirens that were supposed to alert residents throughout the building of imminent danger never sounded. That's when the short, 7-minute window for the ticking time bomb began. Most residents continued in their slumber, never having a fair chance before the northernmost wings collapsed! Just like that, over 1/3 of the apartments were wiped out. Had the alarms rang throughout the hallways and individual units as they were supposed to, 98 souls could've had the chance to fight for their lives rather than free falling to their death.

First Response

By 1:30 am, the first Miami-Dade rescue vehicle, Engine 76, arrived at the deadly scene. Within minutes, the site was so immensely petrifying that when Miami-Dade Fire Rescue Battalion 1 was asked for confirmation if this, in fact, was a "Mass Casualty Incident," they responded over the radio waves, "Affirmative, this is gonna be an MCI level 4, level 5, 6." To give you perspective, a level 4 MCI means between 100 and 1,000 potential casualties. But a level 5 MCI translates to greater than 1,000 deaths. A level 5 is as big as it gets! Given that a level 6 doesn't exist, it spoke volumes to the gravity of the situation. It wasn't long before hundreds of first responders throughout dozens of Miami-Dade County agencies arrived at the disaster scene. Early reports estimated there could be as many as 150–200 people missing.

For the first 5 hours, they heroically rescued 37 fortunate residents stranded on balconies, stairways, and the flooded parking garage within the remaining unstable tower, which could've toppled down at any moment. However, it quickly became apparent that the police officers, firefighters, and rescue workers didn't have the heavy machinery, such as a crane, necessary for a disaster of such monumental proportions! All 8 of Florida's Urban Search and Rescue teams from Miami to Tallahassee were deployed for duty on-site.

In the following hours, highly trained search dogs confirmed signs of life mixed between the rubble multiple times. Hundreds of rescue personnel worked 24 hours a day, tirelessly, against all odds with the existing available resources, in 12-hour shifts. Search and rescue efforts persevered against insurmountable obstacles like the dangerous instability of the structure, underground flooding, random fires, electrical shocks from using jackhammers in wet conditions, clouds of smoke, lethal carbon-monoxide levels, razor-sharp metal fragments everywhere, and gas leaks from crushed vehicles.

At roughly 6:30 am, one of the search and rescue dogs picked up the scent of a live victim underneath the wreckage that filled the parking garage! As we watched the commotion break out, we hoped it was Kima. It was later reported that a female "voice in the rubble" was faintly crying out for help. Rescue efforts were led by the Assistant Fire Chief of Operations for Miami-Dade Fire Rescue Department, Raied Jadallah. He subsequently released an 11-page public memo stating, "Rescue crews explained that the only times they could communicate with the woman was when all operations ceased, and everyone was silenced." It also stated, "Even the faintest whisper from the rescue crews or sloshing in the standing water negated any ability to hear the woman." The giant slabs of concrete between them made it impossible to save her. About 10 hours after the condominium building crumpled, rescue crews lost voice contact with the last recorded victim crying for help at 11:05 am.

Jadallah concluded the memo, "They stayed on until they no longer heard the voice anymore… I think it was one of the things that was most upsetting to them. They never gave up on this person despite the conditions being so precarious"[20]. It was later revealed the faint voice was of 36-year-old Theresa Velasquez, whose body was recovered on July 8. The LA-based Live Nation Entertainment music executive had flown in the day before to visit her parents, Julio and Angela Velasquez, who were residents of unit 304. All 3 of them died in the collapse[21].

A frenzy of media coverage spread the story like wildfire, making the little-known beachside town of Surfside instantly famous—for all the wrong reasons. The emotional burden grew intensely with every passing moment, as families like mine wanted answers for the devastation and confusion. Although the town of Surfside's Community Center became the official family reunification center, it was way too small to accommodate everyone and lacked privacy. The Grand Beach Hotel, just 8 blocks down the street, became the official reunification center for displaced families to rendezvous and served as the information hub for briefing updates.

Chief Jadallah was tasked with the monumental burden of looking distraught family members in the eyes while briefing them daily in the weeks to come. Miami-Dade Mayor Daniella Levine Cava immediately requested a state of emergency for additional resources, reinforcements, and funding to maximize relief efforts. Florida Governor Ron DeSantis did not hesitate to sign an executive order, declaring a state of emergency for Miami-Dade County. The very next day, an Emergency Declaration authorizing federal assistance promptly mobilized to support the search operation and provide support for survivors and funding for the emergency operations, as well as an investigation into the cause of the collapse. Manpower flooded in!

Worldwide Response

It felt like every national governmental agency imaginable was sent to Surfside. The National Institute of Standards and Technology (NIST) initially deployed a team of 6 scientists and engineers to facilitate the collection of hundreds of pieces of evidence, such as columns and concrete slabs, which were then transported off-site for evaluation. OSHA (Occupational Safety and Health Administration) employees helped ensure that agencies equipped their teams with necessary personal protective equipment to prevent injuries or illnesses. The U.S. Coast Guard contributed emergency vehicles. The FBI sent experts to help with everything from crisis management and victim specialists for survivors, to evidence response units. The FAA (Federal Aviation Administration) issued temporary flight restrictions and sent drone specialists and inspectors to help prevent disruptions in operations. State representatives, mayors, senators, and even Miami-born Lieutenant Governor Jeanette Nuñez and Governor DeSantis were present every day. This was on top of dozens of local and national law enforcement agencies, before collaborating with international rescue teams! At one point I thought NASA might send some astronauts to the scene.

As the Chief of Police for the North Bay Village Police Department, my father's agency was one of the many neighboring municipal police forces dispatched. Given that he chose to remain on-site with his loyal uniformed men and women, my family and I elected to spend most of our time on the front lines with him, rather than convening with the other families at the Grand Beach Hotel. While the families were briefed by Asst. Chief Jadallah with disheartening news daily, my family and I were physically present at the scene watching the information unfold before our eyes in real-time. As professionals carefully scoured the area with listening devices, cameras, and trained search dogs, they methodically removed debris piece by piece, bucket by bucket, to avoid creating a disturbance that could cause a collapse within the collapse.

Holding on to Hope

Tension ran high in the hotel briefing room as daily reports of how many individuals were still missing, how many were found dead that day, and how many souls were still unaccounted for. After 3 days, only 8 bodies were found. As many crushing blows as Fire Chief Jadallah had to communicate calmly to torn families, probably none of them were as bad as the one he delivered the evening of Saturday, June 26th. He was repeatedly asked why he could not disclose how many victims had been found. But there was no hiding the ugly truth that no one should have to endure. After trying to brace them emotionally, he uttered, "It's not necessarily that we're finding victims, ok? We're finding human remains." The room instantaneously erupted in weeping.

On Sunday, June 27, 2021, the media reported over 150 individuals still missing. We would later learn exactly 101 precious individuals went down with the building, but 3 of them defied death and survived! Given that the last live victim was found at 6:05 am, our emotions were volatile, especially for the families cooped at the Grand Beach Hotel. However, Chief Jadallah gave them the closest resemblance of good news they'd had in three days. Families were allotted 1 hour of private visitation at the collapse site—with the presence of politicians or media forbidden. But the victims' families were sternly warned that it was an active scene, which meant the risk of encountering haunting images, like mangled human remains, or even recovered corpses.

This was slightly optimistic, especially for the large Jewish community within Champlain Towers South, because Jewish culture teaches that honor and respect for a loved one who has passed away is shown by laying them to rest as quickly as possible. They're not to be left alone. This custom is a beautiful act of love for their soul, which is intended to prevent delay in their soul moving on in the spiritual afterlife. Part of that tradition is not leaving a person alone so that it can be carefully prepared with a sacred purification ritual. Visiting the collapse site was the closest substitute and allowed everyone the opportunity to release their grief in their own way... Some sobbed; others prayed, and some mourners even screamed in gut-wrenching anguish toward the abyss of rubble.

That same day, the Israeli Defense Forces (IDF) arrived, bringing valuable experience from similar past rescue operations after powerful earthquakes had rocked Haiti and Nepal. Their presence brought hope. Following the 7.0 magnitude earthquake that decimated Haiti in 2010, Israeli rescuers famously saved a 22-year-old man, after an astounding 10 days trapped under debris! There were other dramatic rescues over a week after the quake. Golan Vach, commander of the IDF National Rescue unit, and his team used their elite expertise and technology to reverse-engineer a mountain of rubble into a building in puzzle form to see where survivors could be. One method developed 2-D and 3-D computer simulations of the collapse to help determine how the building fell and where voids that could sustain life might be located. From the moment Vach and his militant team of warriors arrived in Miami, they worked 72 hours straight. But they only found human remains, marked by miniature red flags, scattered throughout the avalanche of cement.

United as a Community

For 6 grueling days, my family and I helplessly waited on Collins Ave. As we stood on the sidelines in front of the concrete and metal avalanche, unformed men and women worked tirelessly and continuously. It was a waiting game of watching and hoping. Everyone completely disregarded what divided us and focused on what united us—our community's pain. It reminded of me of the united strength our country found after 9/11.

Everyone wanted to contribute toward a solution to a problem that didn't have one. Local surrounding neighborhoods passed out water to officers and firefighters that blockaded streets up to 10 blocks away. Local houses of worship like CASA Church and VOUS Church sent groups of servant leaders that distributed snacks, sports drinks, candy, and cold water to an army of first responders. Local businesses, restaurants, food trucks, and charitable organizations donated meals, desserts, and energy drinks to keep our heroes fueled up and energized.

One individual, Leo Soto, felt a deep calling to form a memorial wall. He tirelessly scoured the internet, gathering images of the missing, and printed them out on sheets of paper. With a heart full of compassion, he reached out to local florists, humbly asking for their support in donating flowers. Their response was overwhelming, as they recognized the importance of coming together during such a trying time. Along the western fence of the Surfside Tennis Center at Harding Avenue and 88th Street, an ever-growing memorial wall emerged.

It quickly became saturated with hundreds of flower bouquets, stuffed animals, candles, handmade posters, religious messages, and flags. Each item held its own significance, representing the love, prayers, and hopes of those who placed them there. This wall became a tangible expression of the community's collective heartache and longing for answers. The "Wall of Hope" became a sacred space, a sanctuary of shared grief and resilience. People from all walks of life gathered there, drawn by a common bond of compassion and the desire to honor the lives that were lost. It became a place where tears were shed, prayers were whispered, and hearts found connection for one another. This movement is now "The Wall of Hope Foundation", which helps to provide communities that have been struck by disaster with resources to begin the healing process, and to organize proper memorials and vigils.

One of the other unsung heroes of this story, is the nonprofit organization Global Empowerment Mission (GEM). They serve as global first responders to natural disasters and humanitarian crises, mobilizing within 2 days of a crisis and staying in the affected area for as long as needed. GEM provides crucial disaster relief, bridges the recovery gap, and works towards establishing self-sufficient and thriving communities.

When the collapse devastated his own local community, GEM founder and Miami resident Michael Capponi was there to respond. He witnessed the multiple layers of trauma experienced by the affected individuals, with many losing not just their homes but also their friends and neighbors. Recognizing the depth of the tragedy, GEM distributed $397,993 from the Champlain Tower Residents Fund, provided additional funds for relocation deposits, and rent amounting to $349,523, and ensured that all survivor units received a laptop computer. Their efforts were truly remarkable.

I hold deep admiration and appreciation for organizations like GEM, not only because my family personally benefited from their rescue efforts, but because they embody God's love. Just like GEM, God's response to rescue is not based on our accomplishments or circumstances. It is an outpouring of unconditional love for all those who are broken and suffering, serving as a beacon of hope and restoration.

Discovery in the Recovery

I'll never forget that sixth day—June 29. After another long, draining day in Surfside, my family and I were exhausted on every level: physically, mentally, emotionally, and spiritually. Our souls had grown weary. My family dispersed, making the mournful car rides back to their own homes. As I was on my way home after finishing an interview with the media, I got a call from my father. He said he'd received the call we had been dreading—the police had some news for us. The twelfth victim was identified. Against our will, we turned around and drove to the Grand Beach Hotel, knowing that our hearts were about to be ripped from our chests. We'd lost our family matriarch.

One of the most devastating of many dreadful Surfside stories emerged on July 2. Urban Search and Rescue Team, Florida Task Force 2 recovered the bodies of 2 family members, Graciela Cattarossi and her 7-year-old daughter, Stella. What made this story even more haunting was the connection to the first responders who were intimately involved in the rescue efforts. Stella's father, a dedicated firefighter with 10 years of service, and her uncle, who was the brother and fellow first responder of her father, were among the courageous individuals assisting in the rescue operations. In a cruel twist of fate, these courageous men found themselves confronted with the unimaginable task of uncovering the lifeless bodies of their own beloved family members.

A spokesman for the City of Miami Fire Rescue, Capt. Ignatius Carroll stated, "When he was made aware that we were close to where his loved one may have been, then he stood side by side with some of his other fellow firefighters." He continued, "We were able to bring her and then at least give him an opportunity to say his farewells." I can't imagine the heart-wrenching terror this man felt, after a week and a half of searching, to physically uncover his little girl's lifeless body. Somehow, he found the strength to stand firm as he painstakingly covered her with the jacket off his back, then placed a small American flag over her. As he picked her up, can you even begin to fathom the anguish that must've torn his heart apart?

Out of respect, every single machine, movement of concrete, and busy worker came to a completely stop, in total silence. He carried the precious body of Stella Cattarossi out of the disaster, as everyone on the scene reverently honored them both in silence. To make the situation worse, the family lived in apartment 501, which housed Stella's grandparents, Graciela and Gino Cattarossi, as well as her aunt who was visiting from Argentina, Andrea Cattarossi. Five family members ranging across three generations were violently taken in such a cataclysmic manner.[121]

The Demolition

As efforts continued, a contorted shift to the crippled, upright structure caused a 15-hour delay due to safety concerns. To make a terrible situation worse, Tropical Storm Elsa, which would soon become a hurricane, was threatening to strike Florida. This forced officials into an ultimatum: either the wind gusts of Elsa could cause the remaining structure to collapse, or hired experts could execute a controlled demolition safely without causing further harm to the site. Rescuers were also hopeful the detonation could create new pathways to inaccessible areas in the parking garage.

The decision was clear: it needed to go. Residents pleaded for their cherished belongings, but no one would risk their life for material things. On the 4th of July, while the nation celebrated America's birth with firework explosions, the Surfside community mourned an explosion that blew away any aspirations of their former lives. As detonations blasted what was left of Champlain Towers South, although many residents lost loved ones, all of them lost their home. The walls that once safeguarded their families now laid in ruins, while the spaces once vibrant with joy were reduced to empty voids, like its fallen predecessor.

Recovery Mission

Crews continued rescue efforts around the clock. Despite their relentless dedication, the grim reality continued to unfold. With the discovery of 64 confirmed deaths amidst the devastating wreckage and no signs of life, a heart-wrenching decision was made on July 8, 2021. What was a search and rescue mission for survivors painfully became a recovery mission for bodies. The transition squashed anyones remnants of hope against all odds. And then, on July 20, 2021, closure finally came for all the families. The last victim, Estelle Hedaya, was discovered, bringing an end to the agonizing wait. It was a bittersweet moment, as the pain remained, but the uncertainty and longing for answers were put to rest.

Mayor Levine Cava confirmed the disaster was "the largest non-hurricane related emergency response in the history of our state." While the catastrophe was still fresh, Senator Jason Pizzo had very accurately stated, "This is an unimaginable tragedy that will require our attention in the hours, days, and weeks to come, and we will provide the needed support and comfort to our fellow neighbors and residents as they navigate this enormously difficult time." It took all of 12 seconds to gratuitously decimate the lives of 98 innocent men, women, and children. So many families have been torn apart with grief. The youngest victim was just 1-year old, and the remaining victims ranged to age 92. My sweet grandmother, Hilda Noriega, was the eldest of the casualties.

I'll never forget the words of Florida Chief Financial Officer/ State Fire Marshall Jimmy Patronis' encouraging speech a year after the collapse: "While we honor and mourn for the 98 souls that are no longer with us, we also pray for the parents, brothers, sisters, and children that were left behind. On this day one year ago, I saw the work of God when 400 of Florida's Urban Search & Rescue Team members fought, and kept fighting, for any hopes of life. On that mound of rubble, I saw hell on Earth. But I also saw God's presence in the men and women that fought with every ounce of their being to save lives."[123] Although I wouldn't hear this word of encouragement for a year and couldn't explain it at the time, I knew this truth deep in my heart.

The cause of the collapse is still under investigation, but one thing is clear: the collapse of the Champlain Towers South was preventable. Initial reports suggested that the building had been experiencing structural issues for years. Some residents had complained about cracks in the building's walls, and an engineering report conducted in 2018 had warned of "major structural damage" to the concrete slab below the pool deck and garage area. The report also found that the building's waterproofing was failing, leading to water damage and corrosion of the steel and concrete. Some experts suggested that the building's location, on a coastal barrier island, might have played a role in the collapse. Others pointed out the age of the building, which was constructed in 1981, and the impact of years of exposure to saltwater and the elements. Some also suggested that there may have been design flaws or maintenance issues that contributed to the collapse.

Regardless, the collapse of the building was sudden, unexpected, and traumatic, yet it has had a profound impact on the residents of Surfside, the wider community of Miami, and the nation as a whole. The lessons learned from this tragedy will undoubtedly shape the way we approach building safety and maintenance in the years to come. The memory of those who lost their lives will be forever etched in our hearts, and we must honor their memory by working to prevent similar disasters from happening again. While the tragedy cannot be undone, it has sparked a renewed commitment to healing, rebuilding lives, and coping with the hole that was not just left in the ground where the building once stood, but the bigger hole that was left in our souls.

As I walked upon the collapsed condo for the first time, I hadn't yet acquired the intel I just shared with you in this chapter. I had no understanding or comprehension of what had just taken place. All I knew was my entire nervous system was in shock, as sensory overload surged through my body. Some seasons are about surviving, not thriving. It's okay to not be okay. In those times, it's all you can do to focus on breathing and crying out for help. When you've entered a crushing season that burdens your soul with sorrow, the key is coming out of that season. But before you make it out, you must make it through the breaking and crushing. It's time to stand in the storm.

CHAPTER 3

Stand in the Storm

Be merciful to me, O God, be merciful because I come to you for safety. In the shadow of your wings, I find protection until the raging storms are over.

Psalm 57:1 (GNT)

When the Storm Strikes

I've lived my entire life in South Florida where storms and hurricanes are routine and don't phase us. We put up shutters, stock up on our favorite snacks, and get amped up for hurricane parties! But heaven forbid the temperature drop below 60 degrees Fahrenheit. We tend to lean on the dramatic side, as if our tropical blood will freeze up. Everyone breaks out their winter boots and Eskimo suits as if a blizzard is coming. The "snowbirds" who temporarily move down here from the North during the harsh winter months find us ridiculous, and I can't blame them since our winter season is about as severe as their summers. But we're fearless in the face of hurricanes, just like the Spartan warriors before battle. Instead of shouting, *'This is Sparta!'*, we shout, *'This is Florida!'*

Once a storm rolls in, the waves of raindrops pound the surrounding areas as their relentless assault drives people to seek refuge while streets turn into rivers. It's as if the heavens themselves weep, releasing their pent-up energy and emotions upon the earth as lightning bolts rip rigid patterns through the darkness. They unleash enough staggering energy to briefly turn night into day. In the moments that follow, the raw power of these electric currents tear the fabric of the sky open, resulting in an earthquake that descends from above. The eruption commands an instantaneous respect that shakes the very foundations of our surroundings with fear. As the wind gusts with increasing intensity, it becomes a force that can uproot trees, topple structures, and send debris hurtling through the air. It can get scary sometimes.

The point is, when thunderstorms or hurricanes threaten us, South Floridians handle it well. It's only a matter of time until the rain pours, thunder rumbles, floods surge, wind blows, and lightning strikes. We understand it's not a matter of *if* a storm will hit, but rather *when* the storm will hit. We don't get cold weather often, just random cold fronts that last a few days at most, during a brief "winter" season. We anticipate volatile weather systems so that when they do happen, we're mentally prepared. It's a part of the Floridian culture. A storm is the norm.

In September 2019, Hurricane Dorian made landfall in the Bahamas, becoming the most powerful storm in recorded history to hit the island nation. The storm sat over Grand Bahama for more than 48 hours, mercilessly battering the island nation with eye-wall wind gusts reaching over 200 mph. Grand Bahama suffered the most significant damage, prompting a group of us from VOUS Church to respond with a mission trip the following month.

We boarded a ferry for a short voyage to Grand Bahama. The devastation we witnessed broke our hearts. A friend of mine, Greg Burgess, addressed one of our teammates who was deeply shaken by the locals' living conditions. He solemnly said, "I think there's a way to allow things to break your heart, but not break your spirit." Without realizing it, his words of wisdom planted the seeds of this book, which later took root in the soil of my heart.

There's a powerful life parallel here. Getting caught in the storm is inevitable. The storm getting caught in you is optional. You cannot control weather systems; you can only prepare for them. A proactive approach prepares you for struggle, but a reactive approach leaves you vulnerable to unnecessary suffering. When thunder, lightning, rain, and winds strike, we have no control over the storm's destruction. We only have control over the destruction within us! Just like how a cataclysm can compromise weak foundations, our lives can be compromised if we are not equipped to handle life's storms.

Betting on the hope of never encountering another life storm is a losing proposition. None of us are immune to heartbreak. It begs the question, "What is the foundation of your life built on?" That's one of the most important questions we will ever wrestle with. It takes way more commitment to build something than to tear it down. The bigger the building, the more you have to work on the foundation. Same with our lives. When the hurricane-force winds of life hit, will your character and spirit stand firm or collapse? And if you collapse, that's not the end. It's time to rebuild rather than remain.

Foundation Complication

There's a direct correlation between the state of your heart and the condition of your spirit. After Greg dropped that truth bomb on me, I realized later that he got the idea from God in Psalm 34:18 and didn't give him credit. The scripture reads, *The LORD is close to the brokenhearted; he rescues those whose spirits are crushed* (NLT). Notice the promise of this passage doesn't indicate the Lord rescues the brokenhearted—because heartbreak is inevitable. None of us can avoid the valley of the shadow of death.

In the dark morning hours of June 24, 2021, the Champlain Towers South Condo Building in Surfside, Florida, suffered a catastrophic failure as 55 apartment units collapsed within seconds. This "Black Swan" incident resulted in incalculable pain and suffering from the loss of so many irreplaceable people. The ages of those who died ranged from 1 to 92, my beloved grandmother being the eldest victim. At the time of this writing, there's no defining conclusion as to why my grandmother's building pancake collapsed in the middle of the night. However, it's clear that the foundation which held the weight of the building ultimately failed. The aftermath of this tragedy, the third-largest structural failure in U.S. history, resulted in the unnecessary death of 98 innocent lives that were crushed to death in homes mistakenly presumed to be safe.

In his book entitled *Crazy Faith*, the best-selling author of *Relationship Goals*, Michael Todd, vividly illustrates a compelling picture of the significance of an underlying foundation:

When I asked the foundation contractor why it was taking so long (because, honestly, I was ready to see some progress above ground), he reiterated that the foundation is the most important phase of construction. They never rush this part of the process because, as he put it in a very matter-of-fact tone, "We can fix a wall and we can repair a window, but once this house is up, the foundation is set forever—that is, unless we tear it down or do major reconstruction." I couldn't help but wonder, What areas of my life have I built on a faulty foundation? Where do I need some major reconstruction?

Have you heard of the Burj Khalifa? No, it's not Wiz Khal-ifa's cousin. It's currently the world's tallest free-standing structure, at a staggering height of more than 2,700 feet-that's two and a half times as tall as the Eiffel Tower and almost twice as tall as the Empire State Building! It cost an estimated $1.5 billion and took six years to build.

More than 110,000 tons of concrete were used to construct the foundation, which is buried 164 feet below ground level. That's twelve stories of building under the building, because it takes a very deep, very sturdy foundation to keep that 500,000-ton tower standing tall.

A foundation may seem insignificant because it's under the surface, but it makes possible the part that's on display for every-one to see. The integrity of the foundation you build your life on determines the type of structure that can be built on it.

It's unbelievable that there were no signs of inclement weather patterns or natural disasters, like an earthquake, that caused the Champlain Towers South building to collapse. It just crumbled under the pressure of supporting its individual weight. This trag-edy is symbolic of what happens when our core beliefs are not built on a firm foundation of truth. You may be asking what truth? I'm glad you asked! The pain of heartbreak is inevitable, while the hopelessness of a crushed spirit is optional. A broken heart and a crushed spirit may seem the same, but there are important distinctions. Consider the stark contrast:

A crushed spirit curses God through the storm.
A broken heart cries out to God through the storm.

A crushed spirit is defeated.
A broken heart is discouraged.

A crushed spirit is a life sentence.
A broken heart is a life season.

A crushed spirit is a hopeless destination you move to.
A broken heart is a season of grieving to heal through.

A crushed spirit adapts pain as its identity.
A broken heart adopts purpose from the pain because of your identity.

A crushed spirit avoids grief for whatever brings brief relief.
A broken heart chooses to heal through the cycle of grief

A crushed spirit believes this is the end.
A broken heart can heal and mend.

A crushed spirit believes God caused this for your destruction.
A broken heart trusts God will use this for your construction.

A crushed spirit is a wounded heart that's contaminated with infection.
A broken heart knows its healed scar will tell a story from a new perception.

A crushed spirit deceives you that you want to die.
A broken heart frees you to mourn and cry.

A crushed spirit is a captive and incarcerated soul.
A broken heart can be made whole and free your soul.

The ultimate difference between a broken heart and a crushed spirit is the meaning you give your pain. A crushed spirit is like a barren well that's run dry. It empties us of faith, hope, and purpose. But you can either let your pain drag you into a pit of darkness or pursue healing and restoration. As we explore the mystery of pain, trauma, and loss during times of existential crisis, we'll confront a deep question that echoes from our souls: *How do you endure a collapsed heart without it crushing your spirit?*

5 Requisites to Restoration

As we embark on this journey together, we'll explore 5 practical steps that have helped me not only navigate heartbreak, but recover from a crushed spirit.

1. **Reveal It: Recognize your Heartbreak.** *Acknowledging your pain prompts your healing.* Awareness initiates healing because exposure brings closure. Think practically. If someone cut you deeply, wouldn't you acknowledge that the bleeding indicates there's a problem that needs to be addressed? You can't address what you refuse to assess! If you don't acknowledge that you need to heal from what pierced you, you'll bleed on people who didn't cut you. When we bury, deny, or pretend our way through pain, we

slowly lose our ability to empathize. Empathy builds trust and intimacy. Without it, your humanity will just wither away day by day. If you conceal how you feel, how can you heal from what you don't reveal?

2. **Relieve It: Respond to your Grief.** *Addressing your pain positions your healing.* If you don't address the cut, you can bleed out or get an infection in the long run. Stop the bleeding. Start the healing. Be your own first responder, but not your only first responder. Even if you're not responsible for the gaping wound, you're still responsible to care for it. Your life decisions direct you to deliverance or deviate you toward destruction. Like the ocean, the deeper we go, the darker it gets. But the pain of healing is worth the hurt. Unaddressed pain doesn't get better; it enslaves you. Determining your response positions your restoration.

3. **Release It: Relinquish your Anguish.** *Surrendering your pain processes your healing.* You can't always care for your wounds by yourself. There comes a point where you must surrender to the care of a medical professional. When you're in pain, it's easy to feel like a prisoner to your emotions or circumstances. Breaking free from those chains begins with releasing your pains. Surrender isn't a sign of weakness. It takes courage and humility to recognize you can't heal yourself and that you need help. Even a doctor needs a doctor. Forgiveness also takes courage and humility. Whether you need to forgive yourself, an enemy, or loved one, forgiveness is always an inside job. It frees you, not them. The forgiveness you receive is linked in direct proportion to the healing you'll achieve. The more resistive you are to forgive, the higher the ceiling on your healing. It's a paradox. The freedom we seek is found in the surrender we avoid. Relief can be brief. But releasing is unceasing.

4. **Reframe It: Rename your Pain.** *Receiving your healing replaces your pain.* A wound that's healed is no longer a wound. It's a scar. Scars don't bleed, nor can they get infected. Scars are reminders of battles fought and won. But scars don't just happen. They're the result of a transformation process, which takes time and effort. Pain doesn't define us. It transforms us. It's the application of information that leads to transformation. Romans 8:28 reminds us that, "…God works all things for the good of those who love him." That doesn't mean He causes bad things to happen or that everything that happens is good. It means that even in the worst situations, God never wastes our wounds and can use pain to transform us into who we're meant to be. Renaming your pain means that with His help, what we may call weakness, God calls strength.

5. **Renew It: Redeem your Sorrow.** *Draw purpose from your pain to pursue the promise of healing.* This stage is no longer about yourself, it's about inspiring others to find freedom in their healing! Our perception of purpose is often tied to success and prosperity, but true purpose often hidden within our suffering. How do you know that you're passionate about something? You're willing to suffer for it. The enemy knows the power of purpose, often trying to paralyze you with fear, but it's time to reclaim your power. Positive thinking alone cannot overcome spiritual strongholds. Your purpose emerges when you're healed, transforming the deep pain that once broke you into the passion that awoke you. Your passion is rocket fuel, propelling you on a mission of healing and serving others.

Stand in the Storm

As we explore these 5 requisites to restoration in Phase 2, each upcoming chapter is exclusively dedicated to a deep-seated Surfside story of a person or family. Although we'll begin walking together through the valley of the shadow of death in the pages ahead, we won't end there. We're not going to look in reverse at our pasts to regress, but to accelerate forward toward future progress. Deep valleys are the unrealized pathways to the mountaintop. That's why it's so important to *walk* through the valley of the shadow of death, not camp out in it! Don't dwell in a destitute situation that was never intended to be your destination! Take your desperation and turn it into your aspiration. How will you respond to the wound? Will you nurse, rehearse, curse, disperse, or reverse it?

There's a song called "Standing in the Storm" by Skillet that brings great language to the endgame of this book:

> *I'm standin' in the storm like never before*
> *The pressure builds around me*
> *Let the winds surround me*
> *Whatever comes, I'm not givin' up*
> *Fearless as a lion*
> *Not afraid of dyin'*
> *I still got some life in me*
> *You can try to shake me*
> *I still got some fight in me*
> *But you can never break me*
> *I'm standin' in the storm like never before*
> *The pressure builds around me*
> *Let the winds surround me*
> *I'll stand in the storm*

A powerful storm can be a terrifying experience that assaults all our senses. It feels as though we're at the mercy of something reckless that's beyond our control. It can trigger fear that invades our souls, crippling us from the bewilderment of feeling powerless, helpless, and trapped. We hear the fear in the terrible things we say to ourselves, fueling our despair in a toxic feedback loop that cycles dread. However, just like a storm eventually passes, so too does the grip of fear. That's why you can stand in the storm.

As I share my personal and public experiences with a broken heart and crushed spirit, I hope to inspire you to adopt the promises of restoration through your own processes. May the words of hope on these pages come alive in your heart and stir up your faith. May the struggles you face today become your strength tomorrow. May your restlessness become your story of redemption. May your current test become your future testimony. May your heaviest burden now become your greatest blessing. May what feels like a mess at this moment become a miraculous message later. May the cries and confusion of your harshest crushing season become your highest calling. Through it all, may the comforting presence of the Lord draw near to your broken heart, providing refuge and strength to rescue your spirit from crushing, so that your soul is made whole. May your heart heal in the refuge of His love, bringing renewal to your spirit that makes your soul uncollapsable.

A Collapsed Community: Crushing & Healing

CHAPTER 4

Reveal It:
Recognize Your Heartbreak

*You are my refuge and defense; guide me and lead me as
you have promised.*

Psalm 31:3 (GNT)

The Call That Changed It All

It was a typical, muggy summer evening in Miami, and I had
recently returned from the cool, dry climate of Colorado, my
body hadn't fully readjusted to the abrupt change in time zones
or the contrast in weather, but I hoped that exhaustion would take
over and lull me into a good night's rest. Crawling into bed, I rel-
ished in the familiarity of my surroundings. The softness of the
mattress welcomed me, as I snuggled under the coolness of my
sheets. Before I closed my eyes to drift off, I indulged in one of my
guilty pleasures – a sci-fi cult classic, Alien. I grabbed the remote
and started the movie, entertaining myself in the suspenseful tale
of intergalactic horror. Little did I know that true existential terror
was already waiting for me, and it had nothing to do with aliens.
Those few moments of drifting off would be the only taste of rest
I'd experience in the days ahead, as my peaceful night turned into
a waking nightmare.

My phone buzzed at 1:45 am, startling me out of a half-sleep. It was my mom. Seeing my mom's name on the screen wasn't surprising at first, given her job as a nurse practitioner, admitting patients overnight at a hospital. She knows I tend to be a night owl, so when things were slow, she'd call me every once in a while. However, I quickly realized she wasn't working that night. At that moment, I knew it was going to be one of those middle-of-the-night phone calls that nobody ever expects to receive, even in their worst nightmares.

"Hey Mom, is everything okay?"

She was frantic, "Michael, your father just got a phone call from someone in Kima's building! She was hysterically crying and kept telling us that something happened to the building, and we need to get over there *now*! Something about an explosion. Your father already left. Your brother is on his way to pick me up, and then we're coming to pick you up. I need you to be ready in 10 minutes." I confusingly responded, "Mom, what do you mean an explosion? What happened?! What did this lady tell you?!". "I don't know, she was distraught and crying in hysterics, we just need to get there. Please be ready!" She responded.

Although Surfside was a 30-minute drive from my location, I couldn't shake off the fear and curiosity that seized me. Determined to uncover the truth, I contacted the Surfside Police Department to find out what was going on. When an officer answered my call, I repeated my mother's story and inquired about the situation at my grandmother's building. He responded that he couldn't go into details, but it was a bad situation. The lack of reassurance left my mind racing with scenarios. I asked him if it was serious enough to warrant a trip there. Without hesitation, the Surfside police officer urged me, "*Absolutely!* You should get down here."

It just got real. *What the heck happened in my grandmother's building?!* Was it an electrical fire that erupted into a devastating explosion? Or could it have been a mishap caused by a gas stove or a propane tank? I quickly got dressed as I began convincing myself that one of the groggy residents probably sleepwalked into the kitchen for a midnight snack and accidentally microwaved a metal container that caused an "explosion." Or, perhaps, a tired parent left the stove on, causing a small fire, and all the smoke in the building was misinterpreted as an "explosion."

Confusion In the Chaos

It wasn't long before I jumped in the car with my mom and brother. We screeched off like bats out of hell! I started asking questions immediately, to which my mother told me, "Your father is there already there. He's on the phone and isn't speaking… he hasn't said anything in the last 15 minutes… all he keeps saying is that the building is gone." I frantically rebutted, "What are you talking about?! What happened?! What do you mean the building is gone?!"

My dad remained eerily silent. I couldn't even tell if he was on the phone. My mom was as confused and clueless as I was. We made endless unsuccessful attempts to get my dad to utter a response that would hint at what was waiting for us in Surfside. We began to hear him silently sobbing. The longer the silence, the more intense the tension became. I started doing Google searches, checking media outlets, and my Instagram feed, but nothing had been reported yet. The anxiety building up in me was enough to make the baby hairs on the back of my neck stand up.

We arrived in Miami Beach, parking our car a few blocks south of Champlain Towers South in the dead of night, around 2:30 am. It was the closest we could get due to the sea of red and blue strobing lights blocking the street. My mother, younger brother, and I began our northbound trek on Collins Avenue, heading towards 88th Street—the boundary dividing Miami Beach from Surfside. Every step was punctuated by the pounding of our hearts, bracing ourselves for the unknown. The urgency for whatever awaited us matched the apprehensive rhythm of our thoughts.

As we hurried along, the darkness of the night began to recede, giving way to the piercing lights of first responders. The street was filled with a multitude of police cars, fire trucks, and ambulances, their flashing lights illuminated the surroundings in a disorienting display. The street was lined with dozens of stationary vehicles, effectively blockading all three lanes of the one-way street. As we were weaving through all the men and women in uniform, we got close enough to catch sight of the condo building.

A sense of relief temporarily calmed our nerves as we saw Champlain Towers still standing. Thankful that the condo building remained intact, we briefly exhaled a collective sigh of relief. No signs of smoke billowed into the night sky, no evidence of an explosive eruption that my father had alluded to. We continued through the frenzy of rescue workers, our angle shifted as we reached the northern side of the building. In that instant, our world shattered.

There was no building!

Unbeknownst to us at the time, the entire central and eastern wings of the Champlain Towers South condominium collapsed at 1:22 am. The 40-year-old L-shaped building housed 136 apartments and stood 12-stories tall until 40 percent of the apartments instantly disintegrated into what demolition experts would later define as a "pancake collapse." The partial collapse destroyed 55 units, leaving the tower furthest from the beach still standing.

A cold shiver shot down my spine like a bolt of lightning. My mom's face erupted in tears. She began wailing, "Oh my gosh, the building is *gone*. Oh my gosh!" Nothing could've prepared me for what my own two eyes witnessed... I was overcome with confusion, as if my eyes were deceiving me while my brain was in on the trick it was playing on me. My grandmother's building had almost completely collapsed as though it were a controlled demolition! Had I just walked onto the set of a disaster movie? Was Dwayne "The Rock" Johnson about to walk out and announce that we're extras in the filming of *Skyscraper* or *San Andreas* Part 2? Did some sort of sinkhole split the earth wide open and swallow the building? The only place I'd ever seen the tragic terror of this magnitude was in movie productions. It was an absolute war zone, as if the building had been bombed.

Weakness flooded my legs as I fell to my knees at the mercy of one gut-wrenching thought—my beloved grandmother was underneath that rubble. As I gazed at the building's remains, I could see her patio furniture that we'd sat on for treasured conversations over the past 20 years, lying on top of what used to be her balcony. *No, this can't be.* My heart sank into my chest as the tension of knots formed in my stomach. My throat began to tighten. I may as well have been shot in the chest at point-blank range. My bleeding heart began to hemorrhage anguish as I remained on my knees, helplessly succumbing to a hopeless situation.

Earthquake in Miami

The events of June 24, 2021, were mercilessly burned into the memories of those who experienced them, like cattle getting branded. Susanna Alvarez was one of the fortunate few who survived. That night started like any other. Susanna was sound asleep until a rumble abruptly jolted her awake. In a daze, she initially assumed it was a mild earthquake and thought little of it. Little did she know that a historic catastrophe would strike in less than a minute. The entire building shook again, this time, more violently, and Susanna heard a deafening noise that sounded like thunder. Fortunately, she survived to tell of her harrowing experience in the moments leading up to the tragedy.

"I heard what sounded like a very mild earthquake. My first thought was, *Oh my gosh, tomorrow the media is gonna be going crazy… Minor earthquake in South Florida!* And I just went back to bed. I would say less than a minute later that it was horrible… It was like this really loud thunder, and it just went on forever! And my bed started shaking, like shaking from side to side! And my windows opened. I have impact windows, and they just opened to the balcony! At that point, I was like, *Ok something happened!* My first thought was we got hit by lightning because it sounded like thunder. That's when I decided to go investigate. When I opened my door, there was really bad dust all over the place… Then I saw the elevators were gone; there were just piles of rubble! I tried to open the door to the stairs right next to the elevator, and it wouldn't open… So I decided to go around the corner to check out the other door. When I went around the corner, there was nothing there! I could see the sky because I was on the tenth floor—I could see the moon; it was a full moon. It was horrible! I looked down and all I saw was rubble and heard people screaming! That I will never forget in my life ever, ever, ever!"

The call that woke my father up was from Susanna Alvarez. The scene that unfolded before her was nothing short of a nightmare. A haunting mental picture that's almost too horrific to conceive. Susanna's recount is both terrifying and heartbreaking. Her connection to my grandma, a dear friend of her parents, adds a personal and deeply emotional dimension to her story. When Susanna realized that my grandmother was in the tower, she called my father in a state of hysteria. Desperately trying to convey the gravity of the situation, she made her best attempt: *Your mother's building is gone!* As my father received that life-altering phone call, the devastation of the collapse became an indescribable reality, forever altering the course of our lives. But we weren't the only ones.

Judy Spiegel's Legacy

One of Kima's other immediate neighbors, Kevin and Judy Spiegel, were also dramatically impacted by the darkness of that day. They resided in unit 603, just one door away from Kima's. Although the Spiegels' Surfside condo was originally a second home, they relocated to Surfside in 2017 to be closer to their daughter Rachel and her two young daughters, Sloane, and Scarlett. Rachel and I share a unique bond that extends beyond the fact that her parents and my grandmother were next-door neighbors.

There are striking similarities between her mother and my grandmother. The essence of Judy's beautiful spirit reminds me of Kima's radiance. Both souls illuminated a warmth and love that graced others. They were both the matriarchs of our families, with the natural heartfelt ability to connect with extended family and friends, while always going above and beyond with intentional interactions, to make sure everyone felt appreciated. They both embodied empathy.

During the COVID-19 pandemic, Rachel worked a demanding schedule in the medical field, which meant that Judy took on the role of primary caregiver for her 2 young granddaughters. She shared a special bond with Scarlett. During the many days they spent together, she took the opportunity to teach essential skills like reading, writing, and counting. Judy's dedication to her grandkids was a testament to her overall selflessness and love for her family.

Rachel's parents grew up on Long Island and met in New York City in 1978 when Judy worked as a stockbroker. They fell in love and got married in 1982, and started building their family soon after. Kevin had a successful healthcare career, starting as a firefighter and later becoming the CEO of several hospital groups. Judy, on the other hand, dedicated herself to raising their 3 children and pursuing her passion for philanthropy. She volunteered extensively for hospitals, and one project she undertook enhanced the walls of a hospital with art from locals, which replaced the previous dull and generic posters.

Rachel recalled, "My mom was the most loyal wife in the whole world. She worshipped my dad, she loved him. I don't think they ever fought. They were always holding hands. They were very much in love. They were very very happy. My mom was extremely supportive. When my dad throughout his career changed locations or companies, she was always his cheerleader, always dove into the community, always made friends, supported him, and made a mark on that community."

Judy was Rachel's best friend, their unifying force, and the backbone of her family. Sadly, their happy family life was shattered when Judy was alone in their apartment in Champlain Towers while Kevin was away on a work trip in California. Her loss was a devastating blow to her family, who remember her as a kind, compassionate person that never forgot a special occasion and made friends with everyone she met. The loss of Judy was not just a personal tragedy for her dear husband and family, but for the community. The world is a much better place because of Judy's beautiful life. Although Judy's legacy lives on through the many lives she touched, especially Rachel's, the distress of despair remains. Heart collapse strikes a crater of grief in your soul that Rachel shares:

"I never thought, at least not in this stage of my life, I would live without her. I was totally unprepared as was everybody else, but I never saw my life without her in it. I believe that her life was really cut short. When someone says they're in a better place, I don't feel like my mom is in a better place. I feel like her place is supposed to be right next to me or texting me all day long and sending me videos of my kids like I never missed a beat. I don't even understand my own loss you. I don't understand how my mom could not be here. I don't understand how we're planning events without her, but you know I do live my life in honor of her. I am very proud to be her daughter. I'm motivated to live out her legacy and to leave a strong legacy in her children and grandchildren. I'm committed to spreading awareness of the things that she was passionate about and family, but in other aspects of my life and I'm unmotivated. It's hard to balance it all. And it's hard."

As I reflect on Rachel's loss, my heart breaks. I can't help but empathize with her on a deeply personal level. I, too, understand the pain of losing the matriarch who keeps a family glued together. Empathy is not cheap. While sympathy is well-intentioned and feels sorry for the suffering of others, it often keeps us at a distance. Empathy goes a step further—it dives deep into the realm of shared experiences, embracing the pain and sorrows of another with genuine understanding. Sympathy offers cliches. Empathy offers compassion. It's through empathy, not cute phrases like "Heaven needed another angel", that we find the power to build bridges that connect to each other's hearts.

Pain or Injury?

In the personal accounts of Susanna and Rachel, they both exemplified the important first step towards healing in the wake of their traumatic experiences: recognize your heartbreak. This aspect is often underestimated or overlooked, but it puts you in control of taking a proactive role in your own healing, rather than being reactive to your feelings. Invalidating your grief leads to negating your relief. Unaddressed distress doesn't magically disappear or improve over time. The notion that "time *heals* all wounds" is misleading and inaccurate. It may seem comforting to believe that grief will fade away on its own, but that's a myth. A more accurate statement is "time *reveals* all wounds."

Think of the childhood game of peekaboo, where an object is hidden and momentarily forgotten. Just as children play peekaboo and believe that once an object is out of sight, it ceases to exist, we sometimes play a similar game with our pain. We might try to bury it deep, hoping it will fade away on its own. Yet, unrecognized pain doesn't dissipate; it intensifies within the shadow of your life. It hides in the darkness, waiting to resurface and hold you captive. If you don't face your wounds, your wounds will inevitably face you. It can seem counterintuitive and scary to unleash the petrifying truth that has been looming in your soul, especially when despair becomes the puppeteer. But when we summon the courage to face our pain head-on, we reclaim our power. Realizing your grief is what begins to bring some much-needed relief.

For example, I once heard a story of a football coach that had a brilliant method of addressing a hurt player on the field. He would sprint off the sidelines to his downed man and immediately ask, "Is it *pain* or *injury*?" If the fallen player responded as injured, the coach would command, "Get him on a stretcher and in an ambulance right now!" Sometimes the athlete would say they aren't hurt that bad. Being a good coach that showed tough love when they needed it, he'd say, "Then you're not injured. It's just pain. Walk it off. Let me help you up." He wanted his players to recognize the true state of their bodies because that dictated the next steps towards recovery. Remaining on the ground, wallowing in pain, was simply not an option.

All our emotions are God-given. We experience emotions because we're made in the image of God, who expresses a range of emotions, including anger, grief, jealousy, and frustration. These are emotions we often try to suppress or hide, but they're part of our human experience. Sometimes knowing *what not to do* is as important as knowing *what to do*. We must avoid the pitfalls to the dissolution of our souls and replace them with truths that bring long-term solutions towards healing and restoration:

Dis*SOUL*utions: Concealing Your Feelings

Denial is a natural response to overwhelming news, but it's crucial not to remain in denial for too long. Initially, this is good for coping because it has a sort of grace that slows down the pace of shock. The danger of denial is taking it from a stage of grief to a false belief in hopes of long-term relief. Remaining in denial means remaining in confusion, and evil thrives on confusion.

Isolation is a state of involuntary detachment from others that is often rooted in feelings of loneliness or bitterness. It nurses torment. When we isolate ourselves from others, our emotions become more intense and difficult to manage. We may also begin to feel more anxious and depressed since we're not receiving the social support that we need. Isolation is a reactive response to emotional pain that has no end date, nor is there any intention of self-care. In this state, you don't have emotions. Your emotions have you!

Self-condemnation often hides in plain sight in the form of regret. It traps us in a cycle of self-criticism and unforgiveness, holding us captive by our own hand. We become our own judge, jury, and executioner; punishing ourselves for past mistakes and shortcomings. We may blame ourselves for not doing more to prevent the loss. Of course, you could've done more, if you traveled back in time with your current knowledge! We could only make decisions based on the knowledge we had then. The problem with self-condemnation is that it doesn't lead to growth or healing, and keeps us stuck in the past.

*SOUL*utions: Revealing Your Feelings

Acknowledgment is deliverance from denial. Expressing grief is a sign of strength, not weakness. It takes courage to face emotions head-on and allow ourselves to feel. Clarity is key to healing and building confidence. We grasp this concept much more mainstream when it applies to physical injury, but the same principles are true of emotional injury. How do you extinguish darkness? Shine a light on it. Hiding pain in the shadows doesn't make it go away; it feeds it.

Solitude is the opposite of isolation. It's a healthy and intentional investment into our soul care. Taking the time to slow down, reflect, and recharge can help us to heal and build the strength we need to move forward. This means engaging in activities that you find peaceful, such as reading, meditating, praying, worshiping, or spending time in nature. It's a way of taking inventory of what you're allowing to occupy your heart, mind, and spirit. It's important to note that those that practice solitude don't remain in solitude. That's isolation. They reach out to others for support or seek out professional help, such as therapy or counseling. Think of it as *soulitude*.

Forgiveness cures condemnation. It's easy to fall into the trap of self-blame after experiencing loss. We may regret not seeing the signs or not doing more to prevent it. The lie of self-condemnation is that your shame and sorrow define you. The truth is the freedom found in forgiveness refines you. Forgiveness isn't about trying to forget. It's about releasing regret. The things that were a burden in your past can become your story of grace in your present, but only if you acknowledge it.

Memories VS Imagination

Taking strides towards *soulutions* teaches you how to address your past. It's a place we can never return to, and yet, it's something that we carry with us always. Memories and imagination are the 2 things that allow us to hold onto the past, which can equally be a blessing and a curse. Both can be powerful, but they must be used in the right way.

Memories are the remnants of our experiences, the bits, and pieces of our lives that we can hold onto forever. They allow us to remember the good times, the lessons we've learned, and the people that have shaped us. They're essential to our sense of self because our past is an integral part of who we are.

Imagination, on the other hand, is like having memories in reverse. It enables you with the ability to create memories that haven't happened yet. Think of it as a shaping tool. It empowers us with the ability to make decisions today that give us a say in our tomorrow. Consider someone who a fears public speaking. Instead of dwelling on past experiences of failure or getting tomatoes thrown at them, they use their imagination to create desired scenarios. They visualize themselves confidently delivering speeches, captivating the audience, and receiving an applause. By immersing themselves in these imagined experiences, they build confidence, reduce fear, and can prepare in the present.

Imagination can be a tool for overcoming fear and transforming perception, but it can also be a double-edged sword. It's a bizarre superpower that can bring productive change to your present by envisioning a better future. It can equally create emotional worlds of chaos by focusing on the one place it holds no power: your past. That's where imagination becomes a playground for our fears. When the seedlings of fear find fertile ground in the depths of your imagination, they produce a harvest of anxiety. Your imagination is designed to feed dreams and starve fears, but often winds up feeding our fears and starving our dreams! Imagination gets wasted, creating emotional worlds of anxiety filled with regret, condemnation, and worry. You must learn to use imagination wisely.

This is where the wisdom of Proverbs 29:18 becomes so clear: *When there is no clear prophetic vision, people quickly wander astray. But when you follow the revelation of the Word, heaven's bliss fills your soul.* Memories are there to cherish the past, while the best use for imagination is to create new visions. The key is finding a balance between memories and imagination. Memories should be appreciated, but we must learn to let go of bringing our imagination to a place that it can never serve us.

I once heard a leader share this idea: *Why should we hold onto our past within us? We cannot change what has already happened. True spirituality lies in acknowledging the past and questioning its purpose. Is there any benefit to keeping it stored inside of me? The answer is no. It serves no purpose at all.*

Although the intention behind that is noble, it's completely false, other than you can't change the past. It's impossible to forget your past, given that it's essential to also acknowledge that memories and imagination are not mutually exclusive. We can use memories as a source of inspiration for our imagination. By reflecting on your past experiences, you can learn from them and use that knowledge to shape your future. Memories can help create a vision for your future and take steps to make that vision a reality. After all, a car windshield is much larger than the rearview mirror for a reason—because it's important to focus on where we're going, not where we've been. You can use your past.

You're not a floating consciousness from a cosmic accident. You're a beautifully crafted soul. In a world full of brokenness, uncertainty, and confusion, it can be difficult to know which way to turn or what decision to make. When looking back at your past, it's to learn from it. It points you back to God and prepares you to invite Him into your healing journey. The power of empathy isn't limited to connecting us with one another; it extends to building a profound bridge between our hearts & God's heart. God recognizes your sorrow and its beautifully captured in Psalm 56:8 "You keep track of all my sorrows. You have collected all my tears in your bottle. Your Heavenly Father not only sees and acknowledges our sorrows but treasures them. In revealing your broken heart to Him, you invite God into those broken places, allowing His healing touch to bring restoration and wholeness. Revealing your heartbreak to God, unveils his divine comfort with you.

That's why you must face the pain that broke you. If you don't reveal it, God won't heal it. The process of exposure is worth the journey to closure. If you don't face your past, your past will eventually face you. How can you heal from what you won't allow yourself to feel?

It starts with recognizing your own heartbreak, so that your response may bring some relief to your grief.

CHAPTER 5

Relieve It:
Respond To Your Grief

Keep me safe from the trap that has been set for me; shelter me from danger.

Psalm 31:4 (GNT)

Darkest Hour

As I remained kneeling on the street before the devastation, it became increasingly difficult to comprehend the magnitude of the tragedy unfolding before my eyes. Every passing moment blurred deeper into an eternal haze of disbelief. My heart was drowning in a tidal wave of confusion that overpowered me. In an attempt to pull myself together, I slowly rose from my knees, only to remember that my father had been there all along, suffering in silence. I saw my family gathered around him, tear-streaked faces mirroring their wavering souls.

Fortunately, my father wasn't alone to bear the enormity of those critical moments before our arrival. It was the only moment I'd experienced any sense of relief since I received that life-altering phone call. A few of his trusted coworkers from the North Bay Village Police Department had been there to offer comfort and support. Seeing familiar faces standing by my father's side was a glimmer of hope, a lifeline in the sea of despair. But I looked into my father's eyes and saw nothing other than pain and brokenness; the kind that accompanies despair. I could've never fathomed witnessing my dad weeping publicly. Seeing him that distraught was out of character.

It broke me.

In that vulnerable moment, all I could do was rush into his embrace, holding each other tightly. When we finally let go, he began pacing restlessly through the dust and debris-filled street. Still reeling in doubt, he lifted his gaze towards the remaining tower, only to get choked up in a wave of heartbreak, as his eyes returned to the remnants of his mother's once-standing residence. With a pained cry, he exclaimed, "How could this happen? I just dropped her off at home 2 days ago! What the hell is happening right now?" My inability to offer him any hope only made me feel that much worse.

My father's concerns echoed truth. We were plagued by countless unanswered questions that sent our minds spiraling into the darkest realms of imagination. How could his 92-year-old mother possibly have survived this catastrophe? And, if, by some miracle, she was still alive, was she trapped in darkness, burdened by the crushing weight of the concrete? Had she been crushed beyond recognition? How was this even possible? Buildings don't just collapse in the middle of the night. The situation was overwhelming and bizarre; I began to wonder if this was some sort of planned demolition in the middle of the night. All of a sudden, we caught a fresh wind of hope! A frenzy of commotion broke out when two survivors were found.

Clinging To Life

Moments before their home crumbled beneath their feet, 15-year-old high school sophomore Jonah Handler was sitting in his room with his mom, Stacie Fang. Suddenly, concrete layers began to fall as if the building walls were melting apart. According to public records, "They free fell to what they thought was certain death." "Stacie and Jonah landed several floors below and miraculously were still alive." A valiant gentleman visiting from Phoenix, AZ, Nicholas Balboa, was walking his dog nearby when the building suddenly came crashing down. Mr. Balboa vividly recalled, "I can hear somebody yelling and screaming. I saw an arm sticking out of the wreckage. He was screaming, 'Can you see me?' He was just screaming, 'Don't leave me! Don't leave me! Don't leave me!' He said that his mother was in the apartment with him as well, so I couldn't see her or hear her, so I have no idea what her status is, but I do pray that she is all right." Nicholas was the first person to spot Jonah and assisted first responders in rescuing him from the building remains.

Journalist Matt Sullivan wrote a compelling article for *Rolling Stone* that eloquently illustrated the suspense of saving Jonah's life:

Around 1:40 am, over by the beach, dust sparkled in a stranger's flashlight: A man in an Arizona Diamondbacks hat, who'd been walking his miniature pinscher, shouted at Jonah that he could hear him, that he would go find help. "Please don't leave me," Jonah said. "Please don't leave me." The dog walker shouted up at a police officer on the towering heap. The cop shook his own flashlight down at some of the first responders here on the northern edge of emergency, a Miami-Dade Fire Rescue special-ops team known as the Squad. "We got a kid over here!" At approximately 2 am, from beneath the rock and between the clang-clangs of an alarm, at last, the firefighters heard Jonah ask if they could get him out of there.

They could. But the mountain was unstable; a rescue operator, planting his heavy spreader to pry open the slab, felt like he was changing a tire on quicksand. For leverage, his colleague broke up an end table, only for the concrete to wobble back toward Jonah's skull. The Squad sifted through boulders, bed frames, and any debris to steady their jack. They tried to keep the young man's mind steady with small talk while they were at it—the Marlins' fourth loss in a row, Jonah's offseason pitching regimen—and they were dumbfounded when Stacie, out of sight in the cave beneath, told them that his Sweet 16 was coming up. That he was still a 15-year-old boy.

Between 2:19 and 2:24 am, according to dispatch calls and incident logs obtained by Rolling Stone, good news interrupted the chaos of rescue radio: *They have a patient that's gonna be ready to be extricated. They're pulling people out right now.* Jonah's right arm had unlocked. But he held on to his mother's hand as long as he could. Held on tight. "There was a lot of 'Don't worry'—a lot of 'They're gonna get you out,'" recalls the rescue leader. "It wasn't Stacie that was reassuring Jonah. It was Jonah that was reassuring Stacie." He pulled up Jonah by his armpits as a great big barrel of a man, a drive operator from Ladder 46, climbed toward them, waving the boy closer. "Listen, you got no shoes on," he said. "OK if I take you down?" Jonah slumped upon the firetruck driver's shoulder and, as they began to rise from the rubble, called out: "Bye, mom! I love you, mom!" The driver lowered him onto a backboard stretcher. "You made it, man. You made it. You're alive.

Jonah's blue eyes twinkled in the truck light. The big man offered him a fist bump, and the lifesavers sensed—for an instant, at least, as the wreckage revealed itself—a smile. Then they saw the boy's mother trapped inside. The deep end of the tented slab remained connected by rebar to the rest of their old ceiling; it was unmovable. Stacie asked who'd be taking care of her son. He was in good hands, the Squad assured her.

The first responders carried Jonah headfirst to the bottom of the pancaked pile. They walked the stretcher alongside the pool deck and across Collins Avenue for the boy to get some rest. An EMT handed him a phone, and he called his dad: "Where are you?" (Name of Article CITE)

The dramatic rescue carried out by the firefighters was cap-tured on video and quickly made headlines worldwide. Meanwhile, Jonah's dad, Neil, lived close enough to race a few blocks over to accompany his son in the ambulance shortly after 3 am. They rushed Jonah to Joe DiMaggio's Children's Hospital, where he miraculously survived. His mom was also pulled from under the rubble, desperately clinging to life, and rushed to a hospi-tal. However, amidst the rescue efforts, an excruciating sacrifice was made.

The triumph quickly became a tragedy. Frank Rollason, the director of Miami-Dade Emergency Management, confirmed that her leg had to be amputated to free her from the debris. Stacie Fang passed away shortly after arriving at the medical center. While Jonah underwent treatment for twelve compression fractures in his upper spine, Neil faced the heart-wrenching task of delivering the devastating news to his son: "Mommy didn't make it." As her passing marked the first confirmed fatality in the Surfside condo collapse, it cast a dark shadow over the community, forever leav-ing a void in the lives of those who loved her—especially Jonah.

Risen From the Ashes

The magnitude of what Jonah endured is beyond comprehen-sion. He lived through a physical, mental, emotional, and spiritual catastrophe that most individuals wouldn't survive. However, his path to healing had just begun after he was discharged from the hospital. As Susanna, Iliana, and many other survivors have recounted, a thunderous boom preceded the downfall of their homes.

Whenever thunderstorms struck Miami, each roar triggered Jonah's post-traumatic stress disorder, paralyzing him with fear, regardless of his whereabouts. Even when he was outdoors, far from any buildings, the sound of thunder plagued him with the ter-rifying reenactment of a nightmare that had once been his reality. I can only imagine the immense powerlessness Neil experienced as a parent, peering into his son's eyes, only to see a storm raging within him. Yet, his story is far from over, as new chapters are still being written. We'll observe from Jonah's story that he didn't just survive, he persevered by addressing his pain.

Being a devoted parent tasked with filling the roles of both father and mother, Neil became determined to help his son overcome the weight of his experiences. After researching many options, Neil discovered an effective treatment program to address Jonah's PTSD, that proved to be remarkably successful. Jonah's PTSD symptoms were reduced by almost 70%. The incredible progress Jonah made not only transformed his own life but also inspired his father deeply. What began as an unwavering commitment to Jonah's healing, became a pivotal process that ignited a fire in Neil's heart. This new passion burned within him to extend the same transformative restoration to others who'd suffered from similar trauma.

While the world celebrated Jonah's miraculous survival, there was an unrecognized aspect of this tragedy. The first responders who risked their lives to save others had not only witnessed unspeakable carnage but also carried the burden of trauma within. These courageous individuals in uniform, whose struggles often remain unacknowledged, were also victims of traumatic stress. We rarely connect with the idea that these brave heroes are victims because, from my Father's experience, I've heard many of them choose not to seek mental health care treatment. This hesitancy to seek help is often because of the stigma surrounding mental health treatment and concerns about the impact it may have on their role at work, personal records, finances, and insurance.

With this in mind, along with the memory of Jonah's beloved mom and all those who lost their lives that day, Neil, and Jonah set out on a mission to create a lasting legacy of hope and healing through The Phoenix Life Project. This nonprofit organization has emerged as a beacon of hope for victims of catastrophes, ensuring that the needs of survivors, families, first responders, and communities, aren't neglected. Their vision not only provides essential resources for these unsung heroes and survivors of Surfside, but also aims to expand to those affected by future global disasters. This dedication to saving rescuers by offering a lifeline to those who've dedicated their lives to saving others sets them apart. Their website states:

"The mission is to create awareness and provide resources to those in need of mental and emotional recovery from PTSD through establishing a national network of providers to assist victims of trauma, first responders, veterans, their families, and communities. As a strategy to accomplish our mission, The Phoenix Life Project seeks to raise awareness and create sustainability for anyone affected by the Surfside condominium collapse, as well as by any future disasters globally. We strive to educate, advocate, and communicate through developing program initiatives in collaboration with municipalities and their departments (i.e. fire and rescue, police, veterans' associations, etc.). We wish to assist in removing the stigma associated with PTSD and establish a 24-hour, toll-free hot-line that victims and first responders can use to anonymously seek help. In addition, we aim to provide funding for those suffering from PTSD and in need of mental health treatment following a catastrophe or life altering event but simply cannot afford the treatment."

The phoenix, the project's icon, holds profound and timeless significance. This ancient mythological and immortal firebird resembles the majestic appearance of a red and gold eagle. It represents revival, reminding us we can heal after devastation; seeking redemption, which symbolizes transformation. The phoenix also signifies renewal, reflecting our ability to grow through any season of life. Additionally, it embodies resurrection, showcasing that the sting of death around us can awaken a purpose that was dormant within us. It's no wonder the phoenix's imagery of hope and new beginnings, aligns with the mission of "Bringing Serenity to Calamity" and Jonah's real-life story.[116]

Organizations like The Phoenix Life Project understand that, as long as you have a pulse, you still have a purpose because your story is still being written. The only way to have a story of triumph is if you don't give up. You can't stop your story because of a terrible scene. It's often the scenes of struggle that create the most epic stories of victory. Genesis 50:20 states: "You intended to harm me, but God intended it all for good. He brought me to this position so I could save the lives of many people[115]." And the same is true for you.

To find out more information on The Phoenix Life Project, please visit www.phoenixlifeproject.org

Address Your Pain

When Jonah emerged from the depths of millions of pounds of wreckage, he became a symbol of resilience and survival—just like the phoenix. The image of him being carried out of the debris, alive and clinging to life, touched the hearts of people like wildfire across the globe! Just because Jonah made it out of the collapse did not mean his soul was 'uncollapsable'. His dad empowered him to make a choice: the event could define him, or he could transform it into something positive. Neil was inspired by a quote he read from the prolific twentieth-century writer, Aldous Huxley. Huxley stated, "Experience is not what happens to a man; it is what a man does with what happens to him,"[118].

I think Neil was getting at this: We have the power to choose how we respond to pain. Jonah's traumatic experience didn't have to be the end of his story; it became the beginning of a new one. The same is true for you, but it involves stepping forward into your future rather than retreating from your past. Neil's guidance served as a shield for his son's future, instilling the belief that heartbreak doesn't have to define his life, despair doesn't dictate his destiny, and suffering isn't his defining story. Instead, his future is built upon the faith that triumphs fear. Your progress can inspire someone else's breakthrough! Our journeys aren't isolated; they're intertwined with the lives of others. As you reflect on Jonah's story, the power of discovery wouldn't have occurred without his response to it. It's no surprise that the Phoenix Life Project assists in that transformational process by addressing trauma.

Responding to your pain is crucial because relieving it initiates the healing process. Unaddressed pain doesn't magically disappear or improve over time. It'll hide in the shadows and hold you captive because our souls require care and attention, just as much as our bodies do. If you don't face your pain, it will inevitably face you. It can seem counterintuitive and scary to unleash the petrifying truth that's been glooming in your soul. Facing your troubles puts you in control of taking an active role in healing rather than a reactive role in your feelings.

Your identity isn't tied only to your best or worst moments but to the experiences in between. The deep work of understanding your emotions during the in-between brings a liberating revelation: feelings are indicative, not definitive. Pain is an indicator, signaling that something within us requires attention. Experiencing physical pain doesn't define you, just as emotional anguish doesn't define you either. Having sorrow doesn't equate to being consumed by it. Just because your body experiences physical pain doesn't mean you *are* that pain. That is why it's so important not to make permanent decisions based on temporary emotions.

Heart Dialysis

In understanding the power of addressing our pain and shaping our disposition, it is crucial to recognize the parallel between our emotions and the functions of our physical body. Just as our body processes what we consume through digestion, our heart, which is the core of our soul, processes our emotional experiences. What enters our hearts must, eventually, find its way out.

Consider the role of your kidneys in your physical well-being. Kidneys act as filters, removing waste, toxins, and excess water from your body by converting them into urine. When kidneys are unable to function properly, these toxins and waste poison the bloodstream and wreak havoc on blood pressure. In those cases, dialysis acts as a substitute, which filters blood through a machine that mimics kidney function. Those who stop dialysis treatments face deadly consequences. Depending on their overall medical condition and remaining kidney function, their survival is limited to a matter of weeks.[78]

In the same way that unfiltered waste gradually ravages our bodies, unaddressed emotional pain has the potential to pollute and silently deteriorate your heart. The human body relies on the heart to circulate blood to the kidneys for filtration, just as our spirits rely on the heart of our soul to filter yearnings and remove lies. This internal process discerns healthy desires from destructive impulses, removes distorted perceptions, and promotes truth. While we may not always have a choice in becoming septic from kidney failure, you possess the power to prevent your heart from poisoning your spirit. The contamination of a crushed spirit is what leads to a septic soul that eventually collapses.

In the depths of our being, there's a sacred space where seeds of belief cultivate our emotional landscape. Similar to fertile soil, our hearts are *not* neutral. Weeds grow effortlessly, without any attention or dedication. But it takes commitment to grow healthy crops that don't get choked out by weeds. To guard our hearts is to be intentional about the beliefs we allow to take root within us. It requires consciously uprooting destructive seeds and planting new seeds of construction. It's only a matter of time before the emotions we harbor within grow to the surface. Guarding your heart isn't a one-time endeavor, but a lifelong commitment. Simply put, that which you deprive will not survive. But if you want it to thrive, you must be willing to strive.

Guarding your heart is the key to healing. Your heart is the wellspring of life. It's the source where your thoughts, emotions, and actions flow. Remember, the heart's desires don't define your path. Instead, we have the power to shape our desires. If not, the heart's cravings can lead to destructive patterns and unhealthy behaviors, driven by impulsivity and immediate gratification. Jesus emphasized this connection between what enters the body and what comes out of the heart: *Don't you know that everything that goes into the mouth passes into the stomach and then is expelled as waste? But the things that come out of the mouth come from the heart, and it is those things that make a person unclean. It is out of the heart that evil thoughts come, as well as murder, adultery, sexual immorality, stealing, false testimony, and slander. Matthew 15:17-19*[80]

Similar to how hunger can cloud judgment when we're "hangry," emotional pain can distort our perception. Over time, these emotions inevitably erupt through impulsive words and actions. Have you ever shared something hidden that you were scared to say, but immediately felt relief once you finally got it off your chest? That's because your heart, mind, spirit, and soul long for your body to acknowledge your buried trauma. Your body is waiting for your heart to grant permission to face what has broken you. It knows you're lying to yourself when you conceal your feelings, and needs you to release what's poisoning your soul.

Fortunately, we have a pressure relief valve readily available. The only remedy to alleviate it is utilizing your mouth as the evacuation route of your feelings through words. The healing begins by speaking and giving a voice to the silent battles that have consumed you. Open, honest communication alleviates the septic toxicity of pressure built up from within. Your soul is just waiting for your mouth to finally come into alignment with the feelings you've held captive. Don't wait to the point of putting your heart on "dialysis." By courageously expressing our innermost struggles and fears, we invite healing into our lives.

As the words flow from your mouth, they carry the weight of your experiences, the echoes of your pain, and the longings of your soul. With each word spoken, the constraints that bind your heart begin to loosen. This isn't something enchanting I came up with, it's based on the scripture of Luke 6:45 (CSB): *A good person produces good out of the good stored up in his heart. An evil person produces evil out of the evil stored up in his heart, for his mouth speaks from the overflow of the heart. Therefore, confess your sins to each other and pray for each other so that you may be healed.*[77]

The power of life and death lies on your tongue.[75] What your heart conceives, your mind perceives, your spirit believes, and your body receives. What your body receives, your mouth must relieve! It's not until the words echo that you allow yourself to grieve. The longer we contain our pain, the longer confusion will reign. Opening up brings clarity to disparity so you can finally begin to thrive.

I'm an advocate for counseling, therapy, and prioritizing mental health. As we strive for healing, hiring a professional for our mental, emotional, and spiritual health can help. At times, we may feel like we're on top of the world, while other moments feel as if the weight of the world is on us. In the aftermath of the Surfside Condo Collapse, it felt like the weight of the world was on top of me. Shortly after burying my grandmother, I decided to seek professional help. I began attending sessions with both a Christian counselor and a psychologist weekly, in a safe, non-judgmental space. These professionals are legally bound to maintain confidentiality, creating an environment of trust and security. They serve as mirrors, reflecting on what we may not be able to see on our own; offering insights and observations that help us gain a fresh understanding of ourselves. Considering a counselor who shares your values can also enhance your experience.

We often underestimate the power of professional help and how beneficial it is at any stage of life. The notion that seeking help is a weakness or that therapy is only reserved for those in extreme crisis is a misconception that couldn't be further from the truth. In reality, it takes strength and wisdom to acknowledge that we can't become the best version of ourselves on our own. This is something that all the greats understand, which is one of the reasons they're great!

Just as successful athletes, musicians, businessmen, fitness experts, and influential leaders rely on coaches, trainers, and therapists to support their growth and development, we too can benefit from the guidance of spiritual counselors and mental health professionals. Did Michael Jordan think it was ridiculous to hire trainers? Would an Olympic athlete perceive hiring coaches as a weakness? The answer is a resounding, *"No."* It's an investment in yourself. True weakness lies in believing that seeking professional help is a weakness.

As you navigate through your journey of responding to your pain, these same declarations are proclaimed over you. You have the power to pursue healing despite the heartbreak, to surpass the grip of despair, and to emerge stronger from the struggles you have endured. You now know how to initiate healing the overwhelming darkness that's hiding in the shadows of your heart! Shine a light on it! Responding to your heartache begins to relieve internal pressure, but that pressure can build back up. It's only when you develop faith and courage beyond yourself to surrender your anguish that you make space for healing to flow in.

CHAPTER 6

Release It: Relinquish Your Anguish

I place myself in your care. You will save me, Lord; you are a faithful God.

Psalm 31:5 (GNT)

At the beginning of the previous chapter, my family and I found ourselves at the epicenter of the Surfside Collapse, where the devastating news of Jonah's mother revealed the first confirmed fatality. It rippled waves of disbelief and despair across the faces of dozens of police officers and firefighters, amplifying the distress that swept through the atmosphere. Yet, these courageous individuals defied imminent danger to save the stranded residents trapped within the remaining disfigured tower. A sense of urgency hung in the air as the unstable structure threatened to crumble at any moment. They maneuvered a colossal ladder extending from one of the fire engines towards the distorted building, bridging the gap between safety and danger. With each step taken, each life saved, their own lives teetered on the brink of collapse.

From our vantage point on the street, our eyes scanned the daunting two-story pile of rubble that stretched up the exposed side of the severed tower. The rescue workers carefully navigated through the hazards of its treacherous terrain in search of any signs of life. Among the obstacle course of wreckage were mounds of massive concrete blocks, scattered remnants of furnishings, crushed air-conditioning units, shards of shattered cement, razor-sharp scrap metal, and pulverized balconies. The maze of wreckage was intertwined with twisted and jagged rebar, protruding out from every angle.

An alarm composed a repetitive soundtrack that looped from the shadows of the mangled condo building that'd been torn in half. It was as if the building itself was helplessly crying out on behalf of those it had failed to protect. I'll never forget how my eyes were drawn to a stray emergency strobe light on the fifth floor, piercing through the voids of darkness every 2 seconds. Each flash unveiled a frightening scene. It illuminated the skeletal structure of the exposed living space just long enough to haunt us with the spine-tingling reality that this was an inhabited space when it fell. I was immersed in the overwhelming presence of death. The remnants of a once thriving community were now a destructive force that had torn lives and families apart.

Raquel Oliveira was a resident that wasn't home that night. The collapse had spared her life, but her soul was not spared from the unbearable despair that followed. She and her husband, Alfredo Leone, had met in her native hometown of Rio De Janeiro, where they gave birth to a beautiful baby boy, Lorenzo. Their hearts overflowed with love and joy as they welcomed him into the world. The allure of a safer and brighter future led Raquel and Alfredo to make a life-altering move to either Miami or Portugal. In 2017, when little Lorenzo was just 8 months old, they made a move from a seaside city in Brazil to another seaside town, Surfside. Imagine that—they bet their lives on leaving everyone and everything they knew for a "safer" new home.

Unit 512 in Champlain Towers South became their haven, a place where they hoped to build a beautiful life for their family. With its magnificent oceanfront view, it seemed like a blissful sanctuary. As the sun began to rise each morning, 5-year-old Lorenzo began a family tradition. He'd wake up on his own at 6 am and jump in his parent's bed, where they had front-row seats for the sunrise. They'd gaze out the window together, looking towards the horizon, as rays of sunlight emerged through the darkness, illuminating the deep blue ocean waters. As the night surrendered to the glimmering dawn, a breathtaking backdrop of light emerged in full glory as their family began each day.

On the morning of June 23, 2021, Raquel was scheduled to fly from Miami to Denver, Colorado. Filled with a mix of anticipation and emotion, she noticed that Lorenzo hadn't awakened at his usual 6 am. With a tender kiss, she expressed her love for her little boy, unaware of the impact that moment would hold. Walking towards the front door, she held Alfredo in a tight, intimate hug. In that precious memory, their unspoken words conveyed the depth of their love, the bond that transcended distance and time. She opened the door and left in tears. It's not that she was sad. Something about that farewell hug seemed to hold the weight of silent emotions. After all, Alfredo and Lorenzo were going to fly out to meet her in just a couple of days.

As tears streamed down her face, Raquel walked down the fifth-floor hallway, unaware that each step she took was a step toward saving her life. But she was equally unaware that those fleeting moments would be the last she'd ever have with her beloved son and husband. After arriving in Denver, she received a picture from Alfredo, capturing a tender moment of him and Lorenzo enjoying cartoons together on the couch before bedtime. It would become a cherished memory, forever preserved in time within the realm of her heart.

Around 4 am, she awoke to her phone blowing up with calls and messages flooding in. A frantic wave of concern and urgency from loved ones asked if she was alright. Trembling, trembling heart, she learned the unimaginable had occurred. The news hit like a nuclear bomb, obliterating the fabric of her existence. She grappled with the inconceivable, hoping against hope there had been a mistake. The uncertainty tormented her, fueling a desperate plea for answers that consumed Raquel with one sinister question: "Where is my son?"

As the devastating reality of the tragedy unfolded, Raquel was thrust into a realm of unfathomable pain and heartache. The collapse had mercilessly snatched away her beloved son and husband. She lost her entire world. In a matter of several seconds, the life she knew, the dreams she held, were instantly shattered. No words can capture the depths of a mother's anguish as she mourns the loss of her child.

Despite her agony, Raquel found the courage to vulnerably share her story and bare her soul in an emotionally charged interview: "Surviving Surfside: Year One" by investigative reporter Jim DeFede. It was conducted in May 2022, just weeks away from the first anniversary of the collapse. The timing of the interview made the subject more supersensitive.

"Yesterday was my anniversary with Alfredo. We would be 9 years together. Tomorrow is Lorenzo's birthday. He would turn 6."

Raquel's voice trembled with despair as she reminisced. She continued courteously as she gently looked down at two golden bracelets on her wrist right before tears streamed down her face:

"I wear this that says *strong for Alfredo* and *strong for Lorenzo*. And I try to keep strong… with the good memories that I have. But when I think of Lorenzo's birthday tomorrow, I feel very angry… because I only spent 5 years with my son. We dedicated every day of our lives to him since he was born, actually since pregnancy. We studied, researched, reflected, and discussed how to be good parents. How to raise a great child, man, and citizen. Lorenzo was extremely happy, healthy, smart, and loving… and the fact that I cannot celebrate his birthday with him tomorrow really makes me very angry. Very angry. It's the only thing that makes me really angry."

Mr. DeFede curiously responded, "Who are you angry at?" Raquel took one second to reach deep within herself before answering:

"I don't know who I am angry at because I don't know who to blame. I don't have those answers yet. I hope I do have one

74

day, and I cannot assume anything, but I am very angry for not being able to hold my son tomorrow and celebrate his life with him alive."

I'll never forget when I first met Raquel. It was a significant moment in my journey when I had the privilege of meeting Neil Handler and his incredible son, Jonah. The 4 of us gathered at a local pizza joint in Miami, brought together by our shared experiences of unfathomable tragedy. Neil and I had spoken on the phone previously, but I had never met any of them in person.

The truth is, I was nervous to meet the trio for the first time. Although we'd all drank from the same cup of suffering, our journeys through the aftermath were wildly different. We were united in our shared experience but carried different burdens that demanded different responses. For instance, Raquel's life abruptly collapsed without having been in the collapse itself. She not only lost the two most important people in her life but her home and personal belongings to remember them by. Jonah, on the other hand, had miraculously survived the collapse, but his survival came at a great cost. The physical injuries he sustained were likely permanent, and the burden of PTSD weighed heavily on his young shoulders, along with the devastating loss of his mom. As for Neil, he was forced to confront the harsh reality of helplessness as he and his sons suffered in every aspect of his being. I felt like the newcomer in their tight-knit group, similar to a new student walking into class in the middle of the school year. They'd already formed a powerful bond since the collapse.

From the moment we sat down, I was captivated by Raquel's ability to wear vulnerability like a shield. Time became irrelevant as I hung onto every word of her story, inviting us into her world. She spoke candidly of her internal struggles, questioning the purpose and meaning behind everyday actions. The simplest tasks, like, getting out of bed in the morning or going to work, felt empty without her husband and son. The loss of her home, both literally and figuratively, cast a heavy shadow over her spirit, making it difficult to stay motivated with daily routines. The shattered remnants of her former life had ultimately taken her sense of purpose that came with her role as a mother and wife. Her new home provided shelter, but it couldn't bring back the ones that made it home. Despite the sadness in her eyes from countless tears, there was a strength in her that commanded attention in an awe-inspiring way.

As the intensity of Raquel's agony settled within me, I couldn't help but absorb her heartache. As the hours slipped away, I realized I hadn't even placed my order before the restaurant began to close for the night. But it didn't matter. The stories that were shared, filled with transparency, empathy, raw heartbreak, tears, and sweet moments of laughter, were as if we'd known each other for years. Little did I know that it wasn't only my first meeting with Raquel, Neil, and Jonah, but it was also their first time meeting each other in person. The bond that quickly formed between us, despite the circumstances that brought us together, was undeniable. It felt like we'd been lifelong family friends.

I walked out cherishing two particular moments that left a lasting impression. They were beyond the shared tribulations we'd all endured. The first began when Jonah excused himself from the table to use the restroom. Raquel took the opportunity to express to Neil how blessed he was to still have his son by his side. When Jonah returned to his seat, Raquel playfully assured him that she'd always be there for him if his dad ever gave him a hard time. Although her words carried a lighthearted tone, there was an underlying serious, genuine desire to affirm Jonah wasn't alone in his suffering.

During that single interaction, the dynamics of their bond reflected the strength they cherished in each other. It stirred my emotions because, despite the immeasurable desolation of instantly losing her husband and son, Raquel still had the capacity to offer love, comfort, and support to Jonah in a maternal way. At the same time, you have a father and son, where the son deeply longs for his mother. Perhaps it was subconscious, but Neil and

Jonah represented the living embodiment of all that she had lost. Raquel, in turn, represented the nurturing, motherly figure that Jonah no longer had. It was a bittersweet dynamic, but they had each other to grieve, comfort, and strengthen one another. It was such a tender, warm-hearted, real-life Hallmark movie moment with all the feels.

The second moment was initially private, but Raquel later shared it publicly on Instagram. Raquel had originally planned to fly out to Colorado on June 24, 2021, but she stumbled upon a similar flight that was slightly cheaper. It seemed like a practical decision; to take an extra day with her mom and sister while saving some money. Little did she know that this seemingly insignificant choice would be a matter of life and death. In hindsight, Raquel could've waited to fly out with Alfredo and Lorenzo a couple of days later. But this decision played a significant role in sparing her from the devastating fate that awaited those who remained in Surfside. On the eve of Surfside's infamous first anniversary, Raquel shared a screenshot of her airline ticket on social media. Alongside the image, she added a caption that read, "The flight that saved my life on June 24th, 2021."

As we discussed in Chapter 4, memories can feel like an inescapable part of us. Like a shadow, no matter how much you try to distance yourself from it, there it is, looming its presence over your present. Just as it's a natural result of being in the presence of light, our past is a byproduct of living. But, in the same way, a shadow doesn't have substance; our past doesn't have the power to control our present unless we allow it to. When we give dominion to the shadows of our past, we harm ourselves. By acknowledging your past but not allowing it to overshadow your present, it makes space for healing. Creating space for healing isn't about erasing or forgetting your history. You have the power to redefine your relationship with the past by revealing how you're feeling, relieving through grieving, and now relinquishing your anguish.

Renowned author Lois Lowry eloquently portrayed the power of sharing memories. "The worst part of holding the memories is not the pain. It's the loneliness of it. Memories need to be shared." When we dare to share our burdens, something remarkable happens. The load becomes lighter, the pain lessens, and the loneliness dissipates. Sharing a burden helps to lessen that burden. This concept holds true not only for pain but also gratitude. Sharing gratitude increases gratitude. In the case of Raquel, Neil, and Jonah, I witnessed this transformative power firsthand. As they shared stories, their pain wasn't multiplied but instead diminished. It was as if the act of sharing their pain made room to fill the spaces that loneliness had occupied. Sharing each other's pain multiplied their love.

While many aspects of life may be beyond our control, one element we have the power to shape is our disposition. While your position in life may not feel manageable, disposition refers to your outlook, mood, and overall attitude despite your opposition. It's our disposition that determines how we respond to the circumstances that life throws our way. The position provides you with a clear view of the world as it is—the challenges, hardships, and injustices. However, disposition empowers you to see the world as you truly are, beyond the limitations of your circumstances. Even when you're not at fault for your position, releasing your pain is the key to taking charge of your disposition and empowering the prevailing attitude of your spirit. That's how you reclaim control over the narrative and bring meaning to it.

The idea of shaping your disposition might sound corny or cliché if you don't open up often, but you may be sabotaging yourself. Ignoring or neglecting pain only leads to prolonged suffering. Your decisions either direct you to deliverance or deviate toward destruction. There are pivotal moments when you must decide how to respond when you're wronged, betrayed, or crushed by injustice beyond your control. In the depths of despair, it's natural to feel a surge of anger and the burning desire for revenge. The pain inflicted upon you can tempt you to retaliate with vengeance.

Raquel's story is a powerful depiction of how life can present critical crossroads in the face of suffering. The power of passion lies not in the absence of suffering but in the way we harness and transform it into a force for good. If you're not willing to suffer for it, then by default, you're not passionate about it. It's through trials and hardships that you'll discover what you're truly willing to endure. Passion isn't a passive emotion, but it is a double-edged sword. Like fire, it's a powerful resource when harnessed properly, providing warmth and light. But if left unchecked, it becomes destructive, consuming everything in its path. It presents us with a fork in the road, offering two distinct paths that lead to vastly different destinations from the same experiences. The end of that road determines if you'll retaliate with resentment or be revitalized by restoration.

When passion is rooted in resentment, it becomes a destructive force. It fuels our anger and bitterness, keeping us locked in a cycle of negativity and grievance. A bitter heart assumes the position of a victim, allowing past grievances to paralyze your present while blinding you to the possibilities of healing and restoration. The deception of bitterness settles within the lie that surrendering to our outrage will bring relief. It deceives us into believing that nursing our fury, rehearsing our misery, cursing our circumstances, and dispersing our pain will somehow make us feel better. But it's a false promise that will rob you of joy and purpose.

On the other hand, when passion is filtered through restoration, it takes on a transformative power. It allows us to channel our pain into something meaningful, giving purpose to our suffering. It's through the storms of suffering that the dormant embers of passion are reignited, sparking a flame within us that is fueled by empathy. It's often those who have faced exceptional crushing and hardships that inspire us with their exceptional strength. Their empathy flows from their own experiences of suffering, enabling them to connect with others on a profound level. What sets them apart is their disposition to adversity. Instead of allowing bitterness and resentment to use them, they used the pain to drive them toward restoration and transformation.

An example of this transformation can be found in the story of Naomi, a woman who endured immense loss and suffering, that's recounted in the Old Testament book of Ruth. Naomi and her husband, Elimelek, left their homeland due to a severe famine, seeking a better life in a foreign land. Tragically, Naomi's husband passed away, and her two sons, who had married Moabite women, also died, leaving Naomi alone with her daughters-in-law, Orpah and Ruth. Overwhelmed by grief, Naomi decided to return to her homeland, where food had been replenished. Naomi encouraged Orpah and Ruth to remain in Moab to rebuild their lives and find new husbands. Orpah returned to her family, but Ruth stayed by Naomi's side for the journey home. However, the weight of her anguish had already taken a toll on her spirit, leaving her bitter and broken.

When they came to Bethlehem, the entire town was excited by their arrival. "Is it really Naomi?" the women asked. "Don't call me Naomi," she said. "Instead, call me Mara, for the Almighty has made life very bitter for me. I went away full, but the Lord has brought me home empty. Why call me Naomi when the Lord has caused me to suffer and the Almighty has sent such tragedy upon me?"[67]

Naomi's journey was riddled with misery, and understandably, that bitterness had taken hold of her heart. It's in Naomi's disposition that we see the battle between resentment and restoration. But her story was about to take a surprising turn. Through the devotion of her daughter-in-law, we witness a glimmer of hope. Ruth's empathy, born from her own experiences of suffering, enabled her to empathize with Naomi on a deep level.

Ruth's devotion to Naomi led her to work in the fields owned by Boaz, a relative of Naomi's late husband. Boaz, deeply moved by Ruth's character and actions, extended his generosity towards

Naomi and Ruth by going above and beyond to provide for their needs. He not only secured their financial stability by purchasing the land that belonged to Naomi's family on her behalf but also expressed his intentions to marry Ruth. Their hearts found healing, their financial stability and social status were regained, and their overall well-being was restored. In his book, "Single & Secure," Pastor Rich Wilkerson Jr. of VOUS Church elaborates even further on the pitfalls of bitterness.

All bitterness is premature. Why? Because, just like Naomi and Ruth, your story isn't over until your life is over. If you're still breathing, there's still hope. To be bitter is to pass judgment on past events. It means you label those things as wrong, bad, evil, hopeless, tragic-and final. And maybe they were terrible. I'm not minimizing what you might have suffered. But bitterness doesn't just recognize past hurt; it commemorates it. It builds a monument to it. It amplifies it. It drags it along with you. It allows the past to poison your present and sabotage your future. Remember, God turns mourning into dancing and tears into joy (Psalm 30:11). He did precisely that for these two women, and he can do it for you. It's all in his time, though. You don't follow a God who works just in seconds or minutes or days; you follow a God who works in seasons. There are ebbs and flows. The great writer C.S. Lewis calls them peaks and troughs, mountaintops, and valleys. God takes you from one mountaintop to the next mountaintop, but the only way to get to the next peak is to go through a valley. Just because you're in a valley doesn't mean you should feel abandoned, condemned, or afraid. It's only a season, and all seasons come to an end.[68]

In the end, Naomi's narrative is determined by her position, ultimately fueling her passion for resentment. Simultaneously, Ruth filtered her passion through the lens of her disposition, eliciting her faithfulness towards restoration. Her unwavering commitment to staying by Naomi's side demonstrated a disposition that transcended the bitterness that threatened to consume them both. Their story, once marked by anger and grief, became a testament to restoration and legacy. Little did they know that their lineage ultimately led to the birth of Jesus, the Savior whose arrival split the course of history in half. Ruth's decision to relinquish her sorrow and embrace a disposition rooted in love not only brought healing and restoration to her own life but also changed the trajectory of the world!

Just as their story became interwoven with a divine narrative of redemption and restoration, we, too, can rewrite our own stories. Forgiveness is the key that unlocks the chains of resentment, but it's so much deeper than setting your offender free. Forgiveness is the act of freeing the prisoner and realizing that the prisoner was you all along. The healing that accompanies forgiveness is directly linked to the extent to which we embrace this act of grace. The more resistant we are to forgive, the higher the ceiling on our healing.

The freedom we seek lies in the surrender we often avoid. It's by surrendering your grudges and anger that you create space for healing, restoration, and transformation. In a world that often glorifies holding grudges and seeking retribution, it may seem counterintuitive to suggest that surrendering our pain and resentment leads to freedom. However, it is precisely through the act of surrender that we create the space necessary for healing.

Imagine your heart as a container that holds your emotions, experiences, and pain. Just like any container, there's a limit to how much it can hold. When our hearts become filled with unresolved bitterness, there is no space left to receive healing or restoration. It becomes crucial, then, to hollow out that container, creating a void that can be filled with healing and restoration. Relinquishing our animosity isn't about denying or burying our emotions. Creating space for healing is a deliberate act of surrender. Just as we declutter a room by letting go of items that no longer serve us, we declutter our hearts by letting go of grievances that hinder our growth and rob us of joy. Your heart can't overflow with passion if it's bursting with bitterness. It's your responsibility to make room because releasing is a prerequisite to receiving. It's hard to receive gratitude while you are hoarding grievances.

Taking responsibility for your propensity is an integral part of the healing process. While you may not be at fault for the pain you've experienced, you are responsible for how to respond. The word "responsibility" itself alludes to "response-ability," emphasizing our ability to respond. Taking responsibility is acknowledging that you may not be at fault or liable for your situation; you're responsible for choosing how you respond. Bitterness may sway your heart to fixate on blaming those that inflicted your pain, but healing comes from focusing on personal response.

Blame seduces pain to remain. It lures you into the illusion that blame provides a solution when, in reality, it just marinates in the problem. The "blame game" merely assigns who's at fault or liable for an outcome, but it doesn't absolve you of responsibility. Liability and responsibility are two different things, and understanding the difference is essential for relinquishing your suffering. Liability is the legal or moral obligation of being held accountable for consequences. Responsibility is the opportunity to act independently and make decisions. While you may not be liable for the situation, you're always responsible for how you respond to it. The difference between liability and responsibility is obligation versus opportunity! Responsibility overpowers liability.

Imagine you just bought your dream car. As you're cruising through an intersection, a distracted, uninsured driver that's scrolling through social media crashes into your new ride. As a result of their negligence, you're injured. The other driver is to blame for the accident and should be held accountable. However, blaming them shouldn't be your main priority. You're still responsible for getting medical treatment and responding to the aftermath. For example, it's responsible to have liability coverage in your auto policy to help cover damages caused by the uninsured driver at fault. You hold the power of how you respond to problems outside of your control.

Hear me loud and clear! I am *not* saying that you're responsible for the misfortunes and tragedies that happen out of no fault of your own. For example, you're not responsible for monstrous category 5 hurricanes or meteoric earthquakes that obliterate entire cities and take countless lives. You're not responsible for suffering a devastating miscarriage of that precious baby you've prayed many years and tears for. It's not your fault that some bloodthirsty, deranged psychopath walked into a school, fully armed for war, to massacre innocent children. And you're not liable or responsible for a drunk driver killing your loved one in a hit-and-run. Nor am I liable, responsible, or at fault for my grandmother's building crumbling apart in the middle of the night. But here I am because I'm responsible for my response, just as you're responsible for yours.

You are *not* liable for something when it's *not* your fault. But you *are* always responsible for your response, even when it's *not* your fault. Blame points to the problem, but responsibility points to solutions. Responsibility goes beyond fault and focuses on the response. It's about taking ownership of your healing journey, regardless of who is to blame. The fault is never a valid justification to forfeit your responsibility of faithfulness to healing.

Here's a life hack: take your calling very seriously, but don't take yourself too seriously. If you stop laughing, you stop living. If you don't allow bitterness in, you'll keep laughing. It's worth trading bitterness for forgiveness. We live in a fallen, evil world that will try to drag your soul to the pits of hell while you're here on Earth! It starts with a broken heart. If bitterness gets the best of you, it's only a matter of time until you shrink your world down to a destination of isolation. A hardened heart will eventually contaminate your spirit with resentment. If it can harden, it can crack. Unexamined cracks tend to break. If it can break you, it can crush your spirit. Forgiveness softens your heart. Bitterness hardens your heart. But there's a sweet liberation to living with thick skin and a soft heart.

Remember, blame only assigns a name to your pain. Using your energy to name someone to blame won't bring peace. Blame only leads to bitterness and shame that resentment will claim. Will your response lead to your resentment or restoration? Will you allow bitterness to contain your pain and put a lid on your future? Or will you release resentment to make room for the promise of restoration?

So far, we've learned that revealing initiates healing. Relieving initiates grieving. Releasing precedes receiving. It's time to rename your pain.

CHAPTER 7

Reframe It:
Rename Your Pain

*Be merciful to me, Lord, for I am in trouble; my eyes are
tired from so much crying; I am completely worn out.*

Psalm 31:9 (GNT)

Sheltered In

As the time approached 4:00 a.m., those early hours of
Thursday morning were drenched in darkness, both in the
atmosphere and within the depths of our hearts. The night sky was
clear, but there was no clarity to be found. It was still Wednesday
night for my body, as if the day refused to let go. My emotions
were raw, confused, and turbulent. Thoughts ran wild through
my mind, desperately attempting to piece together the fragments
of my reality, each one attempting to unravel the mystery and
find meaning behind the demolition. Just half an hour earlier, the
presence of death and destruction left me distraught, so I sought
refuge from the chaos.

Guided by an instinctive need for peace, I made my way
toward the Solara Surfside Resort, the neighboring building
that had been evacuated. It stood directly across from where
my grandmother's balcony had once faced just 2 hours prior.
Nestling into a small corner beneath the entranceway, I sought

to still my racing thoughts and calm the storm in my mind. An unprecedented thought invaded, flooding it with doubt and fear. Could this building that's sheltering me collapse, too? My sense of security was shattered. Fear was making an all-out assault on my spirit.

In a state of weakness, where anxiety threatened to overpower me, I found myself redirecting my focus, not out of strength, but out of sheer desperation.

I had a desperate need for divine intervention. It's during times of weakness that God reveals His strength. In these moments, I've come to realize that God shows up the strongest. When faith becomes our only option, it becomes easier to fully surrender and trust in His power and provision. I made a choice to change my environment, creating a sacred space where I could seek God's peace and encounter a touch of heaven amid my personal hell.

Placing AirPods in my ears, I began to listen to a song on repeat called "Shelter In" that echoed the promises of God's provision and protection in times of trouble. As the melody filled my ears and the lyrics washed over me, its promises, inspired by Psalm 91, became a lifeline. I clung to them with all my might. The words ushered in my refuge, God's presence, as I poured out heartfelt prayers from the depths of my soul. All I could do was plead with God for a miracle through these words:

[Bridge]
I hear you say because you love me
I will rescue you; I'll deliver you
I hear you say because you call me
I will answer you; I'll fight for you
I hear you say, although one thousand may fall,
ten thousand more, I stand secure
I hear you say no harm will come to your life
I will satisfy, watch salvation rise

[Chorus]
I find refuge, In your love
You're my fortress
My God in whom I trust
I take shelter, in your name
Amazing grace, my hiding place
Amazing grace, my hiding place

—VOUS Worship

I couldn't help but be struck by the irony that the very home my grandmother took shelter in had become a devastating force rather than a refuge of protection. It was a powerful visible representation that placing our hope in anything in this world is ultimately futile. None of it lasts. Yet, in this heart-wrenching truth, a reassurance emerged that brought peace to my spirit. I felt a profound understanding that my grandmother's true shelter, her ultimate refuge, was not in the physical building that had crumbled but in the loving presence of God.

It was as if God's voice struck the depths of my soul, reminding me of His unwavering faithfulness by whispering, "My son, Kima loved me. If she's alive under that rubble, I'll deliver her because my presence is with her. If her body is under that rubble, but her soul is not, I've already delivered her into my presence. I'm her refuge and fortress. Either way, she's safe, sheltered in my presence with me. Do you trust me with either outcome?" The assurance settled deep within, reminding me that she was safe and secure and that He was in control. My perspective shift helped me surrender the outcome to God. I chose to trust in my belief that His love extends beyond the physical realm and into the eternal.

Panoramic Pandemonium

Having gained some composure, I rose from my makeshift sanctuary near the hotel entrance and made my way to where my family had gathered. As I walked, my thoughts were consumed by concern for my father. Although we were all suffering, he was suffering the most. Kima was like a second mother to me, but for my father, she was his last remaining parent, buried somewhere underneath a heap of carnage. My dad is a pillar of strength, a man whose composure rarely wavers. It takes a tremendous weight to break through his emotional armor. As we stood by him, his heart sank further into devastation with each passing moment, like watching ice cream melt away on a hot summer day. Witnessing my father break down in public was a sight we'd never seen before, and it tore at the fabric of our collective strength. Tears streamed down his face, and with each drop, our own tears flowed.

The sheer velocity of the collapse sent a staggering 14 million pounds crashing down in an instant. The impact created a powerful shockwave that sent personal belongings and fragments of lives spiraling in all directions, littering the surroundings. Mundane items and cherished mementos were thrown in disarray. Neckties, credit card bills, portfolio statements, shirts, certificates, documents, and pictures were scattered everywhere. It was a disorganized collage of personal histories torn apart.

Driven by a mix of curiosity and a desire to comprehend the full extent of the devastation, we ventured down the side of the Solara Surfside and looped around the back toward the pool deck for a closer look. In a state of both dread and awe, we locked in on the section of the tower that had crumbled to the ground. We were met with a stretched, unobstructed, panoramic view of a scene that seemed straight out of an apocalyptic nightmare. For the first time, the magnitude of the calamity was revealed to us on full display. It seemed as if a cataclysmic earthquake had struck, releasing a surge of lethal, seismic energy that tore through the very fabric of the building. Half of the infrastructure had been mercilessly ripped apart, leaving an avalanche of debris and ruin in its wake. It was there I took a picture, which is now the front cover of this book.

We cautiously made our way around the pool, drawn toward the area where we believed my grandmother's apartment once stood or whatever remnants were left. That's when my dad spotted her patio furniture mangled around the segments of her broken balcony. Although pulverized, they were instantly recognizable in plain sight. Unbeknownst to us, we were observing the top 6 stories of condominiums piled above ground. The lower half of the 12-story structure was buried, beyond visibility, in the parking garage. Kima's apartment was situated on the sixth floor, right in the center of the destruction. The idea of her whereabouts was downright sickening! How could she possibly be trapped beneath this?! The thought plunged me back into denial all over again. It felt too unbelievable to be reality. That feeling remains even now. The bone-chilling picture you see is our bizarre reality.

An array of red and blue lights splashed an eerie glow on the condemned tower. As we stood in the inferiority of existential terror, all we could do was weep in the wake of the emotional assassination. Positioned on the south side of the pool deck, we found ourselves in a grim front-row seat, silently observing the unfolding tragedy. We were so close but so far from her. He frantically called Kima's iPhone repeatedly, each ring representing a lifeline to the possibility of her survival (yes, my 92-year-old grandmother had a smartphone). It wasn't about the possibility of her answering the call. Any ring or vibration held the potential to shatter the silence and bring hope to our damaged hearts. If her cell phone could've survived, there was a chance she survived. With each passing call, memories curated a montage of cherished moments that intensified my heartache as I fixated on her smashed balcony.

Time For a Throwback

My mind transported me back to a lifetime filled with warmth and love. I could almost taste the mouthwatering, homemade Cuban lunches she lovingly prepared for our family, filling her living room with the timeless and enticing aromas of slow-cooked pot roasts, hearty chicken fracases, or pan-seared steaks. Like any nourishing grandmother, her secret ingredient was love. If I didn't eat more than 2 plates loaded with her delicious cuisine, she'd almost take personal offense. Like clockwork, Kima would ask in her thick Spanish accent, *Why are you not hungry?* Her bright smile radiated joy from seeing our satisfaction as we overindulged. No matter how old we were, even in my thirties, we were still growing grandchildren.

After our satisfying meals, we'd migrate to the balcony, where Kima stuffed us with her beloved cafe con leche and sweet desserts. The balcony was a sacred space where the dining experience seamlessly transitioned into moments of connection and heartfelt conversations. Whether it was just the two of us or our entire family, it was a gathering place for laughter and shared memories. Sometimes, she'd invite friends from her social circle to join us, adding even more warmth to the atmosphere. But the balcony held the most significance **to my dad** since he'd accompany her almost daily during his lunch breaks.

It felt like just yesterday that the sunlight would kiss her face from the reflective backdrop of tropical waves while the fresh sea breeze ruffled through her hair. Kima's excitement to share these special moments revealed her childlike enthusiasm. All she wanted was to be with us. Her heart overflowed with love and care every time we gathered on that balcony because our well-being was paramount to her own. And yet, I struggled to comprehend how those cherished memories in that very place had been reduced to a grisly actuality.

As a child, my grandparents lived on Di Lido Island, a residential neighborhood just minutes away from the Miami Beach Police Department. Due to my parents' busy work schedules, my dad would often drop off my siblings and I at our grandparents' house when we were out of school, and they had to go to work. In many ways, they were like my second parents, that had an equal hand in raising us.

Back in 1985, my grandparents, Joe and Hilda, began the process of buying a condo intended to be their future retirement home in Deerfield Beach, Florida. On August 25 of the same year, their daughter, Kathy, was in a terrible car accident when a pickup truck was involved in a head-on collision course with her vehicle. She was carried to Mount Sinai Medical Center, which is the same hospital I had just been born in 4 months prior. After weeks of Kathy remaining in a comatose state with little to no progress, the hospital filed suit to legally remove her from life support. The doctors and neurosurgeons made the case that her brain damage was permanent, with no possibility of regaining consciousness from a vegetative state. The attorney representing the hospital insensitively stated, "The parents are asking the staff of Mount Sinai to care for a corpse." He continued, "There is no hope in this case."

I can only imagine my grandfather's excruciating despair as he tearfully pled Judge Goderich not to give consent to the hospital to "execute" his daughter. In a spirit of hope, my grandpa begged the judge to grant more time for my aunt. He clung to the possibility of a miracle, citing the gospel accounts of Lazarus, who was brought back to life by Jesus. Judge Goderich ultimately ruled that, under Florida law, Mount Sinai had the power to take her off life support systems. That gave our family a 10-day waiting period to appeal to a higher court before they had the right to pull the plug. My grandfather, Joseph Noriega, boldly proclaimed, "The final decision will come from the final authority—God." Despite their tireless fight and steadfast faith, my grandparents faced the devastating loss of their beloved Kathy. The weight of their grief was crushing, leaving them broken and forever changed.

Through all of their suffering, they continued to press on. In a time of sudden tragic death and misery, my grandparents found a refreshing joy in the arrival of a new life—mine. Amongst tragedy, my existence represented a symbol of hope and new beginnings. Kima took all the tenderness, adoration, devotion, and love for her daughter from deep within the well of her heart and unleashed it toward me unapologetically. Throughout my life, she'd consistently remind me of my profound impact on hers, insisting, "You saved my life when you were born."

At first, I dismissed her words, unable to understand why she attributed such an implication to my birth. After all, I was a usual baby: I made a mess, cried, and loaded my diapers with explosive stink bombs. Over the years, the more she credited me with supposedly "saving her life," the more I'd brush it off. I'd think to myself, *Why does this woman keep telling me this nonsense?* Yet, until her last breath, my grandmother found every opportunity to remind me of the treasured place I held in her life, often becoming emotional in the process. It became a recurring theme, and admittedly, it sometimes felt borderline annoying. But deep down, I knew that her words were a testament to the bond we shared.

At the turn of the new millennium, my grandparents simplified their lives to embrace a new chapter. That's when the promise of condo living captured their interest again. More importantly, it was their second opportunity to fulfill the dream of purchasing a slice of beachfront heaven, which had been cast aside due to the gruesome loss of their daughter. In June of 2000, that dream finally materialized as they became the proud owners of unit 602 in Champlain Towers South. Their new home, with its breathtaking ocean view and nestled in the heart of the tower, symbolized a fresh start. Completely unaware of the fate that awaited the condo building 21 years later, they moved into what would become a death trap.

Message in the Mess

And yet, there we stood, confronting the shattered remnants of her balcony, a sinister reflection of our broken hearts. I longed for a moment to pour a drop of love into her from the boundless sea she'd poured into me. If only she could know how her love inspired me through my despair.

We aimlessly wandered, drifting like lifeless zombies. Eventually, we stumbled our way back to Collins Avenue, in the heart of the commotion. It was then that my father's foot stumbled upon something hidden. Beneath the layers of grainy dust, he discovered a rectangular object. Leaning down, he retrieved it from the ground, carefully blowing away the dust that clung to its surface.

As my father held the mysterious object in his hands, his face drained of color; a mix of astonishment and disbelief washed over his face. It was an envelope with an enchanting butterfly design delicately printed in the bottom left corner. And there, in careful handwriting, the name "Hilda" graced the front of the envelope. Without hesitation, my father tore open the envelope, his hands trembling with anticipation.

Inside, a surge of emotion overwhelmed us as we beheld the contents—a birthday card that had been lovingly given to my grandmother a mere two weeks prior. Each word on the card radiated warmth and affection, bearing the signatures of her dear friends from the prayer group. *Happy Birthday* wishes intertwined with heartfelt words of encouragement, a testament to the deep bond they shared.

In that awe-inspiring moment, we couldn't help but be struck by the sheer improbability of the encounter. Not only were butterflies printed on the envelope and card, but someone had also lovingly hand-drawn additional butterflies on the cover. Undeniably, it was a message in a mess.

Curiosity got the best of us as my sister Michelle, brother-in-law Joe, and I scoured the area for other buried treasures. I overheard Joe calling my father's name with a sense of excitement while holding 2 items. They were photographs, fragile relics of a time long gone. Dust particles clung to their surfaces; as if they were guardians of cherished memories waiting to be unveiled.

The first photograph depicted my grandparents, frozen in time, with my father as a child by their side. It evoked a flood of nostalgia, a glimpse into a bygone era filled with innocent laughter and shared joys. The second photo revealed a more recent chapter, capturing their radiant smiles during a tropical getaway. Seeing their happiness preserved in those images brought a bittersweet blend of warmth and sorrow. We knew these snapshots held profound meaning, but without closure, it was too soon to fully grasp their significance.

However, our journey through the remnants of my grandmother's apartment took an infuriating turn when we came upon an item that had once been securely housed there. It was a personalized certificate addressed to "The Noriega Family" from Kima's church, boldly displaying the words "God Bless This House" at the top. The irony of the situation struck me like a slap in the face, igniting a surge of rage within me. Reading those words felt like a sick joke! I felt an overwhelming urge to tear the paper into shreds and unleash a torrent of profanity toward the heavens. Thoughts raced through my mind, questioning the very notion of God's blessings. How could this be considered a blessing when it resulted in the crushing loss of my grandmother? How could God have allowed such a tragedy to occur? My trust felt betrayed.

Little did we know that it'd take 6 long days of relentless efforts to find Kima's body. That fateful Tuesday, June 29, 2021, she became the sole person who was recovered. Exactly 1 week later, our beloved Kima's memorial service was held on July 6, at her local church. It was the very place she'd met her prayer group that wrote the iconic birthday card. Hundreds showed up to pay their respects to Kima as my dad delivered his final words, entitled, "My Amazing Mom."

June 24th, 2021, was followed by a flood of emotions, unlike anything I've ever experienced before, although I have personally been impacted by tragic events in the past. Nothing even remotely close to this, though.

To make matters worse, feelings of guilt began to surface in just about every imaginable area, including the fact that her apartment was being sold, and she was finally getting ready to move in and live with us. Then with this tragedy, miracles started to occur soon after that we didn't even begin to process until later. While standing on that street corner, I happened to look down at an envelope by my foot. The envelope had my mom's name, "Hilda," handwritten on the front. Inside was a birthday card signed by a group of her friends, who had celebrated her 92nd birthday with her a week or so earlier. I believe that was a message from my mom to say goodbye and trust that she was fine. I'll refer to a few more miracles in a bit.

My mom was 92 going on 73. No one could believe that she was anywhere near her actual age. She was as sharp as a tack, always on the go, and as active as the energizer bunny. She was adored and loved by just about everyone she ever met, no matter how brief that encounter may have been. A perfect example of that was the dozen or so realtors who showed my mom's apartment to potential buyers. Almost all of them contacted our realtor, my daughter, to convey their condolences, some of them in tears and a few wanting to help by even offering to search through the rubble. That was the connection they made with my mom in just the few minutes they spent with her. A realtor actually asked my daughter after a showing if my mom "came with the sale of the condo.

Here is another miracle, one very interested couple with 2 children would have perished in that catastrophe if they had bought that apartment sooner. My mom did so instead, and that's the way she absolutely would have wanted it."

The eulogy captured the essence of Kima's life, but there's one compelling detail that's not included. Another miracle.

When the call came from the homicide detectives, we were instructed to gather at the Grand Beach Hotel without disclosing why. But we knew. Our family reunited for the second time that day, bracing ourselves for the worst. As we gathered in front of the reunification center, it was unfamiliar territory for us, even though many displaced residents and Surfside families found temporary refuge in the hotel. For vacationers, it was a tropical paradise. For displaced survivors, it was a temporary home. For the rest of the Surfside families, such as us, it signified a funeral home where we'd confront the harsh reality of death. How ironic. A family reunification center that became a hub where countless families would never reunite again.

Miracle in the Mess

They herded us upstairs like cattle to the slaughterhouse as we entered the living room of a lavish suite, complete with lush new furnishings, a full kitchen, panoramic beach views, and plenty of space. The contrast between its comforting ambiance and the impending news was almost deceiving. We were greeted by Miami Beach Police detectives in business attire. Their eyes reflected the weight of their duty, and their measured words were filled with empathy and sensitivity. And then, they confirmed what we'd dreaded, like a death blow to our already wounded souls.

Hilda Noriega was the 12th confirmed fatality among the many others whose fate had yet to be discovered.

My entire family erupted in tears, their grief pouring out like a torrential downpour. As whimpers filled the room, I felt numbed by a different kind of burden. During their collective mourning, I didn't shed a tear. In the days leading up to that moment, the weight of my responsibilities as the family's spokesperson had thrust me into the spotlight.

For as long as I can remember, my father, Chief Noriega, had a long history of somewhat effortlessly dealing with media relations. Earlier on in his career, he'd led the investigation for the manhunt for Gianni Versace's murder. He later worked his way through the ranks of the Miami Beach Police Department before taking on the role of a top cop as Police Chief. With my father's extensive experience in the public eye, it wasn't natural for the weight of communication to fall on my shoulders. Since he'd worked almost 30 years before retiring and eventually moving on to North Bay Village, he'd naturally be the one to handle our public affairs. But he couldn't. The enormity of the situation, the grief that consumed him, and the demands of the media were overwhelming. He didn't have the strength or composure to handle it, so he made the decision to bestow me with the honor of designated spokesperson for the Noriega family.

My life had become a whirlwind of media inquiries and interviews, keeping me preoccupied with responsibilities that overshadowed my sadness. It was a role I never anticipated or sought, but one I accepted out of a sense of duty and loyalty to my family. Suddenly, I was fielding media inquiries and conducting interviews while shouldering the weight of my family's public representation and my grandmother's legacy. My own personal feelings were secondary to the demands of the role.

Deep down, I didn't believe I deserved the right to mourn for her yet. It was a self-imposed punishment. My regret smoldered with rage deep in my bones. Self-condemnation consumed me, fueled by the knowledge that I'd missed what should've been my last shared family memory with Kima. Just a few days before her home crumbled, our family had gathered together to celebrate Father's Day. A part of me knew I shouldn't have gone on that trip once I realized it conflicted with the holiday. Although I contemplated canceling, I didn't. But I ultimately paid the price for it. Fury drove me, but I harnessed it into making atonement for my disgrace. I couldn't change the past, so I became fiercely devoted to honoring all that was left of Kima: her legacy.

Through the tears streaming down like a suffocating fog, the detectives patiently granted us space to process the emotional death blow they'd just delivered. They remained composed and stoic, as if they were responsible for holding our fragile emotions in their hands. In a tender gesture, a detective extended a brown paper bag toward my father. "We found these on your mother when we found her body. They were clenched in her hand on her chest. These belong to you now." ·

As soon as he left the room, we gathered around the mystery bag as if we had stumbled upon an ancient, buried treasure. The contents served as a bridge between the realm of the living and the realm of the departed. The tears subsided as curiosity got the best of us. My younger brother Stephen, a fellow first responder, had a pair of latex gloves on hand. With utmost reverence, he proceeded to delicately open the bag. He withdrew its contents, revealing a collection of 6 rosaries. These were the same rosaries that Kima carried with her everywhere, using them for prayer, especially before bedtime. It was such a full-circle moment! Allow me to share the meaning.

When a loved one passes away, their belongings become cherished keepsakes, serving as tangible reminders of their presence. Everything my grandmother owned was crushed to smithereens, no thanks to her forsaken building. Kima's priorities in life revolved around her faith, family, and friends. Consequently, each item we salvaged instantly became a priceless treasure, infused with newfound significance.

The birthday card she'd received not only carried a comforting message embodied by butterflies but exemplified the depth of her friendships. The 2 family photos became impassioned displays of the mighty love she had for us. As for the rosaries discovered tightly clasped in her hand, they were precious mementos that dramatically represented how her unwavering faith in Jesus formed the unshakable foundation of her life. All 3 revered icons felt like divine gifts, providing a tangible connection to her spirit and reassuring us that she found safety in God's refuge. They're lasting symbols that solidified her legacy, bringing us comfort during our grief.

It became clear to me that the presence of the "God Bless This House" certificate was not a cruel, cosmic joke. It was a testament to the power of God to bring transformation to a terrible situation. As Hilda Noriega fell asleep that night in prayer, her body fell to its demise. In that same breath, her soul was freed. She awakened in the full radiance, splendor, and majesty of the Heavenly Father. Although her remains were recovered, Kima's spirit was rescued. She experienced a resurrection, entering into a new and eternal existence of the triumph of life over death. This message in a mess transcended what initially seemed like a loss into a testament of legacy. It brought serenity to an obscenity.

Metamorphosis in the Mess

The end of her life on earth didn't mean the end of her soul. It was her metamorphosis, similar to a butterfly. Butterflies hold deep symbolism due to the breathtaking journey of their existence—a journey that parallels our own human experiences and resonates with our souls. Like the butterfly, you choose to either *go* through the change or *grow* through the change.

From the humble beginnings of an egg, a caterpillar commences the passage of a butterfly. As the caterpillar progresses through its life stages, it undergoes a mind-boggling mutation. With each passing day, it grows and undergoes a series of molts, shedding its old skin to make way for new growth. It squirms around, eating voraciously, driven by an innate desire to feed and fuel its future conversion. But the true marvel lies in the next stage, after retreating into a self-imposed solitude, encasing itself within a protective cocoon.

Inside this gloomy space, a mysterious makeover takes place, unseen by the outside world. Its body undergoes a complete restructuring as the cells dissolve into a fluid-like substance, reshaping and reforming into an entirely new being. Eventually, the cocoon splits open, unveiling a remarkable creature no longer called a caterpillar. It's renamed to a butterfly. Why the name change? This name change signifies not just a restructuring but a rebirth. The butterfly is a new creation that defies the laws of gravity, capable of soaring to new heights at unimaginable speeds in its previous form. Its metamorphosis is so miraculous that it borders on the realm of magic.

Butterflies symbolize renewed hope because they demonstrate that even a creepy crawler can emerge from its darkest and loneliest place with the confidence and expectation of transformation. And if they can do it, so can you.

The butterfly exemplifies the essence of transformation in its most radical form. Change and transformation are often misinterpreted as synonyms. *Transformation* is not merely a change in appearance but a comprehensive reorganization of your being. *Change* implies a temporary modification or a reversible alteration. Like changing clothes, change can be just a phase. When we say someone is going through a phase, we are implying that it won't last. We never say that someone is "transforming" clothes because that would imply permanence, and that would be kind of weird.

The Formation of Transformation

Renaming your pain is about *transformation*! It's not just about shedding old skin or adopting new behaviors; it's about undergoing a fundamental and permanent shift in your identity and way of being. Transformation is a complete metamorphosis from the inside out. Transformation empowers you to reach new destinations that your previous self was unequipped to sustain. You can change without transforming, but you can't transform without changing. Change is mandatory. Growth is optional. Transformation is forever.

If you've done any adulting lately, you know that change is not only guaranteed, it's mandatory. But transformation is optional. Scripture is clear about this in 2 Corinthians 4:16-18[126] *"Therefore we do not lose heart. Though outwardly we are wasting away, inwardly, we are being renewed day by day. For our light and momentary troubles are achieving for us an eternal glory that far outweighs them all. So we fix our eyes not on what is seen, but on what is unseen since what is seen is temporary, but what is unseen is eternal."* Change is an external action, while transformation is an internal process. Simply put, change is something you do, while transformation is who you become! Transformation begins with what is unseen. Your heart.

How do you not lose heart when your heart is broken? It begins with recognizing that your beliefs serve as the blueprint for your life. These underlying beliefs, deeply ingrained within us, shape our thoughts, emotions, and actions. To experience true transformation, you must first examine and challenge these underlying core beliefs because they're formed through the lens of your perspective. That dictates the choices we make, the actions we take, and the outcomes at stake.

Rename Your Perspective

The way you *perceive* is the way you *receive*. Perspective is your input that predetermines how you will receive the output! Reception doesn't alter perception, but your perception ultimately shapes your reception. Embracing a perspective shift can lead to a transformative shift in reception. That's why the wrong perspective can cost you a hefty price. NASA can tell you firsthand.

During NASA's manufacturing of the Hubble Space Telescope's primary mirror, a 2-foot metal rod was accidentally inserted upside-down in a measuring instrument, leading to a flaw that blurred the telescope's view. The error went unnoticed at the time, with the worker unaware of the mistake. The flaw, known as spherical aberration, caused a 1.3-millimeter spacing error, resulting in blurred images from the telescope. NASA officials attributed the error to technical mistakes made under pressure during the manufacturing process. To rectify the flaw, the wide-field planetary camera of the telescope was replaced during a space mission in 1993 for an additional $15 million cost.

Nothing was fundamentally wrong with the telescope outside of a small misalignment. Just like the Hubble Space Telescope resulted in a blurred grand perspective, our hearts can also become misaligned, distorting our perception of reality. Psalm 51:10 beautifully captures the essence of seeking a renewed perspective "God, create a pure heart in me, and renew a right attitude within me." Our hearts have the power to blur our perspective, leading us astray and causing us to perceive deception instead of truth. Just as the Hubble Space Telescope needed correction to regain its sharp vision, we, too, must allow God to recalibrate our hearts.

The flow of perception:

Perception -> Belief -> Faith -> Hope = Reception

Oftentimes, we find ourselves praying for God to change our external circumstances, unaware that He is working to transform our hearts from the inside out. When we rely solely on ourselves instead of God, we end up blinded by our limited sight. However, true transformation begins when we allow God to change our hearts and shift our internal perspective. It is not about waiting for God to align with our desires; rather, it is about aligning our hearts with His divine wisdom and guidance. It takes practice and intentionality to reframe your perspective. Sometimes, what you receive as deception is from misguided perception. It only takes a minor shift in perspective to transform our entire outlook on life.

Here's a practical example of perspective. It's a myth that you get stronger in the gym. When we engage in weightlifting exercises, we intentionally subject our muscles to stress and resistance. This process results in microscopic tears in the muscle fibers, temporarily weakening them. Although that is a fact, what is also a fact is if you were to use this as an excuse not to go to the gym, that would be from a blurred perspective that's not based on truth. It may seem counterintuitive, but it is through this intentional breakdown that the foundation for true strength is laid.

However, true growth and strengthening occur during the recovery period that follows. It is during this time that our muscles rebuild and repair themselves, becoming stronger and more resilient than before. To support this process, our bodies require adequate rest, proper nutrition, and hydration. The soreness is a sign of muscle recovery. Your growth is tested when you lift the weight again and can lift more reps and more weight. The paradox of strength lies in the understanding that true growth occurs during the recovery phase, not within the confines of the gym.

This is also true of your soul. You don't get stronger in the breaking; you get stronger through healing. But you must rename your pain to the promise attached to healing. What you see as heartbreak can be renamed to healing. What the caterpillar called dark and isolated, the butterfly called free and reborn. When your muscles become weak and fatigued, they are actually getting stronger and recovering. What we called Kima's death became her transformation.

Lasting transformation is not about behavior modification. Changing your behavior is not the answer to lasting transformation because your underlying beliefs will remain the same. Your beliefs determine your behavior, which is why behavior does not transform until your beliefs do. Changing behavior without transforming beliefs is like addressing the symptoms of a problem without addressing its root cause.

We must recognize that true growth does not occur within the confines of pain itself. Rather, it is through navigating and embracing the healing process that we find the strength to overcome and emerge stronger than before. Just as muscles repair and become more resilient, our souls can heal and grow in ways we may not have anticipated. The pain we experience is not an endpoint but a catalyst for transformation.

Wouldn't it be so much easier if we knew upfront how long we'll be lingering in a season of suffering? I wanted God to fast forward through the storm and show me calm. God's deliverance may come in different forms. Sometimes, He will guide us through the storm, providing strength and resilience to face each challenge. Other times, He may choose to deliver us from the storm, bringing an end to our pain and ushering us into a new season of healing and restoration.

There's a message in your mess because God promises the pain we experience is not an endpoint but a starting point. It is through facing the pain that we may find healing to rename it to our purpose. God promises that our pain is not in vain. In the book of Proverbs, it is written, "You can make many plans, but the LORD's purpose will prevail" (Proverbs 19:21). Our suffering is not meaningless; it has a purpose in the greater story of our lives.

Reveal it to recognize your Heartbreak. Relieve it to respond to your grief. Release it to relinquish your anguish. Reframe it to rename your pain.

Now it's time to renew your purpose, redeem your sorrow, and bring purpose to your pain.

CHAPTER 8

Renew It:
Redeem Your Sorrow

I am exhausted by sorrow, and weeping has shortened my life. I am weak from all my troubles; even my bones are wasting away.

Psalm 31:10 (GNT)

Edgar Gonzalez's Story

In 1976, Cuban Prime Minister Fidel Castro became president of the Council of State and Council of Ministers. A young couple, Maria and Jose Gonzalez, had just given birth to their firstborn child, Edgar. The evil regime held the new father, who was a physician, captive in prison. By the time Edgar was four years of age, their family had escaped the clutches of communist Cuba and made the journey to the land of opportunity, where they eventually settled in Miami. His mother, Maria, encouraged him to study law since it was a career she had always wanted to pursue, but the Cuban government did not allow her. Edgar knew that he had a duty to fulfill, and with that, he decided to study law, just as his mother had dreamed.[31]

At the age of 13 years old, Edgar met his childhood best friend, Rolando Moreno, on their high school football team—right after playing an intense scrimmage. During their senior year, Rolando endured a devastating injury that blew out his knee. After a week in the hospital and three surgeries, Edgar visited him every day. He also took Rolando to physical therapy appointments, which gave Edgar a prime opportunity to lovingly remind him, "Now, you will never beat me at basketball." Every guy knows you can't have a best-friend bromance without talking some smack!

Just weeks into recovery, Rolando got the worst news of his life. His father was killed in a car accident on the Julia Tuttle Causeway while driving over Miami's Biscayne Bay. He was so devastated that Edgar spent the night in his room so his best friend wouldn't suffer alone. After 3 days, Rolando wasn't able to get any shuteye. Not because he was sad but because Edgar snored too loudly. In a season when Rolando thought his life was over, it was Edgar who encouraged him to continue. Edgar lived the full manifestation of Proverbs 18:24, "A man of many companions may come to ruin, but there is a friend who sticks closer than a brother."[33]

Years later, Edgar encountered "one of the rarest of specimens in Miami: a blonde non-Latina" at Rolando's birthday party in 2002. That rare beauty was none other than his wife-to-be, Angela. However, Edgar had twice the love to give, as he also embraced Angela's daughter, Tayler, as his own.

By Moreno's own account, "Edgar embraced fatherhood from day one. He'd speak of Tayler not like his stepdaughter but as his own." Edgar and Angela were blessed with a second daughter when "a little angel by the name of Deven Marie Gonzalez was born."[34] Moreno continued, "After Deven was born, he never attended another dolphins game. Never played paintball with me. Or attended another concert. I've never seen a more devoted father to his children than Edgar Gonzalez. Every weekend was about Tayler and Deven and their extracurriculars." These heartfelt words were spoken in honor of Edgar's beautiful soul at his "celebration of life" service, held after his tragic passing in the Surfside Collapse.

5-Story Fall

That dreadful night, the Gonzalez family settled in at home late from a long day. Deven played volleyball at a high level and had just finished a workout, vertical training, private practice, and beach practice that evening. Edgar, Angela, and Deven decided to unwind with a pizza and movie night. It was Wednesday evening of June 23, 2021. After finishing a scary movie at 12:30 a.m., 16-year-old Deven didn't want to sleep alone that night, so she drifted off with her parents. Not even an hour later, a loud, thunderous rumble jolted Angela out of bed! Having no idea what was transpiring at the moment, her life-or-death motherly instincts instantly kicked in as she yanked her daughter out of bed, shrieking — *"RUN!!"*

In what seemed like a millisecond, Angela's adrenaline was pumping enough epinephrine-infused maternal superpowers through her body to frantically carry her dazed daughter the first few steps before Deven caught her footing. But it was too late. As they stumbled a few steps out of the bedroom, another colossal roar struck! It's not far-fetched that the initial rumble that awoke Angela was the deathblow of failing foundations giving out in the parking garage, which initiated a chain reaction. There was a minuscule snippet of a moment between the structural supports giving way down below and the colossal BOOMING roar of the building shattering all around them. They "lost their balance," but in reality, the floor caved in as they fell rearward.

Angela & Deven held one another for dear life as they free fell with the building 60 feet below. Angela landed on her back just before the collision of her daughter's body crashed on top of her. The impact sent Deven rolling down the rubble 20 feet away and left Angela with a big gash on her back, a shattered pelvis, a lacerated liver, and a lacerated bladder. After miraculously surviving the 5-story fall, Deven was still conscious. She removed a piece of concrete that landed on top of her left leg, realizing she'd suffered a compound fracture to her femur so severe that both ends of her snapped bone were protruding through her flesh! She was bleeding out. While in excruciating pain, Deven yanked out a metal rod caught in her hair and tried to get her leg to a less elevated level, minimizing blood loss. That's when she started screaming out for her mom, who was falling in and out of consciousness.

"This Could be it."

A heroic trio of Miami-Dade firefighters—Tyler Tomsic, Scott Walker, and Lieutenant Corie Jones, emerged on the scene, ready to face death. As they began climbing the unstable, 5-story mound of building remains, the warped lingering tower was still shedding debris. Furniture, air conditioning units, concrete blocks, and flooring were dangling freely. Walker stated, "This could be it," knowing full well that they could die from the dangerous conditions above, beneath, and beside them. Despite the dangerous environment, they proceeded valiantly with caution until they spotted a girl staring down in shock. She was covered in dust and blood. It was Deven. Once all 3 fire-rescue workers made their way to her, Deven infamously remarks, "I have a tournament this weekend; I play volleyball."

They began working on getting her out for medical attention, but Deven informed the firefighters they needed to save her mom. Since Angela wasn't in their line of sight, the first responders said that a search and rescue team would get to her. But Deven insisted they find her right away. She pointed them to where Angela was, roughly 15-20 feet above. Walker left the pack and located Angela as she was going in and out of consciousness. There were signs of internal bleeding and not much time to save her.

Meanwhile, Deven mounted Tomsic's back for a quasi-piggyback ride, where she held tight with her right arm and leg. Lt. Jones provided support to her mangled left leg as they made their way down the wreckage. Despite her throbbing agony while still bleeding, Deven only screamed one time through all that movement to save her life. Once they made it to safety, an ambulance was summoned before quickly returning to the ruins for Angela.

Angela's location was dangerously close to the landing zone of falling projectiles from the erect tower. They tried to get Angela to stand, but her body couldn't support any pressure on her shattered pelvis. It had been roughly 45 minutes since the collapse, and there was no time for negotiation. The threesome of fire-rescue workers encouraged her to fight through the pain. With all four lives lurking in the valley of the shadow of death, they mimicked what they had just done for Deven and piggybacked Angela between Tyler and Scott as they pioneered back down. About halfway, they discovered a rectangular piece of wood that resembled a tabletop or door. They were able to lift it out of the rubble and place Angela on top, carrying her the rest of the way on a makeshift stretcher. The three selfless, valiant warriors successfully rescued both Deven and Angela to safety before they were rushed off to the hospital for treatment.

Tayler arrived "home" to the devastation shortly after her mom and sister were taken to the emergency room. Tayler had been out that night and hadn't realized what she would be coming home to. As she gawked in horror at the sight, she burst into tears. That's when a police officer gave her the worst news imaginable—anybody that was in her wing of the building hadn't made it out. For a solid hour, Tayler wailed and screamed in mourning on the side of the road as she entertained the unfathomable nightmare of losing her family in an instant! Thankfully, her aunt called her with the good news that an ambulance had taken Deven to the hospital. Once Tayler arrived at the hospital, she learned that her mother was still alive and felt a wave of relief come over her.

Road To Recovery

Angela was in a coma for 5 days and came back to consciousness on her birthday. Although she was re-given the gift of life, her husband was still among the missing. Two excruciating weeks later, on July 8, his body was recovered. Edgar's "Celebration of Life" service was held on July 23, 2021, at Christ Fellowship Church. The service commenced with his favorite passage of scripture found in Joshua 1:9... *Have I not commanded you? Be strong and courageous. Do not be afraid; do not be discouraged, for the Lord your God will be with you wherever you go.* Angela, Deven, and Tayler honored him with loving, sweet, and heartfelt dedication.

Angela:

My husband was "my person." We complemented each other. We were perfect for each other. He had so much love for me, his daughters, and his family. Edgar's love language was acts of service. For the last 10 years, he's woken me up at 7 a.m. with a fresh cup of coffee and a kiss. Once a week, he'd wake me up even earlier to put gas in my car. He'd laugh because if I forgot to put gas, it wouldn't even occur to me to check the gas gauge. I will miss his hugs, his love, and his constant reassurance of God's love. He was an exceptional father and somehow understood how to survive in a house of three women! Finding the right words was something hard for him. But his bear hugs said enough for all his girls.[92]

Deven:

Sometimes describing Daddy in words is so hard because he was so amazing. I remember how passionate he was when I would go to his law firm after school—How he would start talking about politics, and we would go back and forth, or ease into his work with phone calls, feeling impressed with how smart he was. I remember the morning talks we had heading to school—about the world's problems, about school, about me, or just small talk. I remember his hugs. I will miss his hugs and the safety and warmth they provided, and how it felt so strong that nothing could penetrate it or break it.[92]

Tayler:

Once I moved out, he made a point to call and ask me how I was doing and remind me that he loved me. He would make sure we still had our daddy-daughter dates by having lunch with me even after I had moved out. One time he found out I was sad on Valentine's Day. He called and took me on a special daddy-daughter date. Daddy was a morning person; he'd sing the nerdiest songs or joke around until I was no longer cranky.[92]

Pastor Rick Blackwood followed up on Tayler's words with simple statements that held a profound message. "That's how you live a great story. You love and serve other people—Jesus first, and family right behind." Edgar's story was great because he lived each day with that idea in mind.

On December 16, which would have been their 17th anniversary, Angela took to Instagram to reveal her cherished final memory with her beloved.

"That night you reached over, Deven, grabbed my hand and said " I love you". Deven poked me as I wasn't paying attention and said, "Mom, Daddy said he loves you". I looked over at you, squeezed your hand and said "Sorry honey I didn't hear you, I love you too".....and then we all just fell asleep. Those were our last words to each other. I've thought of 1,000 things I wish I could have told you that night. But nothing will ever be more perfect than I Love You. Happy Anniversary My Love! I Love You. Today

would have been 17 years. Remembering us and the beautiful life we created together."

There's a big difference between FEELING like your world is collapsing versus when your world *has* collapsed. The Surfside Collapse was a literal outer manifestation of the devastation that occurs when our inner world is crushed, resulting in emotional injury. Of all the professions in the world, Angela understands this as a trauma therapist better than anyone.

In September 2022, she posted a hilarious reel on her Instagram page. It's a reaction video of her and Edgar sitting down, watching footage of their wedding. They were reliving the moment the bride and groom were about to seal the deal at the church altar with a kiss. The reel zooms in toward the tv, just as the newlyweds are pronounced husband and wife, where Angela goes in for a deep, shameless, wet kiss. As they're undoubtedly sharing a good, old-fashioned, passionate French kiss on screen, an explosion of laughter (probably Deven and Tayler) fills the family room—followed by, *"WE WERE IN CHURCH! WHOA!!"* The camera quickly zips to Angela, cringing in laughter while covering half her face in embarrassment, while Edgar grinned proudly behind her. Then the camera zips back to the tv just as the newlyweds unlock their lips. As much joy as you can feel from the love and laughter that was present in that short clip, her captions will sober you right up.

Missing my person, my best friend, my husband. Missing the laughter and closeness within our home. I realize the past few days haven't been "good days". I've only zombied through, disconnected in an effort to numb the pain. Grief can be so confusing. The very thing I need to heal is also what hurts the most. I allow myself to remember, and I'm heartbroken. I miss you. The loneliness without you is unbearable. I vividly see your smile and yearn to smell your scent. I miss how you'd look at me, and could still make me nervous. My mind knows you're gone, but my heart is passionately in love with you. Will this ever get easier?

I found strength today in my own journey as a trauma therapist. As I prayed for God to ease the pain, I was reminded of my own words to clients in the past, to numb pain means to numb it all, the love, joy, and laughter today. I remembered their courage to face pain, and now it's time to do the same.

Reminding myself-It's OK to not be OK! There's no expected grief timeline. Nothing has to happen or be wrong today; Im grieving all my losses. #SurfsideStrong

Broken Heart Syndrome

The same part of the brain that processes physical pain is the same part of the cerebellum that processes emotional pain. That's why the intensity of a broken heart is as real as the pain of a broken bone. When you go through a particularly traumatic experience, your body produces protein compounds and hormones, such as adrenaline, that are meant to help your body cope with stressful events. The massive hits of adrenaline can cause smaller arteries to narrow, resulting in a decreased blood supply that overwhelms your physical heart muscle. The medical term for broken heart syndrome is *stress-induced cardiomyopathy*. That means the loss of a loved one, a divorce, betrayal, abandonment, breakup, or other traumatic events can literally break your heart and put you in the hospital for treatment.

Although symptoms of this physical condition can be treated, no hospital treats the source of these ailments within our soul that torment the spirit. There are so many ways to go through internal crushing that is not seen. Yet, none of us can escape it. I believe that many people who are suffering in their soul are misdiagnosed—or worse, undiagnosed, with a broken heart when the underlying condition is "internal bleeding" of a crushed spirit. When Angela's pelvis was smashed and bleeding internally, she couldn't just walk it off and get some rest. But more often than not, that's exactly how we respond to the pain of emotional injury because there are no 911 calls for your heart. Some battles are not violent. They're silent. Your body can feel emotional pain just as intensely as physical pain. However, what if we treat emotional wounds the same way we treat physical wounds?

When you go into a season of crushing, you must decide to come out of it. Ernest Hemingway has a famous quote that says, *"The world breaks everyone, and afterward, many are strong at the broken places. But those that will not break, it kills."* Yes, the world breaks everyone in one way or another, but it's not always the case that brokenness automatically leads to strength. Some people are crushed by their pain and never recover. However, a more accurate statement is, "The world breaks everyone, and afterward, many are strong in the healed places that were once broken places. But those that will not heal after breaking, it collapses and crushes." That's why you must face the pain that broke you. True perseverance comes not from simply enduring our pain but from actively pursuing healing and restoration. But how can you be redeemed once the damage is already done and the pain has spread like wildfire?

Faith Forged by Fire

Just as Jonah, Angela, and Deven inexplicably survived the Surfside Collapse, in ancient times, there lived three honorable, young Jewish men who had a near-death experience. During the reign of King Nebuchadnezzar of Babylon in 587 B.C., he erected a 90-foot golden statue that required all people of all ranks and status to worship it. Refusal to obey this decree would result in being thrown into a blazing furnace. The king's intention may have been to project himself as a deity to be worshipped. After all, humanity has a long history of worshipping pagan gods, the most common false god being the pride of our ego. Tim Keller said, *"If your God never disagrees with you, you might be worshipping an idealized version of yourself."*[96]

Despite their high positions and the risk of being betrayed by their jealous colleagues, they bravely stood up to the king and refused to worship the golden statue. The three Hebrews, known by their Babylonian names, Shadrach, Meshach, and Abednego, only worshipped the one true God of Israel. They were highly respected officials in Babylon but were betrayed by jealous executives hoping to get rid of them. Despite the consequences, the trio stood firm in their faith. They boldly stood up to the king and refused to worship the golden statue.

Nebuchadnezzar, filled with rage, ordered the furnace to be heated seven times hotter than usual and had the 3 men thrown into it. However, Shadrach, Meshach, and Abednego stood firm in their faith, declaring that God could rescue them from the furnace, but even if He did not, they wouldn't serve the king's gods. The flames were so intense that the soldiers who threw them in were killed. However, Shadrach, Meshach, and Abednego were miraculously saved and unharmed by the fire.

Nebuchadnezzar was astonished to see that they were walking amongst the flames unharmed, and he even saw a fourth person with them who appeared to be a "son of the gods." He called for them to come out of the furnace, and when they did, it was clear that not a hair on their heads was singed, and their robes were unaffected by the fire. Amazed by the sight, the king called out to them to step out. When they emerged from the fire unscathed, everyone present, including the prefects, governors, and the king's advisers, saw the fire didn't affect them. They were completely unharmed. Nebuchadnezzar praised the God of Shadrach, Meshach, and Abednego, acknowledging that they'd risked their lives rather than serve or worship any god except their own.

The power of redemption in this story is truly remarkable. Life can be like a blazing furnace at times. There are seasons in our lives when the situation is 7 times hotter than anything we have ever faced before, where the fires of life may consume us entirely, leaving us with no hope or way out. Scripture doesn't downplay the severity of a situation, but it also does not downplay God's power to redeem. They had more hope in their rescue than the heat of the fire.

But as the story of Shadrach, Meshach, and Abednego shows, the presence of a fire in our lives does not mean an absence of God's presence. God didn't just rescue them from the fire; He rescued them *in* the fire. Rescue is not always God removing you before the fire; instead, it's His presence with you in the fire. The story demonstrates God's ability to rescue you, even after you feel that it's too late. It shows that redemption is possible even in seemingly impossible circumstances.

Renewed by Redemption

Redemption is a picture of God's ability to rescue us, even after we feel that it's too late. The story of Shadrach, Meshach, and Abednego shows us that we can have faith and hope amid the most difficult circumstances. It reminds us that God can rescue us from the fires of life and that we can emerge stronger and more resilient as a result. No matter how hopeless our situation may seem, God's power to redeem is always present. We need to have faith and trust in His ability to rescue us. It's through God's purpose that we begin to understand the unique calling He has placed on our lives.

In the previous chapter, we explored the power of perspective in leading to our transformation. Redemption trades the problem for the promise of purpose and, in doing so, prompts impassioned action. It's in the promise of God that He can bring the good out of anything, even pain, if we trust Him. My life verse is anchored in Romans 8:28, *"And we know that God causes everything to work together for the good of those who love God and are called according to his purpose for them."* I filter every situation through it, especially the bad ones. However, it's important to see the true meaning behind this verse since it's often misquoted and misunderstood.

Romans 8:28 doesn't claim that all things that happen to us are inherently good. Atrocities such as disease, racism, starvation, genocide, rape, divorce, suicide, hate crimes, mass shootings, war, and disasters, like the Surfside Collapse, are not good. It also doesn't guarantee that every story will have a happy ending. Not every injustice is corrected, and not every pain is removed. Although God allows these things to happen because of free will, He doesn't deliberately cause them to happen.[128]

When sorrow attempts to overpower our spirit, we have a choice: to run to God or to run from Him. God promises that He not only possesses the power to bring forth good from any situation but also to produce joy from our painful experiences if we place our trust in Him. The key to discovering purpose in our pain lies in seeking His purpose and aligning ourselves with it. In doing so, we can find meaning, benefit, and even joy in our suffering.

To be clear, joy is not cheap. Each tear shed in sorrow becomes a seed that will be redeemed for a harvest of joy. That's not a cliche; it's a promise. The Passion Translation (TPT) expresses this pledge in Psalm 126:5-6, *"Those who sow their tears as seeds will reap a harvest with joyful shouts of glee. They may weep as they go out carrying their seed to sow, but they will return with joyful laughter and shouting with gladness as they bring back armloads of blessing and a harvest overflowing!"* Joy is not a fleeting or superficial emotion. Rather, it's a deep-seated and profound state of being that transcends our circumstances.

Have you considered those who are most on fire have gone through the most heat? It's through the refining fire of adversity that your character is shaped, faith is deepened, and purpose is unveiled. Redemption isn't just a one-time event but a continuous process that requires faith, trust, and perseverance. It isn't always a straightforward process, either. Redemption may not always come in the form of a rescue from the flames. Instead, it may be a refining process of transformation and growth that occurs during our struggles. It's the process of being rescued in the trials by fire rather than being rescued from them. I can think of no greater example of redemption and restoration than Deven Gonzalez.

CHAPTER 9

Restore It:
Rescue Your Spirit

He heals the broken-hearted and bandages their wounds.
Psalm 147:3

Scuba Diving Story

When I was a teen, I worked up the courage to go scuba diving on a family vacation, where we explored a sunken ship 60 feet below. One of my biggest fears has been the deep abyss of the ocean. After jumping into the water, I'll never forget the shiver that tingled up my spine as I gazed down at what looked like the Titanic a mile beneath my dangling flippers. It made me feel uneasy and anxious. Once we made it down to the sunken ship, large square-shaped man-made holes were conveniently carved out of its body for scuba divers to seamlessly glide through.

While swimming through one of the areas, I accidentally kicked the top off of a metal object, causing it to slash cleanly through my fin and into the back of my heel. As I squirmed in pain, panic overcame me as I witnessed my blood clouding the water. Desperately, I rushed to the surface in search of medical assistance, and a tour guide promptly guided me onto the boat. It became apparent that there was a combination of black debris and rusty metal shards caked into my nasty cut. The grime in my bloody gash prevented medics from stitching me up. At first, glance, avoiding stitches seemed like a victory until they had to clean my wound manually. The pain I experienced was not from the initial cut on the back of my foot, but rather from the intense scrubbing of my raw wound, like scrubbing a dirty pan in the kitchen sink.

The Promise of Process

As much as I detested the process, I understood that the scrubbing was a necessary first step toward my healing. The alternative would have been a certain infection, prolonged healing, prolonged pain, and potential complications in the future. If you're anything like me, you may have wished for a sprinkle of magical fairy dust that could instantly relieve the burden of grief. However, just like everything else in life, healing is a gradual process. Our human nature tends to seek pleasure while avoiding pain.

It would be fantastic if we could go to the gym just once and achieve our dream body. Imagine eating a couple of kale salads with chicken and instantly becoming ripped. If that were the case, the inverse consequence would also hold. Would you want to eat just one Twinkie that makes you obese? Would you want to lose all your gains after missing the gym for a day? Do you see the dilemma? We all want the promise without having to go through the process. Yet, deep down, we understand there can be no victory without adversity, no testimony without a test, no promotion without devotion, no triumph without trials, and certainly no glory without a story.

Deven's story isn't just about surviving against all odds but achieving a remarkable triumph through restoration. Despite undergoing multiple leg surgeries, her journey to recovery was far from over. Previously an active athlete devoted to training, conditioning, and practicing volleyball, her injuries left her temporarily bedridden. To regain strength, she had to undergo many months of physical therapy, as her muscles had deteriorated from being immobile. Surgery resets and repairs the bones. Physical therapy restores and regenerates the muscles.

The healing process required intentional effort and hard work, and Deven was committed to turning her setback into a setup for a comeback. However, she didn't go through the journey alone. She had the guidance and support of Dr. Kelly Terry, a Certified Strength and Conditioning Specialist, and Coach Dave Palm, a five-time National Volleyball League pro tour titleholder and 2015 MVP award winner. Their expertise not only helped restore Deven's body but restored her belief in herself. Almost a year after her injuries, Deven posted an inspiring video update on social media, describing her progress through the pain as she practiced beach volleyball on June 14, 2022:

It's hard to push yourself when you feel the weight of the world on your shoulders. My mind wants to step faster and play harder, but my body is not what it used to be; it's weaker and slower. Today I just couldn't get under that ball as fast as I wanted to. I'm learning to be kind to myself and accept that some days I'm stronger than others. And even on those weak days, that doesn't stop me from getting up and going to practice. I love you, Daddy, today was a hard day, and all I wanted was you. I miss you always and forever. Thank you, Coach Dave, for pulling me through today's practice. You have continually pushed me and believed in me since the beginning of my recovery; I'm so thankful for that.[61]

Deven's wisdom is truly impressive, and her choice of words when contrasting pushing versus pulling is particularly noteworthy. She harnesses her father's love and coach's support to "pull" her through tougher days when she doesn't have the strength to "push" herself. She completes this thought loop by thanking Coach Dave for "pushing" her. It's clever how she understands that her coach pulls her to help her push herself, as this contrast is profound. While you can "push" someone up or down, you can only "pull" someone up. When you have a vision attached to a compelling purpose, you don't have to "push" your vision. Your vision pulls you. Good coaches like Deven's get the best out of their players because they pull them up! They bring out the best in their players because they pull them up.

Her caption served as a prelude to two of the most challenging days she would encounter during the first year of her post-collapse life. Merely five days later, she faced her first Father's Day without her dad. On June 19, 2022, Deven's heartfelt tribute to her hero was captured in a beautifully curated TikTok. Through her words and in the video, you can sense Edgar's tender-hearted and irreplaceable presence:

Happy Father's Day, Daddy. I miss you so much words can't describe the pain in my heart. I would give anything for one more day with you. I want one more bear hug, one more forehead kiss, one more morning lecture from you, and I wish I had one more tournament with you. I miss you doing your dog bark for every kill I got, you getting me breakfast every morning tournament, and especially you giving me a thumbs up in between plays. I still don't think it's fair, and you not being here is a complete sham, but I know you would be saying, "god has a plan for us all, and your plan is the greatest of them all" I love you with every fiber of my being. You were the Goose to my Maverick dad; I love you forever.[62]

The Surfside Condo Collapse impacted every family differently, and each holiday served as a painful reminder of the loved ones lost. As the first anniversary approached, the countdown began, and the weight of the impending date hung heavy on everyone's hearts. There was no escaping the grief that came with it. Deven chose to share her journey of recovery and remembrance through a series of photos on Instagram. The photos chronicled her journey from being bedridden and bandaged in a hospital bed to undergoing physiotherapy, training for volleyball, and finally, visiting the memorial site. Her emotional caption captured the profound impact that the tragedy had on her and the community:

It's crazy to think this was me a year ago. A year ago, my world fell apart in a matter of moments. I suffered injuries I can't even begin to describe and was filled with so much sorrow, pain, anger, and fear. I was confused about why this happened to me and what I did to deserve it. My mother didn't deserve this; I didn't; my sister didn't; my dad didn't, and as well as the 98 lives lost didn't deserve this. My heart is filled with so much grief, even today, as it was the night I woke up in that rubble. People don't get to see that side of me. However, you do see one thing. Progress and healing. These photos show the progression I had from June 24th to right now currently, and all I can say is, "Wow, I have come so far, and I am so proud of myself," and I know my mom and sister are, too and I'm so proud of them. Daddy, I miss you so much. It will never be fair towards you or us. You are supposed to be here with us, celebrating that we survived, but you aren't. I will always have a gap in my heart; nothing can fill that used to be yours. I know you are watching me, and you are just waiting to give me that bear hug again and scratch your peach fuzz against my face, and I would always complain about it. We miss you, and we love you. Always and forever your Goose to your maverick deven[63]

The captions in Deven's story provide a beautiful progression that tells a full-circle narrative of her restoration. When Deven suffered the excruciating pain of a compound fracture, the most significant priority was to stop the bleeding. Deep wounds are a double threat because they can cause large amounts of blood loss and increase the risk of infection. The first step to healing is to stop the bleeding by applying intentional pressure. Secondly, the wounded area needs to be disinfected. If an infection occurs, it can cause serious ailments, such as cellulitis, that prevent healing. Then, the bone, or bones, needs to be set back in place. In this case, a surgeon would reallocate each fractured bone back to a normal position, keeping them in place with the help of pins, rods, screws, and plates. Lastly, the bone is bound up in a cast for weeks or months.[44]

Even though you can't see or feel it, the new tissue gradually strengthens as it undergoes calcification and transforms into strong, healthy bone over months[45]. The process of healing a broken bone can teach us valuable life lessons about compound fractures and the three-stage process of restoration.

Stage 1: Inflammation

The inflammation stage is characterized by swelling, redness, and pain after an injury. The body's immune system rushes cells to the wound to begin repairing the damage. This can be compared to the immediate reaction we often have in the face of adversity or trauma—we may feel overwhelmed, scared, or angry. Just as our body responds swiftly to an injury, we cannot ignore the problem or hope that it will go away on its own. However, just like the body's immune response, this initial reaction is necessary for healing to begin.

Stage 2: Repair

During the repair stage, one must be patient and remain faithful to the body's ability to heal itself without seeing immediate results. The regenerating tissue is soft and fragile at first, which is why it needs the protection of a cast. Just like a broken bone needs to be bound for months, we need to be patient and allow time for healing to occur in our lives. This prompts us to slow down for self-care. We may need to seek support and give ourselves grace, just as we would for a broken bone. Remember, healing takes time, and rushing the process can delay healing.

Stage 3: Remodeling

The final stage is remodeling, which is where the real transformation occurs. As the body calcifies new bone tissue, the bone becomes sturdier and thicker than before until it's made whole. Think of this as a metaphor for how we can emerge from debilitating experiences stronger and more resilient than we were before. It may take longer than we expect for emotional wounds to heal. We're capable of rebuilding from even the most severe injuries and setbacks. Remodeling doesn't just take place within our bodies but also within our souls. The beauty is we won't be the same person we were before, but we can emerge stronger.[45]

Restoration is the ultimate goal of the healing process, whether it's a broken bone or an emotional wound. It's the process of returning to a state of wholeness, but it is important to note that it is not the same as returning to the way things were before the injury occurred. The healing process transforms us, and restoration can mean something different than simply going back to the way things were. We can use what we've learned to help others going through similar struggles and to live more purposeful lives.

Through the 5 steps to healing outlined in the book, Deven was able to overcome her pain and live a restored life.

The first requisite in this process is: *Reveal It: Recognize Your Heartbreak.* Deven's injury was so traumatic that she had to recognize the mental, emotional, and physical burden of her world falling apart. She was honest with herself about the range of emotions she felt, including sorrow, pain, anger, fear, and confusion. However, she didn't stop there and moved on to address her pain.

The second step is: *Relieve It: Respond to Your Grief.* Deven didn't allow herself to remain stagnant or isolated in her suffering. Instead, she took full responsibility for her healing. Deven also recognized the response of support and encouragement from her mom and sister, further fueling her journey. Just as Deven embraced her responsibility for healing, we, too, can seek out resources, support, and tools to alleviate our pain. But she didn't settle for temporary relief of grief. She was in it for full restoration. After addressing her pain, she began the process of surrendering.

Thirdly, *Release It: Relinquish Your Anguish.* Deven surrendered to the care of first responders, doctors, therapists, trainers, coaches, her volleyball team, and, above all, her family. Not just once for relief, but repeatedly, for as long as it took. The impact of the supportive community of "responders" she formed is so profound that Deven wrote a heartfelt tribute of gratitude, which comes later in this chapter. Their unwavering encouragement reminded her to show kindness to herself and embrace the process. Despite her "mind wanting to step faster and play harder while her body was weaker and slower," she remained committed to healing. Even on her weakest days, she got up and recommitted to her recovery and renamed her pain.

The fourth step is *Reframe It: Rename Your Pain.* This requisite is about reframing the situation through a new lens and taking ownership of your perspective. Deven exemplified this by renaming her pain from "pain and grief" to "progress and healing." Despite being a victim of a tragic event, she refuses to identify as such. Instead, she embraces her identity as a victor! Renaming your pain from wounds to scars isn't about forgetting the past. It's about recognizing that your pain is a part of you, but it doesn't define you. It's about writing the story of your future with hope rather than being stuck in despair. Deven's final step to restoration was to draw purpose from her pain.

The last requisite is: *Renew It: Redeem Your Sorrow.* The ultimate reward of redemption is restoration. It extracts purpose from the pain by redeeming tears for joy, heartbreak for healing, and suffering for passion. When you're no longer wounded, your scars tell a story of strength that helps others. Deven discovered purpose in her pain by honoring her father's legacy. She held onto her fathers' words, "God has a plan for us all, and your plan is the greatest of them all." Healing is about you; purpose is about others. By honoring her father's legacy, placing trust in God's plan, and drawing strength from her family, Deven found meaning and purpose, despite the immense pain she overcame.

Sweet Redemption

That's why I was beyond ecstatic when Angela extended a personal invitation to Deven's senior night at Miami High on Oct. 10, 2022. It was a special occasion, as Deven would be honored while playing her first official volleyball game since the tragic night of the collapse. Being part of the close-knit inner circle, including her mom, sister, Edgar's parents, coaches, trainers, therapists, and other members of the Surfside family, like Raquel Oliveira, made me feel like a distinguished guest of honor.

It was humbling to have a front-row seat, witnessing a defining moment in Deven's life. Defining moments are rich in emotion because they're typically comprised of great mountaintops, deep valleys, and major pivots. I believe that Deven was experiencing all three of these elements on that remarkable night.

As Deven played her heart out, she was acutely aware that her mind envisioned a level of performance that her body couldn't fully deliver. She deeply felt the absence of her father, longing for his presence and the cheers he should've been there to offer. Yet, it was also a pinnacle moment, serving as a poignant reminder that she'd been granted a second chance at life and a second chance to bring all her healing progress, hard work, and passion back onto the volleyball court. She played with pride, knowing how proud her father would have been, while her mother and sister cheered from the bleachers, surrounded by loved ones who believed in her.

It was also a pivotal point as she confronted the limitations imposed by her post-collapse body, while her senior night marked a substantial transition into the next chapter of her life—a chapter that her amazing father wouldn't physically be present for. As her team secured victory, an overwhelming wave of emotions flooded over her. Tears streamed down her face as the conflicting forces of triumph and defeat clashed within.

It was the moment her world of grief and pain collided with the opposing world of progress and healing. Edgar, the heart of her inspiration, couldn't be there to cheer her on like the rest of us. The game itself, driven by her love and passion, faced a barrier as her body didn't perform to the potential she envisioned. It felt as though the same love that propelled her progress also left a void in her heart. Deven found herself torn between mourning the distance she'd fallen from her previous life before the collapse and celebrating the remarkable ascent from the depths of despair. The anguish of missing her beloved dad, who would've been so proud of her, added to the complexity of it all.

Gain Through Pain

Deven's heart was broken. But her spirit was not crushed. I know this, not because she told me, but because she didn't pull herself out of the game. She didn't give up. Once the injury healed, she still played, although she still hurt. Being healed doesn't mean there's no more pain; it means there's no more injury! She demonstrated that being healed does not guarantee a pain-free existence but rather a state where the injury no longer controls or limits her abilities. It signifies a transformation that goes beyond physical healing, encompassing emotional, mental, and spiritual restoration. Deven's journey surrounds all these aspects, reflecting a profound transformation and a victorious spirit.

By embracing her pain and persevering through the healing process, she not only healed her wounds but also nurtured her spirit. Deven bears a large scar on her left thigh, a reminder that she not only endured the crushing experience but emerged from it. And so can you if you dare to redeem grief and pain for a scar of healing and restoration. Often, it is the pressure of breaking that pours out the provision of blessing if we allow it.

The Burden in Blessing

It's daunting that sharp pain can still reside in the very place that has healed. In *The Dark Knight Trilogy*, there's a powerful message that what we truly fear lies within ourselves. To conquer fear, we must become fear. Lean into it. The presence of a burden doesn't diminish the blessing that's attached. Just as a burden may feel heavy, it's often through carrying that burden that you discover purpose in the very thing you avoided.

The great American abolitionist Frederick Douglass said it well: *"If there is no struggle, there is no progress. Those who profess to favor freedom and yet depreciate agitation are men who want crops without plowing up the ground. They want rain without thunder and lightning. They want the ocean without the awful roar of its many waters. This struggle may be a moral one, or it may be a physical one, or it may be both moral and physical, but it must be a struggle. Power concedes nothing without a demand. It never did, and it never will."*[94]

Blessing can accompany the weight of fear because it has a heavier burden:

- The heavier the weight, the stronger your muscles grow.
- The farther back you pull the bow, the further and faster the arrow will fly.
- The more time a toddler falls, the faster they learn to walk.
- The darker the night, the brighter the stars glow.
- The better a plant is pruned, the more fruitful it becomes.
- The deeper you dig a foundation, the more stable and secure the building.
- The hotter the fire, the purer the gold.
- The higher the mountain, the more breathtaking the view from the top.
- The more failures faced, the sweeter the victory
- The harder the test, the better the testimony.
- The greater the crushing, the greater your calling.

Proverbs 24:16 says, *"For a righteous person falls seven times and rises again, But the wicked stumble in time of disaster."* This challenges our misconception of failure. Falling is not the problem; staying down is. Only the dead stay buried. In contrast, we plant something alive that is meant to grow and flourish, transforming into its purpose. Yet, beneath the surface, something incredible is happening. The seed is transforming, taking root, and preparing to sprout new life.

Similarly, there are moments when we may feel buried, obscured, or unseen. Those are the times when significant growth and transformation take place within us. To truly embrace the power of transformation, we must refuse to have funerals for things that are planted. The idea that even the most undesirable and unpleasant circumstances can serve a greater purpose in our lives isn't a new concept.

Funny enough, cultivating productive crops takes manure. Stool serves as a rich source of nutrients for the soil, creating fertile ground for planting new seeds. "Crappy" situations help break down our pride and false beliefs that hold us back, allowing us to cultivate healthier soil within our hearts. Drawing purpose from pain is about helping others plant seeds of new life. And planted seeds rise! Everyone falls, but not everyone rises. Like Deven, you can rise.

The journey Deven experienced is a remarkable example of the transformative power of restoration. The large scar on her left thigh is a constant reminder that she not only went into the crushing but that she was able to come out of it. She overcame physical and emotional pain but also found a way to turn her suffering into a source of inspiration for others like me. She exemplifies that healing is possible, no matter how challenging the circumstances. Although Deven suffered from a collapse, her soul is uncollapsable. By recognizing, responding, relinquishing, and renaming your heartbreak, you, too, can redeem your spirit and restore your soul. You can transform your wounds into scars that inspire hope and healing.

Deven's Tribute

Thank you to Allan Africa, my Performance Coach, and The Miami Perimeter for reigniting the fire in my heart, allowing me to refocus and push myself to the next level. Thank you, Lauren Santos, Performance Coach, for pushing my mom and reminding her how fierce she is!

My physical therapist Kelly, Barwis Physical Therapy. Thank you for getting my body where it needed to be and encouraging me during our sessions.

I'm so grateful for my volleyball coaches, Dave Palm, Palm Coast Volleyball Academy, and Brian Coughenour, Program Director/Recruiting Coordinator of Tribe Volleyball. Thank you for your patience, for pouring into me after my injury, and for helping me become the athlete and volleyball player I am today.

My new coach is Donald Suxho, 2X Olympian and IMG Volleyball Director. Thank you for believing in me and giving me a second chance at competitive volleyball!

I love you, Mommy; you've gone through so much and still put us first. There's no words to describe how much I love you! To my sister, Mimi, I love you. Thank you for supporting me and loving on me every day.

Daddy, you are my rock and my number one fan. I know you are watching and cheering me on. I love and miss you every day.

PHASE 3

Beyond Surfside:
Why Do We Fall?

139

CHAPTER 10

Receive It:
Soul Made Whole

But I know the loving God will redeem my soul, raising me up from the dark power of death...

Psalm 49:15 (TPT)

Seasons Spare No One

Miami is known for its year-round warm climate, but it still experiences four distinct seasons. First, there is sunburn season, brought on by blazing sunshine that feels like solar flares; followed by sticky season, an even hotter and more humid sunburn season that leaves you feeling clammy, as if you walked into an outdoor sauna. Then comes the brutal "winter" season, which typically consists of a week-long cold front where Miamians find themselves bundling up in scarves, jackets, and snow boots. Finally, hurricane season arrives, which is the only real season we have out of the above.

We Miamians often hear stories of other areas on the planet where a strange phenomenon occurs every year. Apparently, seasons change the environment. I'm lightheartedly pointing out our preference for long summers instead of long winters. While Miami's seasons may not be as dramatic as those in other parts of the world, they still serve as a reminder of how seasons can teach us valuable lessons about life, growth, and change.

Spring is the season of new beginnings. As snow melts and flowers begin to bloom, we're reminded of the hope and promise of new life. Summer is a time of warmth, abundance, and joy. The long days and sunshine bring us out of our shells, encouraging us to embrace life and enjoy the beauty of creation. Fall is a season of change, reflection, and preparation. The leaves change color; the air cools, and the days grow shorter; signaling to prepare for the coming winter. Winter is a season of rest, introspection, and solitude. The trees are bare, the ground is frozen, and life seems to slow down.

Just as the earth experiences seasons of change, life has a way of imposing change upon us. Scripture captures life's seasonal cycles of the human journey quite literally. It speaks to the reality of seasons of pain and seasons of prosperity and that we must learn to surrender and steward each season as it comes. Seasons transition with unyielding certainty, reminding us of the impermanence of all things in the human journey in Ecclesiastes 3:1–11:

"There's a time for everything and a season for every activity under the heavens: a time to be born and a time to die,
a time to plant and a time to uproot,
a time to kill and a time to heal,
a time to tear down and a time to build,
a time to weep and a time to laugh,
a time to mourn and a time to dance,
a time to scatter stones and a time to gather them,
a time to embrace and a time to refrain from embracing,
a time to search and a time to give up,
a time to keep and a time to throw away,
a time to tear and a time to mend,
a time to be silent and a time to speak,

a time to love and a time to hate,
a time for war and a time for peace.

What do workers gain from their struggles? I have seen the burden God has laid on the human race. He has made everything beautiful in its time. He has also set eternity in the human heart; yet no one can fathom what God has done from beginning to end." Ecclesiastes 3:1-11

The heart of this passage is the idea that life is ever-changing. It highlights that there are seasons of pain and prosperity. It encourages us to embrace the full spectrum of experiences and not cling to any one emotion or event. We cannot control the seasons of life any more than we can control the changing of the seasons on Earth. We can get lost in trying to change what's happening around us that we miss the transformation God is trying to make within us.

In the grander picture of life, there's an inherent beauty woven into every experience, moment, and struggle. It's a beauty that unfolds in its own time, often revealed to us when we least expect it. These pairings highlight the duality of human experience, suggesting that we shouldn't cling to any one emotion or event but rather embrace the full spectrum of experiences. It reminds us that just as the seasons change, so too does our experience of life. Yet, as we reflect on the words that follow, we are reminded of a profound truth: God has made everything beautiful in its time. It's at this intersection that the hope of my Romans 8:28 kicks in again: We know that all things work together for the good of those who love God, who are called according to his purpose.

We may wonder if our efforts are in vain, if the trials we face hold any purpose beyond momentary hardship. God, in His infinite wisdom, has set eternity in the human heart. It is a divine spark within us, a longing for something beyond the temporal. It's a reminder that there is more to life than what meets the eye; that our journey extends far beyond the boundaries of this earthly existence. This longing for eternity shapes our perspective and gives meaning to our struggles. We cannot grasp the intricacies of His plan from beginning to end. And perhaps that is where faith enters the picture. It's in surrendering to the mystery of trusting God.

Faith It Til' You Make It

Faith is a concept that often requires us to venture into the realm of the unknown, but it's an essential ingredient to make your soul whole. The concept of faith is often misunderstood, but we'll demystify it. To illustrate the power of faith, we turn to a scene from the 1984 cult classic film, *The Karate Kid*, to capture the essence of its transformative potential. There's a hidden gem within one of the scenes that is a powerful illustration of the role faith plays in our healing journey. If you haven't seen the movie, I encourage you to watch it. You'll thank me later.

In the movie, Daniel LaRusso is a hot-headed, bullied teen who moves to a new town in California. He has no father figure and gravitates toward an older, humble Japanese repairman, Mr. Miyagi. During a brutal beatdown, Mr. Miyagi shows up and saves Daniel, revealing himself as an unassuming martial arts master. Daniel is amazed and begs Mr. Miyagi to train him. He reluctantly agrees, with the condition that Daniel follows his instructions without questioning his methods.

That brings us to the scene where Daniel begins his "training," which consists of performing menial labor such as washing cars, sanding walkways, and painting fences. Despite specific instructions, including arm motions and breathing patterns, Daniel quickly becomes discouraged, believing that Mr. Miyagi is exploiting him as his slave. Take 4 minutes to watch this powerful scene online.

Mr. Miyagi insists that Daniel "sand the floor," shows him "wax on, wax off" (a circular motion, as though you're detailing a car), and "paint the fence." These seemingly pointless tasks frustrate Daniel, but in reality, each one is practical training for karate self-defense moves. Without realizing it, he puts in enough hours over four days for countless repetitions, creating subconscious reflexes from muscle memory. The resistance of sanding, painting, and waxing makes him quick, and he soon realizes that each chore has a purpose.

Miyagi suddenly yells a battle cry and attacks him with the same sequence of punches and kicks they'd rehearsed. Daniel is forced to action and easily blocks them using the motions he'd just been unknowingly taught. He couldn't believe it. Each chore was training for karate self-defense moves, and he didn't even know it. The resistance of sanding, painting, and waxing made him quick. Daniel's beliefs were initially limited to his feelings from what he could touch, taste, see, smell, and hear. But his perception changes, and with that change comes his belief, faith, and hope, in that order.

Belief is the acceptance of one's perception; faith is putting trust in those beliefs with actions; and hope is the fuel of faith. Losing hope is a common theme among those who lose the will to live, as hopelessness is a prerequisite to a crushed spirit. When we rely solely on our physical eyes for sight and not on the eyes of our soul for vision, we end up blind. Mr. Miyagi conveys the lesson of faith by saying, "Ah, not everything is as it seems."

But Daniel couldn't see it because he was in his feelings. We tend to see the world for who we are, not for what it is. And the same is often true of ourselves. The scenario didn't change. Neither did the chores. The results didn't even change—but the meaning of the outcome awakened a sleeping giant within him!

A shift in perspective can bring about a shift in reception. That is the power of positioning your heart toward a change in perspective. You may be reading this, praying for God to alter your external circumstances while He is answering your prayer by transforming your spirit from within.

A perspective of faith is as crucial to the spirit as muscles are to the body. Muscle memory occurs through practicing or rehearsing physical motions and movements that become automatic. Similarly, muscle memory in your body is what I call a "faith flex" for your spirit. Muscles develop memory through repetitive physical practice and movements that become automatic. Likewise, what I call a "faith flex" for your spirit is the muscle memory that forms through the intentional reframing of your perspective. It requires practice and deliberate effort. If you can train your body to have lightning-fast reflexes for self-defense against attacks, why not train your spirit to do the same? Embracing the uncertainties of faith necessitates intentionality.

According to the biblical definition, faith is confidence in what we hope for and assurance about what we do not see (Hebrews 11:1). Many people mistakenly believe that doubt is the opposite of faith. However, that is not true. The opposite of faith is visibility. If something is visible or perceptible, faith is not required (Romans 8:24). Faith begins where understanding ends. Hope that is seen is no longer hope. Who hopes for what they can already see? Having a solid foundation of faith during your darkest moments can make the difference between mere survival and true transformation.

New York Times Best-Selling author Mark Batterson ingeniously phrases it this way in one of my favorite books, "Chase the Lion."

"If doubt is putting your circumstances between you and God, faith is putting God between you and your circumstances. Faith is unlearning your fears until all that's left is the fear of God. Faith is the willingness to look foolish. And I've already mentioned it, but it's worth repeating: Faith is taking the first step before God reveals the second step. Let me give you one more. Gratitude is thanking God after He does it. Faith is thanking God before He does it."[65]

When we face suffering, our natural inclination is to react like Daniel LaRusso, rather than trusting in God's plans for us. We often become so convinced that our expectations are not being met without realizing that our needs are indeed being fulfilled. I imagine God listening to us like Mr. Miyagi, thinking, "Stand up, show me 'sand the floor.'" God doesn't always meet our expectations because He wants to exceed them. His faithfulness in the past allows us to trust Him in the future, even when it doesn't align with our perceived notion of devotion.

Faith transcends our feelings. It is normal to have more questions than clarity. The truth may be that you feel tired, but faith declares that you are not defeated. You may be facing a significant setback, but faith believes that there is a setup for a comeback. The facts may indicate your struggle, but your faith reminds you that you are growing through the struggle. While you may be grieving a great loss, it does not signify the end of your story. Oscar Wilde once said, *"Experience is the hardest kind of teacher. It gives you the test first and the lesson afterward."* There is purpose in our pain if we choose to view it through the lens of faith. The world often advises us to "fake it till you make it," but we are called to have faith in it until we make it. Faith reminds us that it is a new chapter, not a conclusion.

What is Your Soul?

Before you can begin to heal from a broken heart or overcome a crushed spirit, it's essential to understand the importance of acknowledging that you may not know how this will work out, but it will because God is in control. We are more than just flesh and bones. Just like there's an order to your physiology, there's an order to the intangible parts of you. Psychology refers to "the self" as the totality of your identity as an individual, consisting of all mental and physical characteristics, including conscious and unconscious attributes.[109] "The self" is the very existence of your soul. It's the grand totality of who you are as a person. The French scientist and philosopher, Pierre Teilhard de Chardin, explained it this way; *"We are not human beings having a spiritual experience. We are spiritual beings having a human experience."*[11]

The Scottish poet and author George MacDonald wrote an enlightening dialogue that breaks it down with great clarity. *"YOU won't die. Your body will die and be laid away out of sight, but you will be awake, alive, more alive than you are now a great deal." And here, let me interrupt the conversation to remark upon the great mistake of teaching children that they have souls. The consequence is that they think of their souls as something which is not themselves. For what a man HAS cannot be himself. Hence, when they are told that their souls go to heaven, they think of their SELVES as lying in the grave. They ought to be taught that they have bodies; and that their bodies die; while they themselves live on."*[10]

So what's the difference between your spirit and soul exactly? The spirit of a person is not the soul, but it's a vital aspect of your soul. The late American philosopher, Dallas Willard, contrasted the soul from the spirit with so much wisdom; *"It's important to distinguish the soul from the spirit, or will, because the will or the heart or the spirit is the executive center of the self. In other words, the spirit is the part that is supposed to consciously direct everything in the person, including the soul"*.[112]

Historically speaking, the two Hebrew words for "spirit" are *ruah or pneuma*. They're written hundreds of times, referencing wind or even breath. Just as the wind can effortlessly yet vigorously make its presence known in such an intense way that it can demolish entire cities in a storm, bring a 220-ton piece of metal to flight, aka an airplane, or use its energy to power wind turbines that distribute electricity to entire cities, it is unseen. But most often, they are used interchangeably to describe variations of the powerfully divine, mysterious life presence of God or the vital strength and willpower within humanity that keeps us alive. Here's an example in James 2:26 of the *pneuma* word being used interchangeably for the same verse:

For just as the body without the <u>spirit</u> is dead, so also faith without works is dead. (CSB)

Just as the body is dead without <u>breath</u>, so also faith is dead without good works. (NLT)

Spoiler alert, this isn't to give you a random vocabulary lesson. I'm revealing something much more profound so you can understand the unseen parts that form you. All 3 interpretations of "spirit" (breath, human life force, and God's presence) are very powerful because they share 3 commonalities.

1. They're invisible to the naked eye. You can't see them, only the evidence of them.
2. The source of life. Your body needs breath in its lungs to live. Your spirit is the essence of your presence. And the only reason we have either is God's provision.
3. Live within us. Your body houses the breath in your lungs. Your soul houses your spirit. And there's a hole in our soul that can only be made whole through his presence.

At the very core of your being, you don't have a soul. You are a Soul. You have a body. After all, God is the author, designer, and giver of life. Your spirit is the engine of your life. And breath is the sustainer of your life. In other words, if you were a car, God would be the creator, designer, and builder of it. Your spirit would be the engine. And the breath in your lungs is the fuel. All of it put together, builds your soul! Now that you understand what your soul is, how do you take care of it?

Guard Your Heart

The beginning of your being is your heart. Guarding your heart is all about intentionally choosing what you allow to rent space in your soul.

Think of it as the center of your soul. Your heart feeds your spirit with desires. Those urges of your heart are brought to the consciousness of your spirit, which transcends to your mind in the form of thoughts. Thoughts are a prerequisite to forming beliefs. Those beliefs lead to feelings within our bodies. And lastly, those feelings lead to our actions, which form our social environment. In return, our social life also forms us! Interrelating all the dimensions of your heart, spirit, mind, and emotions so that they form one person functioning in a flow of life.

Soul corruption also begins with the heart. *A glad heart makes a cheerful face, but by sorrow of heart the spirit is crushed (Proverbs 15:13)*[124]. If left unchecked, we drift away from governing the desires of our hearts. That's when our heart begins allowing sorrow to invade our spirit. The wisest king that ever lived, King Solomon, explains how to prevent this: "Above all else, guard your heart, for it is the wellspring of life."[76]

A wellspring has 2 definitions, both of which equally apply. It's the *"head or source of a spring, stream, river, etc."* or *"a source or supply of anything, especially when considered inexhaustible."* In other words, your heart is the source of everything else in your life, which overflows into thoughts, words, and actions. That means every decision in your life is a byproduct of what you've incubated in the confines of your heart. But it will fool you if you're not careful. So why should you guard your heart?

Your heart is your source of life force. It's the originating place of your desires. But it also governs those desires. Think of it as a kidney for your emotions. Losing that filter means losing the ability to nourish the rest of your being with pure hydration that refreshes the spirit. King Solomon recognized the importance of a cheerful heart, which he likened to good medicine, while a crushed spirit dries up the bones[83]. Interestingly, the human body can only survive 3-4 days without water, as every living cell needs it to function, and dehydration can lead to the drying up of bones and eventual death. In the same way, failure to guard the wellspring of dreams, desires, and passions that reside in the very core of your being will eventually dry up your spirit until it is crushed.

Your heart reveals the measure of what you treasure. We guard what we value, not worthless things. Your heart is a reflection of what you treasure, revealing your attachments and motives. It's the core of your being, connecting your relationship with God and others. If your spiritual heart dies, everything else dies with it. Jesus taught, *"Your heart will be where your treasure is"*[85] because our hearts reveal what we're attached to. Trauma and tragedy can awaken us to realign our hearts with their true design. Love is the only treasure that lasts and connects our entire being. Having too high a measure of any other treasure fades away as a loss. Michael Hyatt said it this way—*If your heart is unhealthy, it threatens everything else—family, friends, career—everything!*

The Enemy will try to steal your zeal. Zeal is a strong passion or great enthusiasm devoted to a cause. Our hearts are constantly under attack as the enemy seeks to take our souls or crush our spirits. Our hearts are the battleground where our desires and thoughts are constantly being tested by messages that oppose God's promises. *For our struggle is not against human opponents but against rulers, authorities, cosmic powers in the darkness around us, and evil spiritual forces in the heavenly realm*[88]. This war within us is perpetual, just like white blood cells fighting viruses and bacteria in our bodies. Zeal is a superpower of the heart, and we must protect it from attacks that can crush our spirits.

The heart is extremely valuable & precious, the source of everything you do, and is under a perpetual state of attack. That's why the worst advice anyone can ever give you is the adage, "Follow your heart." Instead of blindly following your heart, it's essential to seek guidance from a higher source. *Proverbs 3:5-6 advises us to trust in the Lord with all our hearts and lean not on our own understanding.* This biblical wisdom reminds us that there's understanding beyond our limited perspectives, surpassing the confines of flawed human understanding.

Our hearts may yearn for instant gratification, seek validation from others, or be swayed by societal pressures. But true wisdom lies in recognizing that not all desires of the heart align with what's ultimately good and beneficial for our lives. Following your heart results in becoming septic sooner or later because *"the heart is deceitful above all things and desperately sick; who can understand it?"*[79]

Imagine replacing the word "heart" with "stomach." Do you ever hear dieticians or fitness experts tell you to follow your stomach? We all know that a diet consisting of fast food, fried snacks, and sugary drinks is not healthy. Our stomachs may crave these foods, but if we follow these cravings, we'll eventually suffer from obesity, heart problems, cancer, diabetes, and other health issues. Similarly, if we follow our hearts blindly, we may end up making decisions that harm us in the long run. Just as we make conscious choices to nourish our bodies with healthy foods, we must also nourish our hearts with the desires of God's heart.

I hope you can see I'm not trying to throw catchy cliches in the form of godly glamour or spiritual sprinkles. In Ezekiel 36:26, God promises, *"I will give you a new heart and put a new spirit in you; I will remove from you your heart of stone and give you a heart of flesh."*[81]. The idea of having a new heart implies that something needs to be surrendered. Our old heart, stubborn and hard, needs to be removed and replaced. These words are both comforting and challenging because they remind us that God isn't content to leave us in our brokenness. They're also difficult because they require us to surrender old ways of thinking and living to embrace His vision for our lives. That requires a new way of thinking.

Renew your Mind

It's not enough to simply guard our hearts. We must also engage in the process of renewing our minds. If we think of our hearts as the gatekeepers to our minds, guarding our hearts is about being selective with what we allow ourselves to be influenced by and dwell on. Our thoughts and beliefs can often hold us back from experiencing the fullness of life that God has for us.

On the other hand, renewing your mind is about taking what you hold in your heart and putting it into daily practice. In essence, guarding your heart is like filtering the input, whereas renewing your mind is about stewarding the output. Heart care is about what we receive internally, while mind renewal is about what we release externally.

If you think of your heart as a garden, then guarding it is like keeping pests and weeds out, while renewing your mind is like planting and cultivating new growth. The seeds you plant in your mind will eventually take root, influencing your beliefs, emotions, and actions. That's why it's so important to be intentional about what you allow yourself to think about, meditate on, and dwell on. Just like a garden needs water, nutrients, and sunlight to thrive, your mind needs faith, hope, and love to flourish.

The process of renewing your mind begins with your words; only when your heart breaks through the barrier of your speech will you experience a fresh start with a new heart. You can't heal from dark trauma that you won't reveal and allow yourself to feel. It's not until you confess what broke you that you can profess freedom over what provoked you!

The key to this transformational process is aligning your thinking with God's truth. That's the reason I've used scripture as the reference point. It provides a roadmap for living a life that's pleasing to God and beneficial for ourselves and others. It's about becoming less like our conflicted, compromised nature and more like God's perfect, loving presence. God desires to renew our minds and transform our thought patterns to be more like His.

The way to renew your mind is to filter it through your God-centered heart. You cannot renew your mind by trying to change the fruit. Instead, you guard your heart by changing what takes root! Focus on the root, not the fruit. Don't focus on controlling the output; just focus on the input. If you want to be *"a good person that produces goods out of the good stored up in your heart,"* start by planting seeds of life. Do this by opening your heart to God and opening your mouth to others.

Pastor Rick Warren, author of "The Purpose Driven Life," which has sold over 50 million copies, breaks it down clearly.

"This is important: You don't have to confess to another person to be forgiven. All you have to do is confess your sin to God, and you'll be forgiven. But many of you have already been forgiven, and you still feel guilty. If you want to be forgiven, you tell God. If you want to feel forgiven, you've got to tell one other person. That's the way God wired it. Revealing your feeling is the beginning of healing. We only get well in the community! You don't have to tell a bunch of people. You really only need to tell one person. If your sin is between you and another person, you go to that person. James 5:16 says, "Confess your sins to each other and pray for each other so that you may be healed" (TLB). It doesn't say "so that you may be forgiven" but so that you may be healed. Forgiveness comes from God. Healing comes in relationships."[89]

Here's an easy way to remember this:

God + Prayer + Confession = Forgiveness
Individual(s) + Confession + Forgiveness = Healing

Soul Restoration

When we talk about our soul being made whole, we often think of it as a one-time event, but in reality, it's a lifelong process. Scripture tells us in Psalm 23:3 that God restores our souls. The idea of your soul being restored to wholeness may seem elusive or abstract, but it's a simple and tangible process that you can choose. It takes surrendering your heart and stewarding your mind.

First and foremost, God wants to heal our hearts. Guarding your heart leads to healing your heart. Psalm 147:3 promises, *"He heals the brokenhearted and binds up their wounds."* Binding up your wounds requires surrendering. However, it is important to understand that guarding your heart does not mean hiding it from the world. That's an isolating response to fear. Instead, it means being discerning about the influences you allow into your life, filtering out what is detrimental to your well-being, and embracing what aligns with God's truth and love. He wants to heal the wounds of our past and mend the brokenness. It's only through surrendering your pain and allowing God to heal your heart that you can experience true restoration.

Secondly, God wants to transform our minds. He invites us to surrender our hearts to Him so that we may steward our minds for Him. This allows His truth and wisdom to replace the lies and distortions that have taken root within us. Romans 12:2 is clear: *"Do not conform to the pattern of this world, but be transformed by the renewing of your mind. Then you will be able to test and approve what God's will is—His good, pleasing, and perfect will."* When we steward our thoughts, we open ourselves up to His transformative work, enabling us to experience true freedom and peace. Stewardship of our minds involves a deliberate choice to align our thoughts with truth. By immersing ourselves in Scripture, meditating on His promises, and allowing His truth to permeate our thoughts, we create space for Him to reshape our thinking.

Through this process of surrendering and stewarding, God can resurrect our spirits. When we're wounded, it's easy to lose hope and give up on life. But God wants to breathe new life into us and give us a reason to hope again. Through His power, He can transform our spirits and give us the strength to keep going, even when life is tough.

But most importantly, God wants to rescue our souls. This means He wants to restore us to the person He created us to be. When we surrender our lives to God and allow Him to work in us, we can experience a transformation that goes beyond our wildest dreams. We can become the person God always intended us to be, free from the wounds that are healed scars of triumph from our past. That's why it's important not only to surrender and steward your heart and mind but also every season of your life.

Surrender your season

The key to surrendering your pain is this: trusting that outcome is God's responsibility, and obedience is *your* responsibility. Instead of focusing on the things you can't control, focus on what God is trying to teach you in this season. Surrender is about releasing. When we're in the midst of a season of hardship, we often want to do everything in our power to change it. Our natural inclination is to try to take control and manipulate the situation, hoping to change the outcome. The danger is giving into the temptation to speed things up; manipulate the circumstances; isolate ourselves from the problem; or even self-medicate through it. Surrendering your season is not about giving up or giving in. It's about releasing the burden of control and trusting in God's plan, focusing on obedience rather than the outcome, and acknowledging that He's in control and we are not. It's resting in the promise that God is the one who holds our future in His hands and promises to work all things together for our good if we love him.

When we surrender our season, we can steward it with a spirit of excellence, managing our attitude and activity. We can trust that God is handling the super while we do the natural. The result is a supernatural collaboration that brings peace and hope, regardless of the season we are in. The 'natural' I'm referring to has been highlighted throughout this book, such as taking steps towards healing, building your faith, and following the 5 requisites to restoration.

It means recognizing that even during our struggles, God is with us and working for our good. It means being willing to surrender our plans and desires and trust that God's plan for our lives is far greater than anything we could ever imagine. As we surrender ourselves to him and allow him to work in us, He has the power to restore our souls in ways that we can't do on our own. God can do so much more with your surrender than your strength. Surrender is reliant on God. Strength is reliant on yourself.

Steward Your Season

After surrendering your season, the next step is to steward it well. It's much easier to steward your season after you've surrendered your season. If not, you'll be too busy comparing your season instead of managing it well. Stewardship is a concept deeply rooted in the understanding of managing and caring for what has been entrusted to us. It requires a prerequisite of a perspective shift from one that is self-centered to one that is God-centered.

We're not the owners of our lives but rather the managers of everything that God has entrusted to us. It goes beyond material possessions and extends to every aspect of our lives, including our spiritual journey. Stewardship involves recognizing that everything we have, including our own lives, is a gift from God. Your parents participated in your creation process, but God formed every aspect of you, including your soul. You may go to work every day to provide for your family, but who gave you the ability to get out of bed and pursue your dreams? We're not entitled to these blessings, but we're called to manage them responsibly and with gratitude.

Stewardship brings rectification. Time, in particular, is an unforgiving commodity that requires careful stewardship. Once it's gone, it cannot be retrieved or reclaimed. Therefore, understanding the importance of who we're becoming today, rather than dwelling on who we were yesterday, is crucial for spiritual formation. Managing time involves setting priorities and boundaries and aligning our actions with our values and purpose. In the fast-paced and demanding world, it's easy to get caught up in the busyness of life and lose sight of the present moment. You may find yourself constantly reminiscing about the past or anxiously anticipating the future, neglecting the opportunities for growth and transformation that lie before us today. Focusing on who you're becoming today involves the courage to face fears, uncertainties, and limitations.

The purpose is why we exist; it gives our lives meaning and direction. When we become what we fear, we're stepping into our purpose from the passion that was produced from what we were willing to suffer for. This means that by facing our fears and becoming them, we can transform them into purpose.

In my own journey, I experienced the loss of my grandmother and went through the grieving process, which led me to understand the significance of my own healing steps in my personal recovery. Recognizing the requisites to restoration, I made a deliberate choice to use my season of loss as a means to support and facilitate the healing of others. It is through these intense seasons of crushing that I found the inspiration to write this book.

By stewarding our lives with wisdom and purpose, we allow God to shape our character, empower our growth, and use us for His greater glory. Had it not been for my most intense seasons of crushing, I wouldn't have written this book. As we steward our lives with wisdom and purpose, we invite God to shape our character, empower us for growth, and use us for His glory.

When your soul is *shaken*, it's an opportunity to *awaken*. I learned this the hard way.

CHAPTER 11

Crushed Spirit

The LORD is close to the brokenhearted; he rescues those whose spirits are crushed.

Psalms 34:18 (NLT)

Journey to My Personal Collapse

Long before the collapse of Champlain Towers South, there was a time when my own life crumbled in the darkness. It was a long season; it shattered my heart, crushed my spirit, demolished my dreams, maimed my mind, sickened my soul, and became the ultimate strife within my life. When we love someone deeply, we're making ourselves vulnerable to being hurt deeply.

The great theologian, C.S. Lewis, breaks it down this way: *"To love at all is to be vulnerable. Love anything, and your heart will be wrung and possibly broken. If you want to make sure of keeping it intact, you must give it to no one, not even an animal. Wrap it carefully around with hobbies and little luxuries; avoid all entanglements. Lock it up safe in the casket or coffin of your self-ishness. But in that casket, safe, dark, motionless, airless, it will change. It will not be broken; it will become unbreakable, impenetrable, irredeemable. To love is to be vulnerable."*[70]

We rely on one another. Perhaps it is because life lacks meaning without relationships, or maybe it is because our deepest desires are rooted in connection and intimacy.

That's why there's no pain quite like heartbreak. I'm not talking about that time you cried at the end of the movie *The Notebook*. I mean the type of pain that comes from the deep, relational loss of our most valuable relationships. The ones where we feel seen, accepted, fully known, and unconditionally loved. That's supposed to be our safe place, just like Champlain Towers South was supposed to be a safe home for all the residents to trust.

Our inner fire alarms go off when we no longer feel safe, whether it's physical, mental, emotional, or spiritual. They serve as warning signals, alerting us to the presence of danger or discomfort in our lives. They can manifest as a deep sense of unease, a nagging feeling that something is wrong, or a profound sadness that weighs heavily. It is during these moments of turmoil that we are often compelled to seek solace, understanding, and a way to overcome the pain.

And perhaps that is the very reason I wrote this. It's born out of my journey through the agony of a crushed spirit. The weight of a crushed spirit has been my unwanted companion, as I've existed in survival mode through the internal torment of hopelessness. Whether your grief is from a romantic heartbreak, a backstabber, or the death of a loved one, they're not meant to fill the hole in your soul. In those dark moments, it's natural to question if it's even worth it to start over, to rebuild the shattered pieces of our lives.

If you find yourself in a season of suffering, where your spirit feels utterly crushed, know that there is good news. Rescue is on the way. I can say this with conviction because I've not only experienced the depths of such despair, but I've also been rescued from it. In my case, it came in the form of divorce because she had an affair, which resulted in the death of the relationship entirely. Without this turbulent life experience, I wouldn't be writing the hope that's spliced into the DNA of these pages.

Divorce is a unique form of loss. It bears a resemblance to the death of a loved one, yet there are distinct differences that make it a complex and emotionally charged experience. One significant distinction is that your ex-spouse is still alive, existing somewhere beyond the boundaries of your life. This realization can bring a layer of denial and rejection, fueling feelings of loneliness and abandonment. Seeing your former partner after the end of the relationship can trigger a flood of emotions reminiscent of reliving the death of that relationship over and over again.

Secondly, unlike weddings or funerals, there are no established support rituals, ceremonies, or comforting traditions that accompany divorce. The absence of these rituals can amplify feelings of isolation, intensify the grieving process, and prolong the healing journey. By no means am I comparing your crushing season to mine, nor am I insinuating the size of my suffering is greater than yours. My intention is to create a connection between the context of my own experience and the similar feelings you may have encountered during your moments of collapse.

In high school, I met a girl who captivated me, but I never had the courage to ask her out. We connected through her older sister, with whom I shared classes and formed a friendship. Our church organized exciting youth gatherings, and one day, her younger sister joined us. She was a stunning blonde with a captivating personality, a warm heart, and an incredible sense of humor. Popular and cool, she seemed out of my league.

Throughout high school, I had a crush on her; silently hoping she would notice me as I walked past her in the hallways. At times, I mustered the courage to exchange hugs, attempting to play it cool, even though I was probably a bit of a doofus. I never made a move. I was blatantly unaware that she held feelings for me, too.

Ignorance is Blind

After graduating, I became a financial professional, starting my entrepreneurial career. Working in sales bolstered my self-confidence, and I adopted personal development as a way of life. I began to believe that I could attain success in all aspects: a thriving business, a fulfilling marriage, a loving family, a spiritually rich life, financial prosperity, and personal growth. Determined and ambitious, I crafted vision boards, set daily goals, and recited affirmations. I prayed as if everything depended on God and worked tirelessly as if everything relied on me. Central to this drive was my desire for a life partner. I longed for a best friend to come home to, a partner who would stand by my side, and together, we could face and conquer any obstacle that came our way.

At the age of 21, I reconnected with my high school crush, who was then 19 and in a toxic relationship. Her boyfriend was cheating on her. She knew it but hadn't broken it off yet. My 21-year-old beardless self saw a wide-open opportunity to step in and man up. I gave her that extra motivation to ditch the zero to get with her hero. I pursued her relentlessly, motivated by a mix of attraction and a desire to rescue her from her poisonous situation. Despite the challenges she faced, including getting a restraining order against her ex-boyfriend, we eventually became a couple on my 22nd birthday, getting engaged just nine months later.

Driven by ambition, I took on the responsibility of helping her navigate various obstacles, whether it was legal issues, family conflicts, or providing temporary shelter. I thrived on her, finding validation and a sense of worthiness through external approval. The more I could prove my manhood by solving her problems and being a provider, the more it fed my ego and fueled my addiction to the high of her approval. I took pride in using a metaphorical "fire helmet," rushing in with my "fire hose" to put out each new crisis. Every opportunity to rescue her gave me a sense of self-esteem and validation. It gave me a hit like a drug to my ego. I was earning her love.

In hindsight, it's clear there were numerous red flags that I failed to recognize. Despite the toxicity being evident to everyone around me, including my family and closest friends, I remained oblivious to the unhealthy dynamics. A relationship is a false sense of security. She was addicted to the need of me. And I was addicted to approval from her. My self-worth didn't come from me; it hinged on her approval. I was so caught up in wanting her to feel secure that I was blinded by my insecurity.

Just because you're not necessarily "wounded" doesn't mean you're a secure person. Projecting security doesn't mean you possess security. A person that already lives FROM security and validation operates very differently than a person living FOR security and validation. One of the crucial lessons I learned from this experience is that starting one's life as a single and secure individual is vital to building a healthy and happy marriage. It doesn't work the other way around. You don't get happily married before you're secure; in hopes of later becoming a secure individual. An external remedy can't solve your question of internal identity! Marriage doesn't solve issues; it exposes them. Most relationship problems are individual issues that couples believe can be solved by a fancy wedding and a brand-new, shiny wedding band. And that's exactly what we did.

Despite my continuous reassurances, my fiancé carried a deep-seated fear of being cheated on, a result of the trauma she had experienced in her past. This fear cast a dark shadow over our relationship, and the topic of infidelity became a recurring theme in our conversations. Each time she expressed her insecurity, I would reaffirm my unwavering loyalty to her. However, her question lingered, "How do I know you won't do the same?"

In one particular conversation, she pleaded with me to promise that if I ever became unhappy in the relationship, I'd communicate it to her rather than betray her trust. She couldn't bear to endure the pain of infidelity again and would prefer the relationship to end rather than be cheated on. Her insecurity was showing, but my immaturity prevented me from understanding why.

I was blind. She was crying for help from a wound that was still bleeding. I failed to grasp the depth of her trauma and the need for healing. Instead of understanding her cries for help, I became frustrated, viewing her insecurities as dramatic. I was annoyed that I was stuck paying interest on a debt that another man charged. Instead of offering patience and understanding,

I grew impatient with her inability to move on from the past. I lacked the wisdom to recognize that my role was not solely that of a rescuer but also a supporter in her journey toward healing.

Ignoring the concerns of my parents and friends, I proceeded with the wedding, convinced of our deep connection. Their resistance just fueled my resolve! I felt they didn't understand what we had in such a short time. In reality, they were trying to hold up a metaphorical mirror to show me all I was not seeing. But I wasn't interested in looking in the mirror because I was in love. The reality was there were so many red flags that I was ignorantly misinterpreting them as green.

Our wedding date was set, and I couldn't wait. Everything was perfect. At the ages of twenty-four and twenty-two years old, I had the privilege of marrying my best friend on the sandy shores, with a majestic golden sunset and the silhouette of the ocean as our backdrop. Since this was going to be our only wedding, we organized an extravagant celebration on Miami Beach, attended by 150 of our loved ones. Our guests couldn't stop raving about it, commenting that it was the most incredible wedding reception they had ever attended. It was a sophisticated black-tie affair, complete with exquisite ice sculptures, skilled cigar rollers, a top-notch open bar, and the best DJ I knew.

Following the reception, our guests bid us farewell as we hopped into a limousine, whisking us away to our luxurious honeymoon suite. My bride and I arrived at our dreamy beachfront hotel room, and in a scene reminiscent of a sappy chick flick, I carried her through the door. The room was full of roses that lay atop the bed in a perfectly put-together heart shape. Stitched onto the drapes was a gold and floral design, and off to the right stood a hot tub looking out onto the beach. At last, the moment I had eagerly awaited for 24 long years had arrived. I presented my bride with the most precious gift I could offer a woman. Our wedding night marked the first time I'd ever given myself to her or anyone. She was meant to be my first and last. I had saved myself for her, a profound way of affirming her immeasurable value as my one and only.

As any married person can tell you, marriage takes work. If we prepared for marriage more than we prepared for the wedding, divorce rates probably wouldn't be as high as they are. It's easy to start things but hard to sustain them. It's easy to get married; it's hard to work on your marriage. Starting something is easy, but sustaining it is difficult. Getting married is straightforward, but nurturing a marriage requires effort.

Until that point in my life, I had never experienced the pain of a broken heart from a challenging season. I hadn't lost a loved one, nor had any close friends betrayed me. My parents and grand-parents loved me unconditionally. Surrounded by a supportive network of family, church, and friends, I lived in a protective bub-ble that instilled in me a natural trust and belief in the inherent goodness of people.

At 25 years old, I believed I had achieved a level of success. My dreams were materializing, and my optimism was boundless. I'd found my ideal partner, my business was thriving, and we owned a beautifully renovated home decorated with her artistic touch. We had accent walls themed with romantic wedding pic-tures, oceanside driftwood, and vintage paintings of beaches and sunsets on the walls. She was employed with a cruise line, and we had a plan for her to retire in a year so we could focus on build-ing our business together. Life seemed predictable and aligned with my carefully crafted plans. Despite my love and support, I'd grown somewhat dismissive, unsure of how else to demonstrate my loyalty and commitment. I didn't realize it, but she was about to bleed all over me from wounds that I never gave her.

Beginning of the End

Three and a half years after we'd been married, I came home one night to my wife's bags packed at the front door. I'll never forget that Thursday night of August 22, 2013. "Listen, I'm not happy and need some space," she stated, "I'm going to leave to spend the night at my mom's house." Confused and scared, I muttered quietly, "What do you mean? Why are you leaving to spend the night at your mom's place? We're not fighting or sleeping in separate bedrooms. We're not even in marriage counseling! Isn't this kind of extreme?" But she insisted. I figured she had a rough day and maybe needed some girl time with her mom. She never came back.

After two weeks of a surprise separation, she made it clear that she didn't want to come home. Despite my desperate pleas for counseling, she remained uninterested and distant. She then revealed the devastating truth: she no longer loved me. The 5-year-old child within me begged her not to punish me. Her words struck me deeply, and I couldn't hold back my tears. I pleaded with her not to abandon us, but she insisted on focusing on herself and her happiness. Although she reluctantly agreed to attend counseling, she also demanded space. It was a crushing moment, and I felt the pain of a truly broken heart for the first time in my life.

The following day, I turned to a married friend for advice, desperately sharing the bizarre situation and hoping for guidance in this unknown storm. His response shook me to the core: "Mike, a woman behaving like this is either cheating on you or has been abused." I vehemently defended both my integrity and my wife's, insisting that I'd never laid a hand on her and that she'd never cheat on me. I pointed out that she had been betrayed in her previous relationship and made it clear that infidelity was her biggest fear. But my wise friend maintained, "I'm just telling you the truth. If you want to discover the truth for yourself, there are ways to find out..."

Broken by Betrayal

Desperate for the truth, I decided to investigate. My life was at a standstill, and I couldn't bear the uncertainty any longer. I accessed our cell phone bill, which documented every call and text message. To my dismay, I uncovered a recurring phone number, with countless text exchanges during her work hours and lengthy phone calls after work. I knew that number. It belonged to a male coworker of hers. A whirlwind of emotions consumed me, but I remained in denial. It seemed impossible that my wife could be cheating on me. She'd carried the pain of infidelity from her past, projecting it onto our relationship. It defied all logic. I needed to confront the truth firsthand.

I confided in my best friend, sharing every detail, and together we embarked on a mission. He understood the support I would need in case my worst fear became a reality. We arrived at her workplace 30 minutes earlier than her usual departure time, strategically parking where we could observe without being noticed. And then, there they were—my wife and him.

My heart pounded heavily as adrenaline surged through my veins. I watched in disbelief as they walked together, exchanging a seamless kiss on the lips before she climbed into her car. It was at that moment that a part of me died, a part that would never fully recover. Overwhelmed with shock, I lost control and spiraled into a state of rage, anguish, and excruciating pain. It felt as if my world had crumbled, mirroring the devastation I witnessed in the Surfside Collapse. Thankfully, my best friend held me back, preventing me from making a foolish decision. I was engulfed in a mixture of betrayal and the same crushing pain she'd once endured.

The next day, I hired a private investigator and instructed him to gather every piece of information. After two days of tracking, he delivered the devastating news. My wife wasn't staying at her mother's house but instead at her lover's. Armed with the address, I confronted her at the location. It was an ugly scene, to say the least. The moment our eyes met, her initial words were filled with disgust, questioning why I was there when she had expressed her desire for space. I won't repeat the exact words that escaped my mouth, but I shouted something like this in disbelief: "You're my wife, and you left me for another man!? Who are you?! When did you sell your soul to the devil!?" I demanded answers, struggling to comprehend how she could abandon our marriage for another man.

She broke down in tears, and I witnessed my wife let her defenses crumble. Gradually, I composed myself and started to seek answers. That night, she confessed to everything, including their sexual relationship. Despite the deep pain and anger I felt, I mustered the strength to respond, "You're still my wife, and we made a sacred commitment. Even though you broke our covenant, I still believe there's hope for us. Let's work together to save our marriage." Her response shattered my hopes as she uttered, "I don't want to save our marriage. I want a divorce."

I learned a hard lesson amongst many that night. Some people are not truly loyal to you; they're only loyal to their need of you, like an addiction. Once the need changes, so does their loyalty. For the first time since we'd been together, she didn't want to be saved by me. She'd found someone else to fill her need. She didn't want me, and I was destroyed. That was the first time she'd directly used the "D" word with me, and I wasn't ready to accept it. How could my life have gone from such joy to utter despair in just under 30 days? It felt like everything had unraveled too quickly. I refused to accept divorce as my fate. I clung to the belief that God had the power to work miracles, even amid my marriage falling apart.

I sought guidance from a counselor, devoured books on marriage and surviving affairs, and sought advice from seasoned couples. One book that resonated deeply with me was, *His Needs, Her Needs* by Dr. Willard Harley Jr. It shed light on how many marriages go through infidelity and, given the right circumstances, anyone could be susceptible to an affair. I was so desperate for answers that I even reached out to Dr. Harley himself and had the privilege of speaking with him over the phone. His insight and encouragement meant the world to me in that difficult moment. To Dr. Harley: if you ever come across this, know that your support was truly invaluable to me.

Crushed by Divorce

My wife attempted to tempt me with a proposition—if I initiated the divorce proceedings, I could keep the house. I refused to take the bait and stood firm in my decision. As her demands escalated, they turned into threats. She made it clear that she'd emotionally moved on and that our divorce was inevitable. If I didn't sign and submit the simplified dissolution of marriage paperwork, she'd take the matter to court and pursue everything I had. Reluctantly, I filed for divorce, believing that the court system would take a considerable amount of time to process it.

To my surprise, I received a notice in the mail stating that our divorce hearing was scheduled just 14 days after the filing. This came as a shock since it'd only been 45 days since my wife left our home to start a new life with another man. It seemed that, contrary to my expectations, the local government operated at lightning speed when I was counting on them to move slowly. Go figure!

On the morning of our scheduled divorce, I was consumed by desperation. Nothing else mattered to me except getting my wife back and restoring our life together. Filled with a sense of urgency, I called her to express my hesitation and unwillingness to proceed. However, the court notice clearly stated that both parties should be present, and this infuriated her. In her eyes, I was an obstacle preventing her from finding happiness in her new path. In her angry outburst, she informed me that she'd proceed with the court hearing regardless, and if the divorce wasn't granted, she'd take legal action against me. Choosing not to appear in court that morning became my final act of faith, creating space for God to perform a miracle. But it wasn't long before I got the death blow to my spirit via text: "The judge granted the divorce."

Up to that point, the cry of my heart to God was; *How he satisfies the souls of thirsty ones and fills the hungry with goodness! Some of us once sat in darkness, living in the dark shadows of death. We were prisoners to our pain, chained to our regrets. For we rebelled against God's Word and rejected the wise counsel of God Most High. So he humbled us through our circumstances, watching us as we stumbled, with no one there to pick us back up. Our own pain became our punishment. Then we cried out, "Lord, help us! Rescue us!" And he did! His light broke through the darkness, and he led us out in freedom from death's dark shadow and snapped every one of our chains. So lift your hands and give thanks to God for his marvelous kindness and for his miracles of mercy for those he loves! (Psalm 107: 9-15 TPT).* Through the brutality and torment, I believed my posture of forgiveness toward her would be met with marvelous kindness and mercy through a miracle because God loves me.

The night my wife left me, my heart broke. The day my wife divorced me, my spirit was crushed. It wasn't just the fact that our marriage, our home, and my life seemed so disposable to her. It wasn't just the suddenness and speed at which everything fell apart. Just like the residents of Surfside and the families who tragically lost their loved ones, including my own, we never anticipated that our home could betray our trust so brutally and without warning. If we had even imagined such a possibility, we would have taken measures to protect ourselves before it was too late. The collapse of my marriage felt like something out of a movie, an unimaginable twist of fate that I never thought could happen to me.

The day of our divorce confirmed my worst fear—I was not worthy of being loved, and I saw no way out of my pain. If being a hero and saving myself for the one I loved wasn't good enough, I would never be good enough. Our divorce validated more than the justification to grieve her. I believed it warranted the right to hate her and hate myself even more for grieving over her. The difference between a broken heart & crushed spirit is the meaning we give our pain. I attached the deep feelings of shame, loneliness, and anguish from my divorce and took on the identity of being a failure, emasculated, and unworthy of love. My emotional disposition had become a spiritual condition.

I didn't just mourn the loss of my wife. I mourned the loss of my life. But it almost felt dishonest to grieve over my beloved. Not because I didn't love her but because I did, and it was all a lie. It was as if I married a person that never really existed—almost like the woman I married who was terrified of infidelity had been cloned and replaced by the unrecognizable person that became obsessed with an affair. Nobody from the wedding celebration was there for the funeral of my marriage. Fear took the throne of my life. It was as if everything I believed that was supposed to lead to my dreams had instead led me to a nightmare I couldn't wake up from.

Where Was God?

Life as I knew it was over. Everything lost its purpose. That's the REAL reason I was able to empathize with Raquel Oliveira so much the first time we met at the pizza restaurant. What was the purpose of trying to build a business? And who would I share it with? Travel with? Why take care of myself? My empty house became a morbid confirmation of my loneliness. Every single square inch of it was a reminder that I wasn't man enough for the woman I loved, but another man was. Going home every night was about as peaceful as going to a cemetery. My house was the final resting place where my marriage was buried. And our bedroom was the tombstone where I mourned. The sum of my life had led me to what felt like a life sentence without parole. So I punished myself for another year and a half before moving out.

For the first time in my life, I'd been completely betrayed, not just by a person, but by God. I held onto faith and hope in a worsening situation. But more than that, I trusted God enough that I saved myself on our wedding night for this woman that ruthlessly gutted me, and for what? Just to be abandoned, betrayed, and emotionally ravaged? How could I be faithful to a God that had not been faithful to me? I had tried it God's way, and it didn't work. I felt betrayed by my wife, by my sense of judgment, and by God. If this was what God's "faithfulness" looked like, I wanted nothing to do with Him. Without warning, my entire life narrative was wiped out.

These words capture the deep distress of abandonment and brokenness from the betrayal that collapsed my world to shambles. Psalm 77:1-10 (TPT) sums up the moment I knew it was over for real. *"I poured out my complaint to you, God. I lifted up my voice, shouting out for your help. When I was in deep distress, in my day of trouble. I reached out for you with hands stretched out to heaven. Over and over, I kept looking for you, God, but your comforting grace was nowhere to be found. As I thought of you, I moaned, "God, where are you?" I'm overwhelmed with despair as I wait for your help to arrive. I can't get a wink of sleep until you come and comfort me. Now I'm too burdened to even pray! My mind wandered, thinking of days gone by—the years long since passed. Then I remembered the worship songs I used to sing in the night seasons, and my heart began to fill again with thoughts of you. So my spirit went out once more in search of you. Would you really walk off and leave me forever, my Lord God? Won't you show me your kind favor, delighting in me again? Has your well of sweet mercy dried up? Will your promises never come true? Have you somehow forgotten to show me love? Are you so angry that you've closed your heart of compassion toward me? Lord, what wounds me most is that it's somehow my fault that you've changed your heart toward me, and I no longer see the years of the Mighty One or your right hand of power."*

I felt so numb from the concoction of sadness, rage, bitterness, anxiety, and self-doubt that I condemned myself as much as I condemned her. How dishonorable, disgraceful, and unloveable must I have been for my beloved to eagerly and unapologetically inflict the same affliction that traumatized her without hesitation? I felt the curse of torment in my bones. It was a venom of SHAME pulsing through my veins. It released a toxin of insecurity that paralyzed my body with guilt, clotted my heart with anger, and plagued my mind with fear. My spirit was crushed with despair, leaving my soul maimed with *shame*. I didn't believe I was worthy of love. So, I acted accordingly, exploiting my insecurity by seeking external validation. I specifically sought validation and affirmation from women as if it were retribution for my ex-wife's actions. It didn't take me long to learn that my raw insecurity was repulsive, so I tried to camouflage it by hiding in my shame.

I believed that building my status, seeking approval, and making a name for myself in Miami's nightlife scene was the best way to escape from my broken self. Being myself was not an option since I saw myself as a rejected, broken loser who drove his wife into the arms of another man. Instead of facing my pain and healing, I drowned it with alcohol, partying, and women. Every social event, club, or outing was an excuse to avoid being alone in my empty house, which used to be home. I lived a life of pretense, hoping to get applause from people who couldn't care less about my well-being. Deep down, I yearned for genuine intimacy, but I settled for cheap perversions that gave me temporary satisfaction. I compensated for my lack of intimacy by projecting false confidence, hoping to be worthy of women's adoration and affection. My manhood had been stripped away, so I overcompensated by trying to impress others. Seeking external validation is the surest way to overthink, use people, and condemn yourself to a life of misery.

While she was alive, I had forgotten my grandmother's example of how she'd shown me unconditional love, just for being born. Love is not performance-based. It's not based on impressing others or achieving the applause of those around you. Nor does love give to get. Love gets to give. By agreeing to this transactional and cheap imitation of love, I was living a counterfeit life from a bankrupt heart. How could I ever love someone else again if I didn't love myself? You can't give what you don't have. Love gives from love, not for love. I couldn't pour water from my empty cup into someone else's because my heart was in a drought. Instead of going to a water source like a faucet, spring, or a well, I just found other people with empty cups and expected them to pour into mine. That wasn't fair to them or me.

I believed my storm separated me from everyone else, and my ego made me delusional enough to think that my pain was unique and unrelatable. At one point, I felt like the world was moving on without me. I had people show up for my wedding, but few were there for me when I was weeping. The church I was a part of at the time was unhealthy and toxic, and I received no support. I had lost hope in counseling because my marriage was already dead, and my family and closest friends were all happily coupled up. Being around them only made me feel more alone and unworthy of love, and it exposed the wounds of my insecurity. I fell into a victim mindset, which only pushed me deeper into a dark hole of isolation.

What cursed me wasn't the storm itself but rather my inability to cope with it. I'd become too focused on my pain, making it into a crutch to justify my pride. My values revolved around external success, self-reliance, and serving my ego. I projected an image of winning in my public life, but in reality, I was losing my soul. It drove me away from God. Being victimized is an event or act that happens to you, but being a victim is an identity shift. My pain became my new identity of pride, which kept me in misery. Divorce crushed my heart, but my own pride crushed my spirit.

Scripture tells us that the sun rises on both the evil and the good and sends rain on the just and the unjust. As mentioned at the beginning of the book, building your life on a weak foundation will eventually maim your heart and cripple your spirit because no one is spared from storms. My pride guaranteed a losing proposition because I thought my peace was found in co-dependency. I didn't just want validation; I needed it. You can only self-administer emotional, physical, mental, and spiritual venom into your spirit for so long until the toxins have an insidious and, eventually, fatal effect. In short, I was losing everything by chasing nothing. What is it to gain the world but lose your soul? I needed a detox. I needed anti-venom. I needed my spirit to be rescued. My spirit needed to be broken.

CHAPTER 12

Broken Spirits

The sacrifice pleasing to God is a broken spirit. You will not despise a broken and humbled heart, God.

Psalm 51:17 (CSB)

Anti-Venom

Eventually, I hit rock bottom. I had spent months partying and receiving external validation. Despite my body being in great physical condition, my spirit was in a state of decay. Ironically, my longing for acceptance led to a consistent motivation to work out and eat clean, but for all the wrong reasons. It was another attempt to prove my value. Although my body grew stronger, my spirit became weaker. I wondered how people could settle for a lifestyle far from the intimacy they desired.

Then, it hit me: if God designed our bodies this way, he must have designed our spirits the same. Just as we tear down our muscles to make them stronger, our spirits may need to experience collapse and tearing to grow. You see, it's only after inputting the right amount of rest, carbs, protein, and water that our muscles can grow back stronger than before. The same principle applies to our spirits —when our hearts and spirits are broken, it may be a sign of growth. Instead of focusing on the pain, we should focus on the recovery and growth of our spiritual fibers. Perhaps when the unseen fibers of our heart are broken and the fibers of our spirit are torn, they are growing. This was the first time I attached hope for a new beginning to my pain.

This realization led me to focus on recovery so that I could grow my spiritual fibers back to be stronger. Just like the physical body requires a healthy and balanced diet to build and maintain muscle mass and overall fitness, the spiritual body also needs nourishment. The thoughts, beliefs, and emotions we consume have a profound impact on our spiritual well-being. If we constantly feed our spirit with negativity, toxic relationships, and unhealthy patterns, it will inevitably become weak and malnourished. This will limit our ability to grow, develop and thrive, just as a poor diet limits our physical potential. In short, just as we are what we eat, we are also what we consume, mentally and spiritually.

Similarly, the toxic substances I was ingesting mentally and spiritually were poisonous to my soul. It's easy to overlook the impact that our thoughts and beliefs have on our well-being, but just like venomous toxins, they can spread throughout our entire being and cause harm. Venomous creatures like snakes, scorpions, spiders, and stingrays come to mind. They produce some of the deadliest poisons on the planet. Poisonous molecules called toxins are what make it such an effective and fatal weapon. When one predator injects another living being with its venom, the toxins circulate within the victim's body and prevent it from functioning normally.

There are several different categories of venoms. Depending on which venomous animal bites its prey will determine how the toxins will disable its targets. Some toxins are designed to attack the bloodstream, causing heart failure. Others invade the nervous system, resulting in paralysis, loss of consciousness, and even brain damage. Some are known to severely damage skin tissue, corrode underlying muscles, and often lead to long-term disabilities if the victim survives.

Cure in the Curse

Here's the paradox: that same venom also contains the cure to save people's lives. The key to life-saving anti-venoms is injecting a minuscule, harmless dose of venom. This prompts the immune system to defend the body by generating antibodies. These proteins fight on our behalf to attack and disable the venom's toxic effects. Scientists have learned how to produce and collect the antibodies, distributing them to effectively treat the infected. Anti-venom is prepared in advance and kept in stock at hospital pharmacies. Snake bites are especially lethal, yet almost all snakebite victims in the U.S. survive simply because medications block the effects of venomous bites and stings. The cure is hidden within the curse.

In the same way, when you're bitten or stung with heartbreak, you must administer anti-venom before the internal corrosion begins to have lasting effects that collapse and crush your spirit. Just as venomous toxins disable their targets, the same is true of traumatic heartbreak. It can attack the bloodstream of your emotions, resulting in heart failure from hopelessness. Broken heart syndrome can invade your nervous system and infiltrate your mind with anxiety. Symptoms are "loss of consciousness" to live in the present, failure to move forward into your future, and internal paralysis derived from internal fear.

Lastly, just as venom damages skin tissue, corrodes muscles, and leads to potentially long-term disabilities, piercing pain that festers into bitterness damages your spirit, corrodes your soul, and potentially leads to the disabling of your purpose! You can make an argument that venom is not very harmful in tiny doses. It's when a lethal amount is administered by a predatory creature that it can kill you. When your world is burning down and collapsing, the overwhelming amount of heartbreak in one dose can be so tremendous that it crushes your spirit. But what if I told you that some of these same things that poison us can also contain the antidote that purifies us?

The cure is not just found in the curse—it's hidden in it! This idea suggests that many of the things we desire, need, or aspire to, are often hidden within things that initially seem negative or unpleasant. It's like there is an inherent duality in many things where the very thing that brings pain or hardship also contains the seeds of its solution or transformation. The delicious fruit is hidden within a small seed, like a kiwi. A butterfly is hidden within the caterpillar. The healing for a broken bone is hidden within that same bone. A majestic oak tree is hidden within a tiny acorn. The tearing of a muscle is the very thing that builds the muscle. Your testimony is hidden in your tests.

These processes may cause temporary pain and discomfort, but they also trigger a process of repair and growth that results in strength and resilience. The idea of the very things intended to harm us simultaneously holding the (often unrealized) remedy to heal us applies not just to our bodies but also to our spirits. When we face difficult trials in our lives, such as illness, loss, or other hardships, it can be tempting to feel defeated and hopeless. However, these struggles can strengthen our resilience, deepen our compassion for others, and help us discover inner strengths we never knew we had.

Broken Spirit

Ultimately, "the cure is hidden in the curse" encourages us to look beyond the surface-level difficulties of a situation and seek out the deeper meaning and potential for growth and healing within it. As you read at the beginning of this chapter, *The sacrifice pleasing to God is a* broken *spirit. You will not despise a* broken *and* humbled heart*, God.* For your soul to heal, your spirit must break. The solution to a crushed spirit is a *broken* spirit. The rescuing is in the breaking.

At first glance, this statement may seem counterintuitive. What does it mean to have a broken spirit? To many of us, the idea of being broken may conjure up feelings of weakness, despair, and hopelessness. But in the context of this Psalm 51:17, a broken spirit is not a negative thing. It is a state of openness and vulnerability, a willingness to acknowledge our flaws and weaknesses, and a recognition of our need for forgiveness and redemption. When we are broken, we're no longer trying to hold it all together on our own. Instead, we are turning to God and surrendering our struggles to him.

This seemingly contradictive idea of finding strength in weakness is echoed in the New Testament. In Matthew 5:3, Jesus says, "Blessed are the poor in spirit, for theirs is the kingdom of heaven." In other words, those who recognize their spiritual poverty and their need for God will be blessed with the richness of his kingdom. 2 Corinthians 12:9 proclaims, "My grace is sufficient for you, for my power is made perfect in weakness." Essentially, it is through our weaknesses that God can demonstrate his strength and work in our lives.

A crushed spirit is a heavy burden that results from the poison of a prideful heart. Proverbs 18:12 (CSB) warns us that, *"Before his downfall a person's heart is proud, but humility comes before honor."* A crushed spirit is the unfortunate consequence of that downfall. Pride camouflages itself in the dark shadows of our pain, preventing us from making progress as individuals. It leads to a sense of entitlement and self-importance, that alienates us from others and blinds us to the truth.

In the name of our pain, we become stuck in our ways and are unable to grow, learn, and change. This, in turn, leads to a sense of hopelessness and despair as we struggle to find meaning and purpose in our lives. We become trapped in a cycle of self-importance that alienates us from others through stagnation, complacency, and sabotage. The poison of pride crushes our spirits and blinds us to the present moment, ultimately leading to a downward spiral to hopelessness.

To put it simply, a crushed spirit is like a water bottle that is already filled with poison. No matter how much water we pour in, it will overflow because the bottle is already full. Our heart cannot receive because it is already overflowing with an excessive sense of self-loathing, self-righteousness, and other forms of self-centeredness, fueled by pride. To put it simply, a crushed spirit cannot receive because it is already full. If you try to pour more water into it, it will only overflow, just as a crushed spirit cannot accept anything new because it is already overflowing with negative emotions. To refill the bottle, we must first dump out the poison and clean it thoroughly.

The downfall of pride can be devastating, but there is hope. The only way to make a vacancy to receive is by evicting our pride. We must dump our hearts of pride and open them up to receive and embrace humility. By cultivating humility and a willingness to take responsibility for our present state, we can begin to heal from the weight of pride. In contrast, a humble heart allows us to acknowledge our weaknesses, learn from our mistakes, and grow as individuals. It enables us to connect with others on a deeper level, fostering meaningful relationships based on mutual respect and understanding. It helps us to become more empathetic, compassionate, and kind towards others. It allows us to learn from our mistakes rather than repeating them out of stubbornness.

Humility also fosters a sense of inner peace, as we no longer feel the need to constantly prove ourselves or seek validation from others. With humility, we can experience a sense of freedom from the chains of pride and the burdens it carries. It is only when we let go that we can truly open ourselves up to be rescued by God's presence.

The message of Psalm 51:17 is just as relevant and important today as it was thousands of years ago. Likewise, a humbled heart is willing to submit to God's will and trust in his goodness and grace. It is a heart that recognizes that we're not in control of our own lives but that God is the one who holds our future in his hands. When we humble ourselves before God, we acknowledge his sovereignty and his power, and we open ourselves up to receive the healing and restoration that only He can provide.

Why Do We Fall?

So why is a broken spirit and a humbled heart pleasing to God? Simply because *"a righteous man falls seven times, and rises again, but the wicked stumble in time of disaster and collapse"* (Proverbs 24:16 AB). It's not the absence of failure or adversity that defines a person's character, but rather their ability to rise again after falling. In the context of this scripture, the terms "rise" and "collapse" refer to the ability of the righteous and the wicked to overcome adversity or succumb to it.

The righteous person falls. The evil, wicked person stays down. This suggests that, when faced with adversity, the wicked are unable to withstand the pressure and ultimately give up or are defeated by their circumstances. In addition, the righteous understand that failure is not the end of the story. The righteous are not immune to failure or setbacks; they're immune to collapse. The mark of an *Uncollapsable Soul* is not that they don't fall, but that they rise.

When we are proud and self-sufficient, we may be able to achieve worldly success, but we are unlikely to find true fulfillment and joy. It's only when we are broken and humbled that we can receive God's forgiveness and healing, and it is only through this process that we can grow in our faith. When we encounter someone who is hurting or struggling, we can offer them the same compassion that God offers us. We can be a source of comfort and support, helping to lift them up and restore their spirit. By practicing empathy and humility, we can deepen our connection with God and with others. My grandmother's impact on my life, which has manifested in this book, is evidence of this connection.

We can spend our whole life chasing a "calling," disguised as prosperity, when in reality, calling chases us in the form of problems. We don't recognize it at first because we can't be passionate about something or someone unless we're willing to suffer for it. Problems reveal what we're passionate about. We just have to be willing to stand in the storm of suffering to produce the passion that's dormant within us. Pain awakens us to what matters most. Your calling might be in what you call a curse. It may feel like you are in a cursed season because you're suffering through a crushing season. But a crushing season does not mean that your spirit needs to be crushed. On the contrary, your calling is usually found where you've been broken and crushed. Your testimony is found where you've been healed and restored.

The path to a crushed spirit is attaching your peace, hope, and faith to outcomes. The danger is that we conclude too prematurely. Living your life attached to outcomes is a weak foundation because you'll always be living only for what can be seen immediately. Your life will be void of joy because you'll be addicted to the outcome you want. There's always something deeper happening that is not seen right away. The difference between those that suffer through a crushed spirit and those that don't is NOT by chance or happenstance. It's a decision made in advance, regardless of the circumstance.

Anything else at the center of our hearts is guaranteed to collapse and crush us. What is taking the center of your life? What are you building your life around? These are the question of what you worship. Whatever is at the center of your life is God or your god. I needed to understand why I had chosen to fill the hole in my soul with a woman. How could I have allowed myself to turn to not only my wife but other women for my sense of masculinity, self-worth, and internal fulfillment?

The DNA of Your Heart

In his book *Wild at Heart: Discovering the Secret of a Man's Soul*, John Eldredge "invites men to recover their masculine heart, defined in the image of a passionate God." And he invites women to "discover the secret of a man's soul and to delight in the strength and wildness men were created to offer." He makes a compelling case that 3 deep, irrefutable desires are ingrained within the masculine DNA of every man's heart: a battle to fight, an adventure to live, and a beauty to rescue. It's part of the masculine journey to be protectors, powerful, and competitive. Men are also drawn to undertake adventurous escapades, pursue exploration, or even a bit of destruction. But nothing measures up to the inspiration that wells up in a man from the presence of a beauty that has him awestruck. A captivating, stunning woman gives a man someone to fight for. He wants to be a hero to the woman that has his heart.

Think about it. Any movie that guys enjoy has all three elements of battle, adventure, and beauty—even if she's randomly thrown in at the end for that heroic kiss that sweeps her off her feet. The book aims to answer the one question every man asks himself—*Do I have what it takes?* This question is paramount because *"Until a man knows he's a man, he will forever be trying to prove he is one, while at the same time shrink from anything that might reveal he is not. Most men live their lives haunted by the question or crippled by the answer they've been given."* (Page 62)

Conversely, Eldredge found the heart of a woman contains a variation of his desires that compliments the masculine heart. The feminine heart uniquely longs to be fought for, to share in adventures, and desires her captivating beauty to be fully unveiled and seen. Her desire is to be desired and pursued, share an adventure with him rather than being an adventure to him, and be captivated by him—fully seen, known, accepted, and loved. As you can see, the male heart complements the needs of the female heart, and vice versa. He wants a battle to fight—she wants to be fought for. He wants an adventure to live—she wants an adventure to share. He wants a beauty to rescue—she wants her beauty to captivate him (this is also why women need to feel known & loved rather than solved). These desires in us make us feel most alive.

They can also destroy us. Just as a fire helps meet essential needs such as cooking food, creating warmth, or harvesting energy, an uncontained fire can just as easily burn down your house or kill you. In this context, although femininity arouses masculinity, it can't bestow it because only masculinity can bestow masculinity. Men need their father or father figure to affirm their strength and validate their identity. This is why it's so dangerous for a man to take his deepest question to a woman. External validation from the feminine heart for the internal question of the masculine heart ends in either addiction or emasculation. (Pg 93). And that's exactly what happened to me.

In my case, the divorce left me with an unhealthy addiction to external validation because I felt so unworthy from a deep sense of emasculation. So what John Eldredge states here is exactly what came to pass for me: *"A man who has married a woman has made her a solemn pledge; he can never heal his wound by delivering another to the one he promised to love. Sometimes she will leave him; that is another story. Too many men run after her, begging her not to go. If she has to go, it is probably because you have some soul work to do. What I am saying is that the masculine journey always takes a man away from the woman in order that he may come back to her with his question answered. A man does not go to a woman to get his strength; he goes to her to offer it. You do not need a woman for you to become a great man, and as a great man, you do not need a woman. As Augustine said, "Let my soul praise you for all these beauties, but let it not attach itself to them by the trap of love," the trap of addiction because we've taken our soul to her for validation."*[15]

Eldredge's work in *Wild at Heart* opened my eyes to the underlying truth that I had never considered in my season of a crushed spirit. His findings point toward a compelling revelation. Our spirits are designed to depend on God. If you take the three unique God-given desires of a man's heart and a woman's heart, it's a reflection of the image of God's heart. From the beginning of creation, God has fiercely fought for his people, even to the point of laying down his life. At the same time, He desires us to seek him first and fight to sacrifice our ways for His. God's entire story is a risky, wild adventure of life. Yet He invites us to share in his adventure on this little blue dot that hangs in the balance of the cosmos. Lastly, God loved us before we loved Him. We are the beauty that He rescued. Yet, He wants us to be fully enamored with the beauty of His love and glory that He unveils to us. In other words, the closest human institution we have that resembles the fullness of God's character is the union of marriage. The fullness of the masculine heart, unified with the completeness of the feminine heart, is a mirror that echos the totality of God's heart. That's why marriage is so sacred. It's an image of his character that symbolizes his love.

Throwback to the Beginning

I want you to see this. Let's rewind it to the inception of humanity. Genesis 2:20-25 says, *"But for Adam, no suitable helper was found. So the Lord God caused the man to fall into a deep sleep, and while he was sleeping, he took one of the man's ribs and then closed up the place with flesh. Then the Lord God made a woman from the rib he had taken out of the man, and he brought her to the man. The man said, "This is now bone of my bones and flesh of my flesh; she shall be called 'woman,' for she was taken out of man." That is why a man leaves his father and mother and is united to his wife, and they become one flesh. Adam and his wife were both naked, and they felt no shame."*

In God's infinite love, he created a partner for Adam, that was such a breathtaking creature that he broke out in praise! He was like, *"WHOA-MAN... Hey, that sounds good; I'll call her woman!"* Eve's feminine essence & exquisite symmetry was the finest artwork he'd ever seen, far beyond his wildest imagination. He felt no shame because they were fully known & accepted by God and each other. Think about that: shame didn't exist! They had perfect unity until the fall of mankind after she ate the forbidden fruit. Although Eve was deceived by the slithering serpent, Adam was not. After Eve took a bite, there was a brief historic moment when Eve was separated from God by sin—but Adam was still sinless. Unlike Eve, Adam didn't fall because he was tricked by the serpent. After all, hiding behind deception or ignorance as an excuse was not an option. It was simply a choice as if to say that he'd rather live without God than without his wife. His fear of losing his romance with her was greater than separation from God's romance. Adam had forgotten that God was his first love, not the woman. He had chosen the gift over the gift giver. Adam gave Eve a place in his heart that was designed for God almighty. That's the moment mankind began to worship creation over the creator. The evils of sin took dominion over the earth, along with the condemnation of shame. So they did exactly what we still do today—try to hide our insecurity in plain sight!

If the intimacy of a woman is the water every man truly thirsts for, why do we remain thirsty after we've had a drink? It's the wrong well. That's why she can't be the source of a man's strength, especially when he was designed to offer strength. We were designed by God, for God, with a desire for Him to be the source of our deepest joy. The problem is most people don't ever discover this revelation. This is why a confident, secure man must discover his masculinity before the woman enters the equation. The foundation of his life should be built on the undeniable truth to the deepest question hidden in his very core: what is that thirst my soul has a deep craving for, and how do I satisfy it?

We were created with the need for love through intimacy. Culture loves the idea of love. Society makes romance a major highlight, if not the center of most creative expressions, like movies, tv series, novels, songs, artwork, and poetry. We are thirsty for passion, acceptance, intimacy, encouragement, romance, connection, beauty, excitement, captivation, ecstasy, fulfillment, and unconditional love. What we do not realize is—are we not looking for the intimate character of God? If you think about it, our obsession with romance is so obvious that we have to wonder how we missed it. Think about the endless paintings, poems, love songs, shows, and films centered around romance, love, intimacy, or losing a lover. Pay attention to the language men use to describe the wonder of her beauty. You can categorize this as obsession, instincts, or even mother nature. Or, could this mystical phenomenon be nothing less than a form of worship? Is union with her not the closest resemblance we have to the heart of God, which makes us feel fully alive?

What pours out of our hearts isn't just a longing for the love of a woman but our longing for who God is. Without the source of God's true love in the heart of a man, a man will try to quench his thirst with the women that came after Eve because nothing else in creation even comes close. As long as God is not in his proper order, our lives will always be out of order. The answer we're looking for is flipping the script of Adam's choice by taking our deepest thirst to God rather than "Eve" and choosing our creator over creation. We must always remember that Eve was not our first romance; God was. It's only in God's love that we find healing and restoration and can love our wives from a place of overflow. After all, how can your heart run dry when the source of your water comes from an endless supply?

That's when it hit me. My heart was broken because I'd lost my wife, but my spirit was crushed because I'd lost my identity. When I got married, I took my deepest question to a woman and made her validation the source of my confidence. We made each other our wells. After the divorce, my insecurity was completely exposed. Over a year of trying to take that wound to other women, I bled all over them. No person can fulfill you. But God's love can. More often than not, he sends us what we need but not who we want because we're so focused on the one that we lost. Part of the healing journey is letting others in to love you.

The Privilege of Pressure

In his autobiography, *The Sacred Journey*, the late author, Frederick Buechner, hits the nail on the head. *"To do for yourself the best that you have it in you to do—to grit your teeth and clench your fists in order to survive the world at its harshest and worst—is, by that very act, to be unable to let something be done for you and in you, that is more wonderful still. The trouble with steeling yourself against the harshness of reality is that the same steel that secures your life against being destroyed secures your life also against being opened up and transformed by the holy power that life itself comes from. You can survive on your own. You can grow strong on your own. You can even prevail on your own. But you cannot become human on your own."*[120]

Everybody has pressure, but not everyone knows how to handle it. You can't manipulate it; you can only learn to manage it in a way that serves you. That's why I believe we can't move forward in confidence and freedom if we're carrying the extra weight of burdens that we were never meant to drag around. It's only a matter of time until you break or drop the extra weight. When I finally sold my house, I subconsciously permitted myself to move on. I stopped punishing myself and allowed for a new beginning rather than reliving the same ending. I'd been injecting so much venom into my spirit that the toxins of insecurity, hopelessness, and bitterness paralyzed me.

The antidote was love, hope, and forgiveness, with a mustard seed of faith. Anti-venom took its course, although feelings don't mend at the same time that you choose to forgive and let go of the chokehold you have on yourself.

My journey of healing from divorce was a difficult one. I felt crushed and broken, like I was carrying a weight that was too heavy to bear. Maybe you feel the same. But looking back now, I can see that this season of my life was preparation for what was to come. It was preparation for me to be strengthened when I needed it most so that when the Surfside Collapse happened, my heart would break, but my spirit would never be crushed again!

I had already learned that my faith is not attached to outcomes but to Jesus. I learned that I couldn't rely on anything in creation, only the Creator. When tragedy struck, I thank God that I was able to draw on the strength that had been gained through my previous struggles. Letting go of burdens is not a one-time event. Forgiveness is a continuous process that requires constant effort and intentionality. But the more we let go, the more Uncollapsable our souls become.

We become lighter, more agile, and more able to navigate the ups and downs of life. The key to letting go of burdens is to trust in God's love and grace. We need to trust that He is with us, that He is for us, and that He is working all things together for our good. We need to trust that He can handle our burdens and that He can transform them into something beautiful. It's about trusting in God's plan for our lives and having faith that he will carry us through even the toughest of times.

Losing my wife caused the collapse of my life. My divorce initially crushed me, but I later realized it didn't have to. I allowed that same pain to break my spirit with humility. What I called a curse in one season, I now call a blessing in another season because my divorce was preparation for Surfside! Had I not learned that my soul was collapsable, then it wouldn't have strengthened my heart, saved my spirit, and refined my soul to become whole for what my future held. If God can do it for me, He can do it for you.

Remember, outcome is God's job; outlook is our job. Order of the universe is God's job. Order of priorities is our job. Control is up to God. Faith is up to you and me. That's how to make your Soul Uncollapsable. Perhaps, this is where some *Cosmic Perspective* may help drive this point home.

CHAPTER 13

Cosmic Perspective

When I look at the sky, which you have made, at the moon and the stars, which you set in their places—what are human beings, that you think of them; mere mortals, that you care for them?

Psalm 8:3-4 (GNT)

A Trek to Space

A life season of suffering can be both humbling and overwhelming. Grief and despair can humble us, make us think about life from a grander perspective, and cause us to question our place in the universe. The pain of loss often forces us to confront our limitations and mortality. There's a deep desire in the human soul to know that there is something more beyond our limited comprehension. It's an innate desire within the depths of our souls to find meaning and purpose in life and to understand why we are here. While some people may turn inward to find meaning and purpose, others look outward, hoping to find answers in the vast expanse of the universe.

This search for meaning and purpose is ingrained in our very being, separates us from animals, and is what drives us to explore beyond our understanding. For many, this search for something greater than ourselves takes on a spiritual dimension. We can look to the heavens and see the handiwork of the God who is responsible for the vastness and beauty of the universe. Even for those who don't believe in a divine creator, the search for something more significant than ourselves is still a fundamental human experience. It's a quest for insight, meaning, and the purpose of the world around us and our place in it.

A crucial aspect of this process for insight is seeking "outsight," looking beyond ourselves to gain a better perspective. When we gaze up at the stars, the infinite expanse of the cosmos reveals our smallness in the grand scheme of things. We realize that our lives are but a blip in the vast universe. Deep space, with its infinite expanse and timeless nature, offers a resemblance of eternity into something beyond our understanding. It can evoke both a sense of awe and wonder in hopes of cosmic relief, as well as a feeling of cosmic despair. This duality reminds us of our brevity in the universe, and yet it also offers the possibility of something greater than ourselves. It's a reminder that there is more to life than what we can see and touch.

The world witnessed an extraordinary example of this duality on October 13, 2021. History was made as the oldest astronaut made his "trek" to outer space. At 90 years, he achieved what many only dream of. This inspirational man is none other than the legendary Canadian actor William Shatner, who has become an icon since he played Captain James T. Kirk in the original Star Trek series that debuted back in 1966. Ironically, a man who's long been fascinated by space and has been a vocal advocate for space exploration, yet has been known for pioneering space for the past 60 years, would finally get to experience what he's always portrayed and dreamt of.

He boarded the New Shepard rocket piloted by Jeff Bezos's company, Blue Origin, to spend ten minutes heavenward in space. In his memoir, *Boldly Go: Reflections on a Life of Awe and Wonder*, Shatner shared his detailed experience of the journey, including his initial fears and concerns as the rocket launched: *"At three g's, I felt my face being pushed down into my seat. I don't know how much more of this I can take. Will I pass out? Will my face melt into a pile of mush? How many g's can my ninety-year-old body handle?"*

Once the rocket pierced through the earth's atmosphere, Shatner found himself feeling different than he had expected. While others onboard took joy in experiencing weightlessness for the first time and celebrated with somersaults, he wanted no part of it. He had only one thing on his mind—to get to the window as quickly as possible to see what was out there. He wanted to witness the mystery of space, the majesty of the universe. Like most of us, he had seen countless images of our planet before, but nothing could compare to the sight of it from space. The colors were more vibrant, the shape more distinct, and the atmosphere was visible like a thin layer of haze around the planet. Shatner was filled with a sense of awe and wonder at the beauty of our home planet.

However, when he turned his gaze away from Earth and looked into the depths of space, he was surprised to find that it was not the awe-inspiring sight he had imagined. *"When I looked in the opposite direction, into space, there was no mystery, no majestic awe to behold; all I saw was death."* Shatner recalled what he saw as a "cold, dark, black emptiness" unlike any blackness you can see on Earth.[102] He continued, *"I had thought that going into space would be the ultimate catharsis of that connection I had been looking for between all living things—that being up there would be the next beautiful step to understanding the harmony of the universe,"* the actor writes.

As he contemplated the view from the spacecraft, Shatner was reminded of a scene from the movie "Contact," in which Jodie Foster's character looks out into the heavens and utters the now-famous line, "They should've sent a poet." Foster's character is struck by the beauty and mystery of the universe, and her words capture the wonder and awe that many people feel when contemplating the vastness of space. For William, however, the experience was different. He realized that the beauty he had always sought was not to be found in the emptiness of space. He described, *"I had a different experience because I discovered that the beauty isn't out there, it's down here, with all of us. Leaving that behind made my connection to our tiny planet even more profound."*[102]

Shatner also testified in his book, *"It (my short time in space) was among the strongest feelings of grief I have ever encountered,"* he added. *"The contrast between the vicious coldness of space and the warm nurturing of Earth below filled me with overwhelming sadness. Every day, we are confronted with the knowledge of further destruction of Earth at our hands: the extinction of animal species, of flora and fauna... things that took five billion years to evolve, and suddenly we will never see them again because of the interference of mankind. It filled me with dread. My trip to space was supposed to be a celebration; instead, it felt like a funeral."*[102]

In his documentary "Shatner in Space," the actor's historic voyage is masterfully recorded, capturing his emotional journey from the moment he boarded the spacecraft to the moment they landed. As the space travelers returned to Earth, Jeff Bezos enthusiastically greeted them with a hearty "Hello, Astronauts!" while they excitedly exited their spaceship with cheers, celebrations, and high-fives. However, Shatner's response was different. You could see the unsettled look of shock on his face as he carefully stepped off the capsule. As he stepped back onto solid ground, Jeff Bezos met him with a warm, heartfelt bear hug, and Shatner reciprocated by embracing him back with open arms. At that moment, Shatner was speechless and could only find one word, "Holy...".

Once everyone disembarked, Bezos turned to Shatner and eagerly asked, "Well?" Shatner appeared shaken, struggling to find the words to describe his cosmic experience. "Well, it's... it's... In a way, it's indescribable. I can't tell you what you have done. Everybody in the world needs to do this. Everybody in the world needs to see the..." Overwhelming emotions got the best of him as he paused, his words momentarily paralyzed by tears, before continuing. "It was unbelievable. Unbelievable. I mean, you know, the little things like weightlessness, but to see the blue color go whip by you, and now you're staring into the blackness, that's the thing. There is mother earth and comfort, but what you see is black."

Overcome with gratitude, Shatner grabs Jeff by the shoulders and quivers the words, "What you have given me is the most profound experience I can imagine. It's odd. I'm so filled with emotion about what just happened! It's extraordinary. Extraordinary." Shatner then says something profound yet perplexing. "I hope I never recover from this. I hope that I can maintain what I feel now. I don't want to lose it."

The Overview Effect

Take a moment to reflect on William Shatner's words and reactions. How can someone go from saying, *"I hope I never recover from this. I hope that I can maintain what I feel now. I don't want to lose it,"* to later writing that it was among his *"strongest feelings of grief"* he had ever encountered? How can someone experience such a dramatic shift in emotion in such a short time? It seems like an abrupt change from the highest of highs to the lowest of lows, but it's important to consider the context of his life experiences that make his words both profound and credible.

Throughout his long life, consider the fact that Shatner has likely been dreaming of exploring space for over 60 years, and he has lived a life that has weathered some significant blows from crushing seasons. Early in his career, he went through a season where he couldn't find work, resulting in him going broke and losing his home. He had to live in a truck-bed camper for some time. Then in 1999, he found his *"beautiful soulmate,"* who had *"meant everything"* to him, lying lifeless at the bottom of their backyard swimming pool. She'd suffered from alcoholism and accidentally drowned after drinking and taking Valium. These are profound experiences that could deeply affect anyone.

Given these experiences, it's hard to believe that a 10-minute joyride to space could bring Shatner to the brink of his "strongest feelings of grief". It seems audacious, but perhaps his spirit was briefly crushed worse than anything he's ever experienced through his space experience. But why? Is he confused or unstable, or is there something else at play?

This cognitive shift in awareness experienced by some astronauts during spaceflight is a concept known as the "Overview Effect". This term was coined by Frank White, a space philosopher and author. White describes the Overview Effect as a transformative experience that creates a deeper understanding of the interconnectedness of all life on Earth. It is the realization that the planet we inhabit is a tiny, fragile ball of life, "hanging in the void," shielded and nourished by a paper-thin atmosphere. Astronauts who experience the Overview Effect often report a deep shift in perspective of Earth and humanity's place in the universe, leaving them with feelings of awe for the planet, a greater understanding of the fragility of all life, and a renewed sense of responsibility for taking care of the environment. They come to appreciate the preciousness and fragility of our existence.

For many astronauts, a trip to space became a journey of the soul, a journey that touches on the deepest parts of the human spirit and challenged them to contemplate beyond themselves. This experience often transforms astronauts' perspectives[103]. In the short film "Overview," which delves into the Overview Effect through interviews with astronauts and experts, philosopher David Loy explains that the experience brings about a unique kind of self-awareness. He states, *"I don't think any of us had any expectations about how it would give us such a different perspective. I think the focus had been: we're going to the stars, we're going to the other planets, and suddenly we look back at ourselves, and it seems to imply a new kind of self-awareness"*[99]. David Beavers of the Overview Institute paraphrases an astronaut who reportedly said, *"When we originally went to the moon, our total focus was on the moon: we weren't thinking about looking back at the earth, but now that we've done it, that may well have been the most important reason we went"*[100].

In the film, 3 other astronauts share their perspectives, providing insight into an experience most of us may never have. Take a moment to live vicariously through them as you read below:

"It really does look like this really beautiful oasis out in the middle of nothingness. And if you have a chance for your eyes to adjust, and you can actually see the stars and the Milky Way, it's this oasis against the backdrop of infinity– this enormous universe behind it."—Ron Garan, former NASA astronaut.

"You look back at it, and it's placed perfectly from the sun to take care of us, and you kind of take that reverse role on about—well, we need be taking care of it too, so it can continue to do that for us. I don't know how you can't have a greater appreciation for it after you see it that way."—Nicole Stott, veteran NASA astronaut.

"You develop an instant global consciousness, a people orientation, an intense dissatisfaction with the state of the world, and a compulsion to do something about it. From out there on the Moon, international politics look so petty. You want to grab a politician by the scruff of the neck and drag him a quarter of a million miles out and say: Look at that, you son of a *****"[104]. —Edgar Mitchell, veteran NASA astronaut, walked on the Moon during Apollo 14 mission in 1971

While the Overview Effect is often described as an experience that shifts one's perspective, it is clear that it's something deeper, more profound. It's an intense spiritual awakening within your soul that rocks every fiber of your being with a *cosmic perspective*. The polarity of cosmic relief and cosmic despair that we can experience makes up an encounter of *cosmic perspective*. In this sense, the Overview Effect is a reminder of the spiritual dimensions of our existence. It reconfirms that there's more to life and that our lives are part of a larger cosmic story that is still unfolding. While the experience is often associated with astronauts, it's not limited to those who have traveled to space. People who have had near-death experiences, out-of-body experiences, or even profound moments of meditation or prayer can also experience the Overview Effect.

Awestruck in Wonder

Whether he realizes it or not, his polarizing responses of deep grief from fear while feeling awestruck in wonder is exactly what scripture describes when you have a real encounter with God. The moment that Captain Kirk returned to earth and was shaken speechless, he could only utter one word, "HOLY." The word holy expresses a sense of reverence or awe for something that has been set apart and is considered divine or has a divine nature. Going to space gave William a cosmic perspective that acknowledges the closest thing to seeing the scope of God's glory and splendor on display. In other words, Shatner was experiencing a deep state of worship.

It's clear from Shatner's experience, and the Biblical scripture describes that encountering God involves both a sense of fear and awe. *Let all the earth **fear** the LORD. Let all who live in the world stand in **awe** of him* Psalm 33:8 (GWT). When we encounter God, we experience a sense of fear because of the power and majesty of the Creator of the universe. The fear of the Lord is not a negative emotion but a healthy respect for the ultimate authority of the universe and a natural response to our smallness in comparison to His greatness.

Furthermore, Psalm 14:26-27 (TPT) brings even further clarity to Shatner's explanations. *Confidence and strength flood the hearts of the lovers of God who live in awe of him, and their devotion provides their children with a place of shelter and security. To worship God in wonder and awe opens a fountain of life within you, empowering you to escape death's domain.* In essence, the psalmist is telling us that living in awe of God and worshiping Him in wonder is the key to a truly fulfilling life. It is through this relationship with God that we gain true strength and confidence, create a legacy of faith for our children, and find the power to overcome death. As we seek to live in awe of God, we discover that He is the source of our strength, the foundation of our lives, and the fountain of life that empowers us to live fully and abundantly.

Invisible Force to be Reckoned With

To truly grasp the revelation behind living in awe of an unseen God, we must go deeper into the vastness of outer space to understand the power of the invisible forces he's created. By recognizing the importance of the Sun and gravity in our lives, we can begin to understand the immense power and glory of our Creator. Without the Sun's heat and light, life on Earth would not be possible. The Sun generates the energy that sustains all living beings, warming our seas and giving energy to the plants that provide us with food and oxygen. But the power of the Sun goes beyond this. Its sheer size and strength are almost incomprehensible. Our planet rotates on its axis once every 23 hours, 56 minutes, and 4.09053 seconds at 1,000 miles per hour, while at the same time, it orbits around the Sun at a speed of 67,000 MPH. Meanwhile, our entire solar system is moving through the galaxy at a speed of 490,000 MPH.

Despite these incredible forces of physics, we're unaware of their existence in our daily lives. Even as you sip coffee while reading this, you're likely sitting in your own world, oblivious to the fact that our planet is spinning at 1,000 MPH, rotating at 67,000 MPH, and revolving at a galactic 490,000 MPH! The power of gravity is what keeps our world in a state of organized chaos, yet we can't even feel it. We have faith in gravity, even though we cannot see, touch, taste, smell, or hear it. We only sense its presence around us from the evidence that surrounds us.

Just as we have faith in the invisible force of gravity that sustains our physical world, we also have faith in the concealed power of Earth's magnetic field. It acts as a protective shield that deflects most of the charged particles from the solar wind. Without this magnetic shield, these particles and radiation would strip away our atmosphere, along with the gases it contains, making it difficult or impossible for life to exist on Earth.

The magnetic field is generated by the movement of molten iron in the Earth's core. This magnetic field has a north and south pole, just like a bar magnet. The magnetic field also varies in strength and direction over time, and there are regions of the field where it is weaker or stronger. One of the most visible yet rarely seen effects of the Earth's magnetic field is the northern lights. Charged particles from the Sun, called the solar wind, interact with the Earth's magnetic field and are funneled toward the polar regions. When these particles enter Earth's magnetic field, they become trapped in the magnetosphere, which is the region of space around the Earth that is influenced by its magnetic field. Upon collision, they release energy in the form of light, creating the colorful and mesmerizing display known as the northern lights. Overall, the Earth's magnetic field and the northern lights are directly linked and protect us from space threats. Yet you can't see this invisible forcefield that intimately hugs the earth.

Wind, like gravity, and magnetic fields, is an invisible force of nature that also sustains our world. The source of wind is primarily the uneven heating of the Earth's surface by the sun. Different surfaces, such as land, water, and vegetation, absorb and release heat at different rates, causing differences in air pressure. For example, when the sun heats the Earth's surface, warm air rises, and cooler air rushes in to fill the space. These differences in air pressure create areas of high and low pressure, and air flows from high-pressure areas to low-pressure areas, resulting in wind. The

Earth's rotation also shapes wind patterns, as it causes air to be deflected and moved in a curved path.

The function of wind is to distribute heat and moisture around the Earth, which helps regulate temperatures and weather patterns. Wind also plays a crucial role in the water cycle by carrying moisture from seas, lakes, and rivers to land, where it falls as precipitation. The wind is simultaneously important for seed dispersal and pollination in plants and the navigation of ocean currents and migration of animals. In addition, wind has been harnessed by humans for thousands of years for transportation, power generation, and various other purposes. In other words, wind is essential to our planet's survival.

Gravity, magnetic fields, and wind are all around us, and yet we cannot necessarily see or touch them. These physical phenomena are invisible forces that not only have tangible effects on the physical world around us but sustain it in a way that's beyond our understanding or control. All of these forces are examples of the mysteries of the universe that we cannot fully comprehend. Yet, they point to a higher power that is beyond us. Just as gravity, magnetic fields, and wind are essential to the functioning of the physical world, so too is a higher power essential to the function of the universe.

Cosmic Perspective

Isaac Newton, one of the most significant scientists in history, has made remarkable contributions to the field of physics. His groundbreaking work still shapes our understanding of the natural world today. Despite all of his successes, Newton recognized the limitations of science. He famously stated, "Gravity explains the motions of the planets, but it cannot explain who sets the planets in motion." This profound observation challenges us to consider the boundaries of science that unlock the secret forces of the universe. But they do not unlock who the source of those forces may be. However, it is worth noting that science can only explain how things work, not why they exist.

Just the fact that we can rely on the laws of gravity to predict the motion of planets and stars shows that there is a level of order and predictability in the universe, which suggests a guiding force. If we can believe in the unseen forces of the universe, such as gravity, is it that much harder to believe in a higher power, such as God? After all, both gravity and God are forces that we cannot see yet sustain our lives. And if God is the creator and sustainer of the universe and all its forces, including gravity, can we not trust in him to guide us through life's challenges? Even in the face of disappointment, disaster, and death, we can find solace in the belief that these experiences are not random or meaningless but rather part of a larger plan.

Colossians 1:15-17 points to the source of all invisible forces that sustain us. *He is the image of the invisible God, the firstborn of all creation. For everything was created by him, in heaven and on earth, the visible and the invisible, whether thrones or dominions or rulers or authorities—all things have been created through him and for him. He is before all things, and by him all things hold together. (CSB)*

This passage presents a cosmic perspective that is both humbling and awe-inspiring. It reveals the ultimate truth about the nature of the universe and our place within it. The earth, our galaxy, and every solar system contained within the vastness of the cosmos are simply resources. Invisible phenomena such as gravity, magnetism, and wind are complex forces. And the creator of every intricate resource and life force is the one who is the source. Ultimately, Colossians 1:15-17 reminds us that we are not alone in the universe. There is a higher power that is responsible not only for the incomprehensible design of the universe but for the elaborate formation of your soul. This realization should inspire awe and reverence for the beauty and complexity of the cosmos and gratitude for the gifts of life and resources that God has bestowed upon us.

When we're in a dark place, hope seems to flicker out like a dying star. When everything seems to be falling apart, when our hearts break, and darkness consumes us like a deep and endless abyss, there's a certain beauty in the stars that shine the brightest in the darkest of nights. When we look up to the sky, we see the stars that seem to appear out of nowhere, their light piercing through the darkness. But what we often forget is that these stars are always present; they just go unseen until the darkness falls.

Much like these stars, hope can flicker out when darkness falls over us through heartbreak. We may feel like we're lost in the darkness, but hope is always there, waiting for us to find it. Hope doesn't disappear; it's something that illuminates into the night, waiting for us to notice it again. The last miracle that once gave us hope may seem like a distant memory, and the next one may feel too far away and uncertain. This is where most of our lives are lived, in the waiting and the uncertainty. But it's important to remember that hope doesn't go to sleep just because it's dark outside. It doesn't disappear just because we can't see it. We might feel like we're wandering in the dark, but if we keep our hope alive, we'll find that God is already there, waiting for us. Hope isn't just about waiting for the next miracle.

The truth is, when darkness falls over us, we are often forced to confront how small we are. We are reminded of how insignificant we are in the grand scheme of things. But instead of feeling defeated by this realization, we can choose to embrace it. It's in the dark places we need Him the most, and it's where He shows up with the greatest power. There is a saying that goes, "It's always darkest before dawn." This phrase implies that in the moments when we are in the depths of despair, when we feel like we are trapped in darkness, that is when the light is most likely to break through. That's why the darkness is both terrifying and awe-inspiring.

Cosmic Grief to Cosmic Relief

William Shatner's experience tells us that our deepest moments of grief should result in our deepest moments of worship, where we cry out to God! When we do that, he is near to our broken heart. When He is near to our broken hearts, he rescues us from a crushed spirit by healing our hearts. It's about finding God amid the darkness, in the places between the miracles, in the middle of our harshest pain and deepest sorrow.

The awe-inspiring part lies in the power of cosmic perspective, the ability to see the bigger picture and to understand our place within it. This is why the curse of darkness brings the gift of cosmic perspective. The darker it is, the easier the light pierces through it. Cosmic perspective sharpens our sensitivity to focus on what is illuminating through the dead of night. It gives us a similar "Overview effect" in space that humbles us to how small we are and how BIG God is. God's love is the light that pierces through the darkness of the broken-hearted. His presence rescues those crushed in spirit. God finds us in the places between the miracles, where our faith is tested and our hope is stretched. He helps us to see the light in the darkness, and he gives us the strength to keep going, even when everything seems lost. It's in this waiting, this anticipation, that we can experience the true power of hope.

When we live in anticipation of God surprising us, we open ourselves up to the possibility of miracles happening in the most unexpected moments. In a way, the darkness itself becomes a kind of light, illuminating the contours of our lives and revealing the hidden beauty that was always there. It sharpens our focus on what is truly important and helps us let go of the things that no longer serve us. The idea that the darker it is, the easier the light pierces through it is not just a catchy phrase; it is a powerful truth. Just as an astronaut in space can see the Earth in a new light, with its fragile beauty and interconnectedness, we too can see our lives from a different vantage point.

When we are faced with the darkness of heartbreak, pain, and loss, it is easy to feel like there is no hope. But in reality, it is precisely in these moments that hope shines the brightest. We come to see that the darkness is not something to be feared but rather a gift that can help us grow and become more fully ourselves. So the next time you find yourself in a dark place, remember that this is where the gift of cosmic perspective can be found. You don't need to go to space for a cosmic encounter with God. Take a deep breath, look up at the stars, and allow yourself to be filled with wonder and gratitude as the God of the universe meets you exactly where you are because he loves you beyond comprehension.

CHAPTER 14

Light into the Night

*The light shines in the darkness, and the darkness can
never extinguish it.*

John 1:5 (NLT)

One Year Later

For the first year anniversary, a gathering was held at the site
where the once-standing beachside paradise stood, now
reduced to a giant open crater of exposed foundation—which
also symbolized the condition of our hearts. The weight of grief
still lingered in the hearts of those affected by the devastating
event since the memories and emotions were woven into the
very fabric of our being. The Town of Surfside held a private candlelight vigil for family members, where we gathered in the early
morning. Standing on the barren ocean front land under the vast
expanse of the night sky, I looked up at the stars, seeking a cosmic encounter with the One who holds it all together.

About 300 family members gathered in the early morning hours
of June 24, 2022. We made our way from Collins Ave towards
the beach, as each step we took on that sacred ground carried
the weight of a year's worth of sorrow. Underneath a large white
tent at the eastern edge of the 1.8-acre lot in Surfside, we stood
united in our shared grief. Separated by metal barricades from the
leftover concrete-and-steel ruins, we formed a solemn assembly

drawn together by the deep connection we shared through this tragic event. The atmosphere was heavy with emotions, yet there was also a sense of strength that emanated from each person present. Some reflected in silence and mourned privately. Others wept publicly. A few attendees wailed from utter shock as they took in the reality of their first post-collapse encounter on the premises.

The evening began with a private candlelight vigil, where the families and loved ones of the 98 souls lost in the collapse gathered alongside the dedicated search-and-rescue team. After a year of mourning, intense legal proceedings, a flurry of emotions, and the arduous task of rebuilding our lives without those who were taken from us by their own building. Now, we stood together, united as one broken community, returning to the very place that shattered our existence—ground zero. No media. No politics. Just us.

As the clock struck 1:22 a.m. on June 24, 2022—the exact moment when Champlain Towers South came crashing down—the ceremony commenced. It was a solemn and sacred occasion, a time to remember not how they died but to honor how they lived. A perimeter fence outlined the foundations that once held the building, and on its boundary, 98 torches stood tall, each representing a life lost. Each one represented each life lost. They were positioned with care and purpose, waiting to be ignited in remembrance.

We each faced the wide open space that used to be filled with so much love. With heavy hearts and tear-filled eyes, the names of each perished loved one were called out in order for first responders to recover their bodies. The night air carried their names, whispering through the silence and mingling with the weight of our grief. No torch was left unlit, for each life held immeasurable value. No family was left unrepresented, as the collective pain and loss resonated through every heart in attendance. And in the act of igniting each flame, we proclaimed that their lives would forever burn bright in our memories.

Meanwhile, on the other side of Collins Ave, in Veterans Park, a separate gas torch was lit, casting its own glow across the landscape. Each passing day, as the torch continued to burn, it served as a reminder of the ongoing search and recovery efforts, the tireless dedication of those involved, and the commitment to bring closure to all those affected by the collapse. It would remain lit until July 20, the day when the last collapse victim was recovered.

Later that morning, the public memorial service took place at the same location, drawing a large crowd of hundreds of people. The televised event featured powerful speeches and tributes from politicians, religious leaders, survivors, and family members of the victims. Each speaker shared their personal experiences and reflections, expressing the profound impact that the collapse had on their lives. Their words were filled with raw emotion, highlighting the immense pain and loss that was felt by the community. The ceremony lasted 2 and a half hours and featured 5 emotionally heavy tributes from surviving family members, along with moving speeches from first responders who persevered through a desperate search that lasted 32 days.

Politicians and public figures from all levels of government were present, reflecting the widespread impact of the event and the recognition of its significance. From local officials like Surfside Mayor Shlomo Danzinger and Miami-Dade Mayor Daniella Levine Cava to Senator Jason Pizzo, and even extending to the Governor of Florida, Ron DeSantis, and the First Lady of the United States, Jill Biden, their presence underscored the magnitude of the tragedy and the importance of collective support.

Regardless of political affiliations, these individuals set aside their personal agendas to offer words of comfort and solidarity to our hurting community. Whether or not you agree with the sources doesn't invalidate the truth spoken that day. Dr. Jill Biden said, *"We honor the light you found in each other, a fellowship that you never wanted to be a part of, but draw strength from just the same. If there is something strong enough to help us carry this burden of grief forward, something able to break its gravitational pull, it's love."*

During an earlier "State of the State" address, a momentous occasion unfolded in the House Chamber of Florida's capitol. It was January 11, 2022, and my family and I were filled with a mix of honor and sadness as we were invited as featured guests. We represented not only our own family but also the Surfside families who had suffered unimaginable loss. Little did we know that this moment would give birth to the very idea behind *Uncollapsable Soul*.

As Governor Ron DeSantis addressed the gathered audience, his words echoed through the chamber, touching the depths of our hearts. *"The loss of the 98 victims who perished in the collapse has been devastating and incalculable. One of the victims was 92-year-old Hilda Noriega, whose son, North Bay Village Chief of Police Carlos Noriega, and grandchildren are with us today. Hilda was the matriarch of an amazing family and was dearly missed by those who knew her. The grief and anguish endured by the Noriega family and the other Surfside families have been overwhelming and remind us that: "The Lord is close to the bro-kenhearted; he saves those whose spirits are crushed." Our state should provide support for an appropriate memorial so that future generations will never forget the legacies of the victims of that terrible event."*

I reminisced how those words resonated deeply as Governor DeSantis took the podium at the one-year anniversary after the First Lady. He shared, *"In a very difficult time, you saw a lot of great parts of humanity coming forward to help those in need."* Desantis continued, *"And I can tell you this: people who've never been to Surfside, people who've never even been to the state of Florida, were inspired by the stories and the lives that those 98 people led. They made an impact on their friends, on their family, on their communities, and beyond. And so, we really thought it was important at the State of Florida to make sure that their memories live on. And so, I was happy in our budget to ask the* *legislature to dedicate an initial $1 million towards a memorial that can be constructed on this site, and I'm happy to report that was included in the budget that I signed into law."* This was just before he designated a portion of Collins Avenue to be renamed *98 Points of Light Road.* This act of commemoration reminded us that although disaster wounded the community, we won't forget that each of the 98 remarkable souls is bright light.

Without knowing it, the themes of light and love in First Lady Jill Biden and Florida Governor Ron DeSantis speeches were in exact alignment with my heart. Although the two Surfside remembrance events brought some measure of healing, they lacked the aspect of spiritual healing. I longed to create something more personal, something that wouldn't only pay tribute to their memories but also bring the Lord's presence near to the brokenhearted. Guided by faith and fueled by a collective desire for healing, a group of us from VOUS Church joined hands with CASA Church of Surfside to organize a unique remembrance event.

Light Into the Night

As the sun began to set, casting its golden hues across the horizon, people from all walks of life started to arrive. That evening, we held our own remembrance event on the sandy shores, just steps away from the dead space where the condo building once stood tall. Hundreds of people from all walks of life showed up, including the family & friends of the victims, local residents, mourners of Surfside, and even beachgoers that were passing by. The public gathering came to be called *Light into the Night.*

Light into the Night was more than just a remembrance event; it was a transformative experience that brought our broken community together. As we gathered on the sandy shores, our purpose became clear: to remember those we lost, honor the lives they lived, empathize with one another's pain, inspire hope, pray together, and bring a touch of heaven to a space that had once represented hell. Prayer became the cornerstone of our gathering. It opened our hearts and brought us closer to the presence of God.

We experienced worship, a cry, and a faith that can't be found on the mountain top. It's only in the pit. Prayer opens up your heart and brings us closer to the proximity of God's presence. Prayer is less about moving God's hand and more about God moving our hearts. Praise & worship are a problem for your problems. We don't praise God because of our situation but because of who He is! But it wasn't just prayer and worship that brought healing; it was the power of community. In times of tragedy, we often find that our greatest source of support and healing comes from those who have walked a similar path of pain. As the saying goes, "Hurt people hurt other people, but healed people help heal others." In coming together as a community, we discovered the resilience that lies within our collective spirit.

As the sun began to set, we arranged a small stage platform and positioned speakers and a microphone facing the ocean, directing the attention of the attendees towards the empty pit that symbolized the shadow of death. With an acoustic guitar in hand, the same Greg from the Bahama's mission trip and his wife Carolina led the gathering in singing 3 praise songs that held significant meaning for me on that very same day 1 year earlier. One of them was "Shelter" In by VOUS Worship.

Pastor Ezekiel from CASA Church, located just a few blocks away, stood with us every day, joined by numerous individuals serving their own community as a mission field. He delivered powerful words of faith, hope, and encouragement. Another dear friend, Kat Rowse, guided us into a time of prayer and reflection, inviting the presence of God to envelop us.

As I stood before the gathering, expressing the depth of emotions was a challenge. How could mere words adequately convey the weight of sorrow while honoring the lives lost in a meaningful way? Instead, I shared my personal journey—a narrative that has become the essence of this book. I recounted my encounter with the collapse, my path towards healing and hope, and how my weakness has been transformed into strength through God's grace.

One lesson I learned was that we all need one another. When the lights black out inside of us without warning, we need a few solid people that are willing to be present and stand with us in the gap. I used to perceive. Whether it's a warm embrace and attentive ears, sharing comfort food and a movie night, staying by your side during a hospital stay, or simply holding your hand and offering prayers as tears stream down your face, these acts of support can make a world of difference.

When Kima perished in the building collapse, her legacy of love emerged from the rubble. Although her life was already a shining light, it was God who illuminated her legacy. As is often the case with victims, especially my grandmother, a person's life cannot be measured only by its duration but by the love they give freely. The quality of life depends on the amount of love one shares. When we depart, those we leave behind will recall two things: the memories we created and the impact we made. People will remember how we made them feel and the effect our love had on their world and beyond. The culmination of all our life's decisions creates memories and impacts that define our legacy. Our legacy takes the form of faith, hope, and love and continues to live on through the lives we touch.

Lighting Up the Sky with Legacy

That's why we released 98 sky lanterns, each one representing a departed soul. As the lanterns soared into the sky, we symbolically released the flame that symbolized their essence. It was an act of hope, reminding us that there's more to life beyond this earthly realm. While our loved ones may no longer be physical with us, the flame of their love continues to burn within our hearts. As we watched the lanterns ascend, we released their souls to the heavens, acknowledging their transformation into the afterlife. It wasn't just a reflection on their passing but a celebration of the everlasting impact they had on our lives. Their flames will never be extinguished; they're just beginning to shine. Darkness does not take over the light. But light overcomes darkness as if it's afraid to be swallowed by its radiance. The community of lanterns emitted a glow in the sky that resembled the bright love of an entire community that may not live on with us, but their glow lives on through us.

The one-year anniversary of the passing of our loved ones was an extremely difficult day for us emotionally. We were all struggling to come to terms with the loss, and it felt like we were caught in the midst of a raging storm. However, we found peace at our Light into the Night memorial gathering. During the gathering, we didn't just mourn but also expressed gratitude for the impact our late loved ones had on our lives. We remembered their kindness, laughter, wisdom, and the love they shared with us. But it was so much more than honoring their memory. It was an intimate time of celebrating their lives and connecting with our creator under the stars.

The Cure of Community

When you belong to a unified community, your personal venture becomes a shared adventure. A tribe becomes your place where your internal quest for meaning converts to shared struggles. Many hands make light work. This is why community is paramount to personal recovery. Its power lies in the ability to uplift, inspire, and carry us through the darkest moments of our lives. I believe there's no more beautiful picture of community than this.

A few days later, when Jesus again entered Capernaum, the people heard that he had come home. They gathered in such large numbers that there was no room left, not even outside the door, and he preached the word to them. Some men came, bringing to him a paralyzed man, carried by four of them. Since they could not get him to Jesus because of the crowd, they made an opening in the roof above Jesus by digging through it and then lowered the mat the man was lying on. When Jesus saw their faith, he said to the paralyzed man, "Son, your sins are forgiven." Now some teachers of the law were sitting there, thinking to themselves, "Why does this fellow talk like that? He's blaspheming! Who can forgive sins but God alone?" Immediately Jesus knew in his spirit that this was what they were thinking in their hearts, and he said to them, "Why are you thinking these things? Which is easier: to say to this paralyzed man, 'Your sins are forgiven,' or to say, 'Get up, take your mat, and walk'? But I want you to know that the Son of Man has authority on earth to forgive sins." So he said to the man, "I tell you, get up, take your mat, and go home." He got up, took his mat, and walked out in full view of them all. This amazed everyone, and they praised God, saying, "We have never seen anything like this!" Mark 2:1-12

This act of faith and determination makes me wonder if these men had seen Jesus perform miracles before. Perhaps they had witnessed Him heal other friends or family members and had seen firsthand the power of His love and compassion. It's possible that their previous experiences with Jesus had given them the confidence to take such bold action. Regardless, this act of determination and faith was not only a reflection of their belief in Jesus' power but also their love and commitment to their friend.

It's important to note that it wasn't the paralyzed man's faith that led to his healing but the faith of his friends. This highlights the power of community and the role that others can play in our own healing and restoration. There are times in life when we are called to be a community of people who have the strength and faith to carry others who may not have the strength or faith to carry themselves. We may be called to tear through the roof and bring our friends and loved ones to Jesus, so to speak. And there are other times when we may need to rely on the strength and generosity of others to help us through difficult times.

In the same heart, we need a community that normalizes vulnerability, transparency, and honesty, where we can share our struggles and be met with compassion and understanding. Why? Commitment lasts better in the community. When we are surrounded by people who breathe faith into our spirits, we are more likely to stay committed to healing. We are also more likely to extend that commitment to others and to help them on their own journey.

This is part of God's divine design of our souls. We were created to live in community and to support one another through life's ups and downs. It's okay to need others and to rely on them for strength and support. In fact, it's essential for our own healing and restoration. As we come together in community, we can shine a light into the void of night and begin to find healing and restoration. It's only by supporting and encouraging one another that we can truly find wholeness and bring healing to the world around us.

When we come together in the community, we bring our unique experiences, perspectives, and gifts to the table. We can support each other in our struggles and celebrate with each other in our victories. We can be a shoulder to cry on, a listening ear, and a source of comfort and strength for one another. We are healed to help others. The paralyzed man was not only healed, but he was also given a new purpose. He was able to walk again and use his newfound strength to help others. The faith of his friends lit his heart on fire with their faith!

A candle loses nothing by lighting another candle. In fact, the light grows brighter and shines even more brightly. Instead, we become a source of light and hope to those around us, and our faith, hope, and love multiply. If you light a log on fire, it won't last very long. But if you put together a cluster of logs, it'll burn for hours. What began as a spark can ignite an unstoppable forest fire! As we receive healing and blessings in our own lives, we are called to share that with others and to be a source of hope and encouragement for those around us. The fire is love, we're the forest, and God is the source of the love igniting us.

God sends us night lights in the form of people. When everything is broken within you, it's not about knowing what to do. It's about the crew that's surrounding you! When we think we want answers, God gives us the presence of his love through others. The stronger the community, the stronger the unity. We need each other because we burn hotter & longer with one another other.

The story of the paralyzed man and his friends in the Bible teaches us that we are meant to go through life with each other and with the healing presence of the only one who can rescue our spirits—Jesus. We must not only seek healing for ourselves, but we must also help others find healing and carry them to Jesus when they cannot come on their own. In this way, we can be a blessing to others and share the light and love of Christ with others. As we do, His bright light will shine greater than any spotlight. As my beautiful grandmother exemplified, there's no greater cause worth living for than a legacy of love.

This event sparked a powerful movement that has led to the new establishment of our non-profit organization, *Light into the Night*. Our mission is "To empower grieving communities that have been crushed by tragedy, through public ceremonial gatherings in natural environments that inspire emotional and spiritual healing, by honoring & celebrating the legacies of those who have deceased." As discussed earlier in this book, this is another example of bringing purpose to your pain. Hidden within the depths of your suffering is a deeper calling to light up the darkness around you. Don't worry about the spotlight. Just be a bright light into the night. As my beautiful grandmother exemplified, there's no greater cause worth living for than a legacy of love.

CHAPTER 15

Legacy of Love

"My soul is crushed with grief to the point of death. Stay here and keep watch with me."

Matthew 26:38 (NLT)

When a Tomb Becomes a Womb

The title of this book, "Uncollapsable Soul," carries a deeper meaning than what meets the eye. It speaks to the resilience and strength that we all seek to have in life. Yet, it's not a strength that can be attained solely through our own efforts. We're limited in our ability to achieve an *Uncollapsable soul* on our own. But, with the power, grace, and love of God, we receive unbreakable spirits so that our souls are Uncollapsable.

The Light into the Night commemoration was a time of worship and remembrance. It was a powerful reminder of the importance of turning our focus to God, especially during difficult times. Worship has a way of taking the focus off of ourselves and, instead, acknowledging all that is right with God. It allows us to remember that God is still good, even when our circumstances are not. It is a way of acknowledging that, even in the midst of difficult circumstances, God is still with us, not because he sympathizes with our pain, but because he empathizes.

In the Gospel, John 11:1-44 recounts the story of Jesus raising Lazarus from the dead. When Lazarus fell gravely ill, his sisters, Mary and Martha, sent word to Jesus, hoping for his intervention. By the time Jesus arrived in Bethany, four days had already passed since Lazarus' death and burial. When Jesus arrived in Bethany, Martha and Mary were heartbroken. They'd lost their beloved brother and were mourning his death. When Martha heard that Jesus was coming, she went out to meet Him, while Mary stayed home. Upon arriving, Jesus met with Martha and then Mary, who both expressed their disappointment that Jesus didn't arrive in time to heal Lazarus. Jesus comforted them by assuring them that Lazarus would rise again, but they didn't understand his context.

Mary and Martha were understandably upset. They couldn't understand why Jesus had taken so long to come and why he hadn't healed Lazarus before he died. But Jesus had a plan, and he knew exactly what he was doing. He was about to perform a miracle that would demonstrate his power and authority over death itself. In Jewish culture, it was believed that the soul lingered around the body for 3 days after death, but after the third day, it was believed that the soul had departed, and there was no hope of bringing the person back to life. They had faith that Lazarus could've been healed, but Jesus missed their timing.

Jesus then asks to see Lazarus' tomb. It's here that we get the shortest, yet one of the most potent passages of scripture, in John 11:35, "Jesus wept." After weeping in front of the grieving crowd, He commanded the stone to be rolled away from the tomb. Martha was hesitant, warning that there would be a stench since Lazarus had been dead for 4 days. But Jesus, unfazed, said to her, "Did I not tell you that if you believe, you will see the glory of God?"

It was at this point that Jesus revealed to her the true nature of his power, saying, "I am the resurrection and the life. He who believes in me will live, even though he dies, and whoever lives and believes in me will never die." These words were a clear declaration of Jesus' divine authority over life and death. In a powerful and dramatic moment, Jesus called out, "Lazarus, come out!"

And to everyone's amazement, Lazarus, who'd been dead and buried for 4 days, emerged from the tomb, still wrapped in his burial cloths. Jesus had done the impossible. Jesus then called out to Lazarus, "Lazarus, come out!" (John 11:43), and to everyone's amazement, Lazarus emerged from the tomb, still wrapped in his burial clothes. Who else but Jesus could turn a tomb of death into a womb of new breath?

The Miracle of Empathy

Martha and Mary wanted a miracle of healing. But Jesus' wanted a miracle of resurrection. It's worth noting that Jesus didn't perform this miracle simply to show off his power or to gain more followers. He performed this miracle to demonstrate that he had power over death itself. By waiting 4 days to perform the miracle, Jesus showed that he had power over death itself, not just the moment of passing. Moreover, the reference to the "stink" of Lazarus' decomposing body underscores the gravity of the situation. He'd already performed many miracles before, including healing the sick and casting out demons, but raising someone from the dead was on a completely different level. Death was not a trivial matter but a horrifying reality that brought with it the decay of the physical body. Yet Jesus was undeterred by this, showing his complete authority over the natural order of things.

But what is perhaps most striking about this story is Jesus' empathy and compassion for those who were mourning. As the passage notes, "When Jesus saw Mary weeping, and the Jews who had come with her also weeping, he was deeply moved in his spirit and greatly troubled" (John 11:33). Jesus wasn't weeping for Lazarus himself, as he knew that he'd soon be raised from the dead. Rather, he was weeping for the pain and suffering of his friends, who were grieving the loss of someone they loved! In fact, when he arrived in Bethany, he was moved to tears by the sight of the sorrow and pain of Mary and Martha, Lazarus' sisters. Jesus wasn't weeping because he'd lost a friend or because he was

powerless to stop death, but rather because he deeply empathized with the pain and suffering of those around him.

Even though he was fully aware of his divine power, he never
used it to dismiss or belittle human suffering. Instead, he fully
entered into the human experience, sharing in our joys and sorrows, our victories and defeats. It highlights the paradoxical nature
of Jesus' divinity wrapped in his humanity. On one hand, he is
fully omnipotent and omniscient, possessing the power to raise
the dead and control nature. On the other hand, he's deeply compassionate and empathetic, able to feel and express emotions
like any human being. He's both God and man, able to bridge the
gap between divinity and humanity. Jesus could've simply arrived
and performed the miracle, but he chose to connect with those
who were grieving and share in their pain. He wept with them and
shared in their sorrow, even though He knew that their sorrow
would soon turn to joy.

His willingness to take the time to mourn with his friends
before performing the miracle shows us that he values our emotions and wants to comfort us in our times of grief. This shows us
a crucial aspect of Jesus' character: his deep love for humanity.
He didn't just come to save us; He came to be with us, to share
in our joys and sorrows, and to show us the depth of God's love
for humanity. It reminds us that even in the face of our deepest
sorrows and greatest fears, we can find hope and comfort in the
knowledge that Jesus has the power to bring new life out of even
the darkest situations. The story of Lazarus' resurrection is also
a reminder that there's nothing beyond the power and authority
of Jesus. He showed them that even when all seems lost, even
when death has claimed its victory, there is still hope.

There's Only One Soul That's Uncollapsable

The love of Jesus is the key to unlocking the Uncollapsable
soul. You can find healing and strength through empathetic intimacy with God that was bridged through the love of Jesus. This

intimacy is the quickest way to healing, and it is through our relationship with Him that we find our source of love and grace. Hear my heart on this. The love of Jesus is the sole reason that my spirit was rescued from the distress and agony of a shattered soul and was able to endure the traumatic experience of losing Kima in the collapse. That's not a cliche; it's the honest truth.

There are many religions and beliefs in the world, and many people question how Christians have the audacity to claim that Jesus is the only way to heaven. Jesus' exclusivity as the only way to heaven is often perceived as arrogance or intolerance. But it's not. It is a matter of love.

When a person sins, it doesn't necessarily mean that they are bad or evil. Rather, sin is a spiritual condition we're born into that makes us dead. It's like a terminal disease that we inherit in the DNA of our soul. Sin separates us from God and leads to spiritual death. God is holy and perfect, and sin is anything that falls short of His perfect nature and character. The Bible teaches that the wages of sin is death (Romans 6:23), and this death is not just physical but also spiritual. Spiritual death means that we're cut off from God's life-giving presence.

In the Old Testament Jewish culture, animal sacrifices were used as a way to atone for sins and restore the relationship between God and His people. The shedding of animal blood was necessary because, according to the law, without the shedding of blood, there is no forgiveness of sins (Hebrews 9:22). It seems weird until you contemplate that throughout humanity's existence, freedom from any form of oppression has never been achieved without the shedding of blood. Regardless, every Old Testament sacrifice was like paying the minimum on a credit card that had a balance way too big to pay off in anyone's lifetime. It may have been enough to get you by for some time, but the massive balance you owed still remains. The sacrificial system was based on works, meaning that a person's relationship with God was dependent on their inability to follow the law.

Out of His immense love for us, God humbled Himself by stepping out of heaven and taking on human form, so He could pay the full debt that we owed but could not possibly pay. Jesus Himself claimed to be the only way to the Father. In John 14:6, Jesus said, "I am the way, the truth, and the life. No one comes to the Father except through Me." This statement is clear and unambiguous. Jesus was not just a wise teacher or a prophet; He was claiming to be the only way to God. Meaning that he was a blatant liar, raving lunatic, or the Lord of all. But he lived a perfect, blameless life and was obedient even unto death.

The Place of Crushing

The Gospels describe the physical, mental, emotional, and spiritual pain He endured during His arrest, trial, and crucifixion. In Matthew 26:38-39[129], Jesus expressed to His disciples, "My soul is crushed with grief to the point of death. Stay here and keep watch with me." He went on a little farther and bowed with his face to the ground, praying, "My Father! If it is possible, let this cup of suffering be taken away from me. Yet I want your will to be done, not mine." The concept of the "cup" in the Old Testament, as referenced in Isaiah 51:17, symbolizes God's wrath against sin. Fully aware of the suffering that awaited Him, He longed for the cup of suffering to be taken away. However, He surrendered to God's will, acknowledging that His ultimate purpose was to bring redemption and reconciliation to humanity.

First, Jesus was betrayed by one of His own disciples, Judas Iscariot, who led a group of soldiers to arrest Him. Jesus was about to be arrested, where He prayed in agony. In the book of Luke, a physician and one of the four Gospel writers, we encounter a powerful scene in the Garden of Gethsemane. It's here that we witness Jesus, the Son of God, in a state of such immense anguish that he sweats drops of blood. This phenomenon, known as hematidrosis, is a rare medical condition where an individual's sweat becomes tinged with blood. The intensity of Jesus' suffering is reflected in this physical manifestation.

In this pivotal moment, Jesus asks some of his disciples to pray and keep watch. His instruction to stay awake is not merely physical, as it carries a deeper meaning. Jesus is urging his disciples to live for him, to remain committed and vigilant because He's about to sacrifice Himself for them. In His imminent death, he called them to carry on his mission and live in the light of his teachings.

The significance of the location, Gethsemane, adds further depth to this scene. The name itself means "a place for pressing oil." It alludes to the crushing and pressing process used to extract oil from olives, symbolizing the intense pressure and suffering that Jesus would experience. This imagery illustrates that our calling, our purpose in life, often comes with its own share of pressures. Pressure can form you or crush you, but that's a choice to make. Like olives being crushed to produce valuable oil, our calling may crush us, but it's through pressing and pressure that power is generated.

In the Garden of Gethsemane, Jesus experienced a depth of anguish and turmoil that is difficult for us to comprehend. He knew that He was about to face betrayal, suffering, and ultimately, death on the cross. In the midst of this intense inner struggle, Jesus demonstrated an extraordinary display of love and grace that continues to astound me. Even in betrayal, Jesus didn't allow his human desires to consume Him. Instead, He extended compassion to those who came to arrest Him. When one of His disciples, in an act of desperation, sliced the ear of a servant, Jesus responded by reaching out and healing the man's ear, demonstrating His divine power yet again.

He was then taken to the high priest's house, where He was questioned, mocked, and beaten by the guards and the religious leaders. He was then taken to the Roman governor, Pilate, who found no fault in Him, but allowed Him to be handed over to be crucified because of the demands of the crowd.

Jesus was then subjected to brutal torture with a whip known as the "cat of nine tails." The Roman soldiers stripped Jesus of His clothing, leaving His back completely exposed, and then tied Him to a post or pillar. The "cat of nine tails" was a whip with multiple strands, each of which had sharp pieces of bone or metal attached to the ends. Soldiers took turns striking the Lamb of God with the whip, using all their strength to cause the maximum pain and damage possible. When the tails of the whip struck, these jagged ends dug into his flesh, causing deep lacerations and ripping off raw flesh and muscles. And this was just one of many forms of suffering He endured leading up to His crucifixion.

They placed a crown of thorns on His head as a mockery and struck Him repeatedly. He was forced to carry His own cross upon his torn, bruised, bloody, exhausted body. It was a grueling and humiliating experience. The cross was heavy, and He had already been beaten and flogged, so He was likely weak and in great pain. As He carried the cross through the streets, He was mocked and ridiculed by the people, adding to His humiliation.

When He arrived at the site of His crucifixion, Jesus was stripped of His clothes and nailed to the cross with His arms outstretched. The nails would have caused excruciating pain as they were driven through His wrists and feet. He hung on the cross for several hours, enduring intense physical and emotional suffering. Perhaps the greatest suffering Jesus experienced leading up to the cross was spiritual in nature. As He hung on the cross, He cried out, "My God, my God, why have you forsaken me?" (Matthew 27:46). This was the moment when Jesus, who had never sinned, became sin for us, bearing the punishment that we deserved as he carried the full weight of humanity's sin upon Him. Despite all of this incalculable suffering, Jesus not only endured the cross but chose it, knowing that His sacrifice would bring salvation and eternal life to all who believe in Him.

Resurrection Power of His Uncollapsable Soul

Most importantly, had Jesus remained dead in the grave, that would've made him a mere mortal. It would have invalidated his claim to be the Son of God and would not have fulfilled the Old Testament prophesies that the Messiah was to fulfill. But Christ did rise from the dead, and that changed everything. His resurrection gives us the assurance of eternal life. The resurrection of Jesus is a sign of God's love and grace for humanity by providing a way for people to be reconciled with Him.

The death and resurrection of Jesus are seen as the ultimate expression of God's love for humanity. As it says in John 3:16, "For God so loved the world that he gave his one and only Son, that whoever believes in him shall not perish but have eternal life." The resurrection of Jesus shows that God's love for humanity extends beyond this life and that He desires to have a relationship with each person.

Secondly, the resurrection is a sign of God's grace. Grace is the unmerited favor of God, meaning that it is not earned or deserved. The resurrection shows that even though humanity is sinful and deserving of punishment, God offers forgiveness and salvation through His Son. As it says in Romans 6:23, "For the wages of sin is death, but the gift of God is eternal life in Christ Jesus our Lord." The resurrection demonstrates that God offers this gift of eternal life to all who believe in Him.

Thirdly, the resurrection of Jesus is a sign of God's power and sovereignty. It shows that God has power over death and that nothing is impossible for Him. This is a reminder to believers that God is in control and that they can trust Him in all circumstances as it says in Ephesians 1:19-20, "His incomparably great power for us who believe. That power is the same as the mighty strength he exerted when he raised Christ from the dead."

Finally, the resurrection of Jesus is a sign of God's promise of new life. The resurrection of Jesus is not just a historical event but a promise of a new life for all who believe in Him. As it says in

1 Peter 1:3, "Praise be to the God and Father of our Lord Jesus Christ! In his great mercy, he has given us new birth into a living hope through the resurrection of Jesus Christ from the dead." Jesus didn't just resurrect. He is resurrection. And we get to share in Jesus' resurrection! That same power that conquered death, hell, and the grave lives in us when we invite him into our hearts.

Jesus assures us that we can find security and hope in him, even in the midst of trials. In John 16:33, he says, "Take heart, for I have overcome the world!" These words serve as a reminder that our calling is not meant to crush us into despair but rather to propel us towards victory. By embracing the crushing and pressing moments of our calling, we can tap into the power and strength that comes from relying on God. While our calling may involve challenges and pressures that seem overwhelming, we can find assurance in the knowledge that Jesus has already overcome the world. He has gone before us, conquering sin and death, and through him, we can find the strength to persevere and overcome every obstacle we face.

The message of Uncollapsable Soul is not to point to William Shatner, myself, or the universe. It points to Jesus. Some question His exclusivity as the only way to heaven, seeing it as a display of arrogance or intolerance. But consider this: if there were only one cure for cancer that treated terminally ill patients with 100% effectiveness, would you view this as exclusivity or celebrate the cure? The real question is not—how could a good God be allowed to hold me ransom because I sinned by making Jesus the only way to heaven? Rather, ask yourself this—how is God so good that he allowed Jesus to become sin and pay my ransom so that I may go to heaven? It is a matter of love. Jesus is the only way to God because He is the only one who can conquer death, providing forgiveness and reconciliation with God that we could have never achieved. He didn't have to. He chose to. You & I are the passion of Christ. And there's no greater love than this.

W.O.R.S.H.I.P. Through Your Grief

The life of Jesus exemplifies how our greatest purpose is often hidden within our most punishing grief. Despite facing immense suffering, Jesus persevered and ultimately fulfilled his purpose on earth. And his suffering through the cross confirms that even in the most ruthless seasons of crushing, there is purpose in the pain. The cross, a symbol of death and despair, was transformed into a symbol of hope and redemption through Jesus' sacrifice. Similarly, we may find that our own struggles and hardships hold within them the seeds of our greatest passion and purpose. This isn't just a lesson that can inspire and guide us in our own lives but an invitation that even in the darkest of times, we can find strength and hope through him. Through perseverance and faith to see beyond our current circumstances, we can overcome even the most punishing grief and find the cure hidden within what feels like a curse—not by our own strength, but by Jesus' strength.

This is why the traumatic experience revolving around the Surfside Condo Collapse and the loss of my grandmother broke my heart but did not crush my spirit. I wouldn't trust a god that sits up in the clouds while throwing lightning bolts at us and wondering what it means to be human. When you and I are deeply suffering, how could this fictitious god comfort us with sympathy and aloofness? But Isaiah 53:3 foretold us the about the Messiah. *He was despised and rejected—a man of sorrows, acquainted with the deepest grief. We turned our backs on him and looked the other way. He was despised, and we did not care.* Who are you and I that God would step into this world as one of us, with the full authority of heaven—yet freely trading himself for the full suffering of what we could never comprehend so that we could live freely in his presence? You see when we are suffering, God does not sympathize with us. He empathizes with us in our pain. He feels our pain. And he is with us in our pain if we allow him. Additionally, 1 Peter 2:24 says, "He himself bore our sins in his body on the tree, that we might die to sin and live to righteousness. By his wounds, you have been healed." This verse highlights the ultimate sacrifice that Jesus made for us, which made it possible for our souls to be healed and made whole.

This is also why the only response to this kind of love is worship. God doesn't want legalism, religion, or traditions. He just wants your heart. He wants a divine romance with you, meaning he wants you to love him with all your heart, mind, strength, and soul! He wants our presence in his presence. Jesus didn't come for behavior modification. He came for heart transformation. In essence, God wants your entire life to be a form of worship. Using a WORSHIP acronym, you can learn how to live in the freedom of his peace.

W – Welcome God's presence into your life
(Hebrews 4:16)

O – Open your heart & confess that Jesus is Lord
(Romans 10:9)

R – Repent of your sins & receive his grace
(1 John 1:9)

S – Seek God's presence daily to transform your heart & mind (Romans 12:2)

H – Hide God's promises and scripture in your heart.
(Psalm 119:11)

I – Include yourself in a community of believers that serves others. (James 5:16)

P – Pour out your praise & pray continually
(1 Thessalonians 5:16-18)

Surrendering our lives in WORSHIP to Jesus exchanges our shame, fear, and sorrow for freedom, love, and gratitude. The byproduct of fear is worry. But the opposite of worry is worship! But the byproduct of love is worship! It's living from a place of thanksgiving for all that God has done for you. *Love never brings fear, for fear is always related to punishment. But love's perfection drives the fear of punishment far from our hearts. Whoever walks constantly afraid of punishment has not reached love's perfection (1 John 4:18 TPT).* Jesus is the perfection of love because he is love.

Salvation stands as a gracious gift from God, a doorway to establish an intimate relationship with Him. You don't have to work for salvation; you simply need to believe and receive it. Salvation is about what He has already done for you—not what you can do for Him. Surrendering your life to Jesus is the greatest decision you can ever make. It starts with believing in your heart that Jesus is Lord and asking Him to be your savior. Through Jesus, you receive a living hope (1 Peter 1:3-6) that you're never alone in your brokenness and that you'll spend eternity in His presence.

The promise of living a life of worship is clearly laid out in Proverbs 3:21-26 (TPT). *My child, never drift off course from these two goals for your life: to walk in wisdom and to discover your purpose. Don't ever forget how they empower you. For they strengthen you inside and out and inspire you to do what's right; you will be energized and refreshed by the healing they bring. They give you living hope to guide you, and not one of life's tests will cause you to stumble. You will sleep like a baby, safe and sound—your rest will be sweet and secure. You will not be subject to terror, for it will not terrify you. Nor will the disrespectful be able to push you aside because God is your confidence in times of crisis, keeping your heart at rest in every situation.*

When you have a radical encounter with the source of all love, there are only two responses: Repentance & forgiveness. Having an Uncollapsable soul does not mean being invincible or never experiencing pain or suffering. An Uncollapsable soul is marked by an unshakable faith in someone greater than yourself. His name is Jesus. In the end, having an unbreakable soul is about being able to weather life's storms with courage, grace, and a sense of purpose. It's about having the trust and hope to overcome even the toughest of challenges and emerge stronger, wiser, and more compassionate on the other side. Not because of who we are but because of God's love within us. He is with us in pain because he took on the full force of it.

God Gets Anxiety

God gets anxious. Let me rephrase that—God understands anxiety. Jesus, the Son of God, experienced the full range of human emotions during His time on Earth. He could've easily bypassed the grief of Lazarus' death. Yet, Jesus wept for his friend, despite knowing that He'd soon raise him from the dead. He also could've chosen to opt out of the suffering of His own death, avoiding the cross and the weight of humanity's sins. Yet, He chose to endure it all and empathized with our anxieties. He understands the depth of your pain and the weight of our burdens. In that sense, God's understanding of anxiety surpasses our limited human comprehension. He didn't simply observe our pain from a distance; He entered into it, experiencing the full weight of our brokenness. God's understanding of anxiety is not distant or detached but intimate and personal.

Jesus, in His perfect innocence, willingly took upon Himself the weight of the world's crimes, bearing the most torturous death imaginable. Jesus gives us gratitude in exchange for our guilt. Everything we receive from God, including forgiveness, grace, and salvation, is not earned but given freely. Guilt loses its power when it has been forgiven. It becomes a choice to hold onto guilt when it has already been exchanged for the grace and mercy of God. The question often arises: How can a good God allow bad things to happen to good people? However, an even more profound question: How could a good God allow His perfect Son to become sinful and condemned as guilty? Both are very relevant and valid questions. Life is unfair in its disgrace, but God's love is extravagantly more unfair in His grace.

Jesus lived out how to endure a broken heart and suffering. His attitude was—God if you're not gonna take it from me, then use it for your glory. In the same way, our attitude should be one of surrender and trust in God's plan. I encourage you to pray, "God, if You're not going to take it from me, then use it for Your glory." In John 16:33, Jesus declared, "Take heart, for I have overcome the world!" In His victory, we find the assurance that we're not mere survivors but conquerors through Him. The path to victory isn't without its challenges.

Prayer becomes not just a preparation for the battle but the battle itself as we seek God's guidance, strength, and comfort in our journey. But the more pain we experience, the closer God draws near to us. Through honest and vulnerable prayer, we connect with God's heart and experience the transformation that comes from relying on His power. As we follow in His footsteps, we learn to navigate our own trials and tribulations with faith and trust, knowing that God is with us every step of the way. May Jesus' love and our journey through His victory be the foundation upon which we build our lives, bringing light, hope, and transformation to a world in need.

As I reflect on Kima's legacy, I'm filled with a sense of responsibility and honor. Her inheritance is what she left FOR me. But her legacy is what she left IN me. The greatest tribute I can offer her is to continue sharing her legacy by introducing others to the source of her boundless love—Jesus. That's what made my sweet Kima's life and legacy so remarkable. In an interview with CBS News, David Begnaud, a Lead National Correspondent, pointed out that had Kima passed away peacefully in her bed many years later, her impact wouldn't have reached as many lives as she has today. I wholeheartedly believe in the truth of his words.

Kima's sweetness, compassion, love, and beauty were a reflection of God's character. I pray that you open your heart to an intimate relationship with Jesus so that you can not only live your life according to His example but also with His love deeply embedded in your heart, just as Kima did. That's how you endure a broken heart without crushing your spirit. You trust God with it because He gets your anxiety. When your world is collapsing, may you pray, "God, if your plan is not to take this cup of suffering away, then I ask that you use my story for your glory."

As you move forward in faith, you'll see that your destiny is not at the mercy of your history. Faith is like a muscle that strengthens through the resistance of failures, within the gym of your fears. Calling often reveals itself through falling. That's when you'll realize your calling has been seizing you, hidden within your fears.

Remember, your pain is bigger than you! If God is the source of miracles, you are the resource of miracles. Someone out there needs to hear your story of how you went from hoping for a miracle, to becoming a miracle! There's nothing more inspiring than a person who suffers through a collapse around them, but perseveres because of the uncollapsable soul within them! YOU are called to be that person.

May love be your legacy.
May the Lord be near to your heart so that your spirit may never be crushed.
Your *soul* was made to be *uncollapsable*.

References

(2022a) *Apple Podcasts: Collapse: Disaster in Surfside (EP. 1)* [Preprint]. Treefort Media & Miami Herald. Available at: https://podcasts.apple.com/us/podcast/collapse-disaster-in-surfside/id1596363315.

(2022b) *Apple Podcasts: Collapse: Disaster in Surfside (EP. 2)* [Preprint]. Treefort Media & Miami Herald. Available at: https://podcasts.apple.com/us/podcast/collapse-disaster-in-surfside/id1596363315.

(2022c) *Apple Podcasts: Collapse: Disaster in Surfside (EP. 3)* [Preprint]. Treefort Media & Miami Herald. Available at: https://podcasts.apple.com/us/podcast/collapse-disaster-in-surfside/id1596363315.

Alexander, C. (2021) *Surfside condo collapse: 3 generations of Cattarossi family die in condo collapse, The Palm Beach Post.* Available at: https://www.palmbeachpost.com/story/news/2021/07/08/surfside-condo-collapse-4-family-members-cattarossi-family-identified/7889016002/.

Apa Dictionary of Psychology (no date) *American Psychological Association.* Available at: https://dictionary.apa.org/self.

Batterson, M. (2019) *Chase the Lion: If your dream doesn't scare you, it's too small.* Crown Publishing Group.

Beesley, K. (2018) *Why it's important to get to the root of your emotions, Psychology Today.* Available at: https://www.psychologytoday.com/us/blog/psychoanalysis-unplugged/201808/why-it-s-important-get-the-root-your-emotions.

Bennett Williams, A. (2021) *Surfside victim Edgar Gonzalez's life was a labor of love, 'acts of service', The Palm Beach Post.* Available at: Surfside victim Edgar Gonzalez's life was a labor of love, 'acts of service'.

Branca, S. and Holly, J. (2021) *Victim who died at hospital following Surfside Condo collapse identified as mother of teen pulled from rubble, WSVN 7News | Miami News, Weather, Sports | Fort Lauderdale.* Available at: https://wsvn.com/news/local/victim-who-died-at-hospital-following-surfside-condo-collapse-identified-as-mother-of-teen-pulled-from-rubble/.

Branigan, T. and Whitaker, B. (2003) *Why was Iran death toll so high?*, *The Guardian*. Available at: https://www.theguardian.com/environment/2003/dec/27/iran.naturaldisasters4.

Brasileiro, A. (2021) *'Not a single drawing': Mom who lost son, husband in Surfside faces life without keepsakes, Miami Herald*. Available at: https://www.miamiherald.com/news/local/community/miami-dade/miami-beach/article252760408.html.

Brice, A. *et al.* (2010) *10 days after Quake, israeli workers rescue buried survivor*, *CNN*. Available at: https://www.cnn.com/2010/WORLD/americas/01/22/haiti.earthquake/index.html.

Cinone, D. and Bradford, C. (2021) *First victim of miami condo disaster is mom, 54, of teen boy pulled from rubble, The US Sun*. Available at: https://www.the-sun.com/news/3159934/first-victim-miami-condo-tower-stacie-fang/.

Cleveland Clinic MD (2021) *Compound fracture: What is it, types, symptoms & treatment, Cleveland Clinic*. Available at: https://my.clevelandclinic.org/health/ diseases/21843-compound-fracture.

Clifford, G.C. (2021) *Phoenix Bird Symbolism & meaning (+totem, Spirit & Omens), World Birds*. Available at: https://worldbirds.com/phoenix-symbolism/.

DeSantis declares state of emergency for Miami-Dade County (2021) *https://www.mysuncoast.com*. Available at: https://www.mysuncoast.com/2021/06/24/desantis-declares-state-emergency-miami-dade-county/.

Douglass, F. (no date) *Frederick Douglass: Selected Speeches and Writings, Goodreads*. Available at: https://www.goodreads.com/quotes/6398-if-there-is-no-struggle-there-is-no-progress-those.

Edgar Gonzalez—Celebration of Life (2021) *YouTube*. Truelife Productions. Available at: https://www.youtube.com/watch?v=i3SMgxbr8rl.

Faith definition in American English: Collins english dictionary (no date) *Faith definition in American English | Collins English Dictionary*. Available at: https://www.collinsdictionary.com/us/dictionary/english/ faith.

Federal response to Surfside Building collapse in Florida (2021) *FEMA.gov*. Available at: https://www.fema.gov/fact-sheet/federal-response-surfside-building-collapse-florida.

Global War on Terror (no date) *George W. Bush Library*. Available at: https://www.georgewbushlibrary.gov/research/topic-guides/global-war-terror.

Gomez Licon, A. and Spencer, T. (2021) *Watch: Search resumes after rest of South Florida condo demolished*, *AJC*. Available at: https://www.ajc.com/news/nation-world/

crews-nearly-done-drilling-for-florida-condo-demolition/4CNST-74K5FGPNIWHLGD3KXNDHU/.

Gonzalez, D. (2022a) *"Happy Father's Day daddy⊠. I miss you so much words can't describe the pain in my heart. I would give...'*, *Instagram*. Available at: https://www.instagram.com/tv/Ce_ge8qDlTV/?utm_source=ig_web_copy_link.

Gonzalez, D. (2022b) *'It's crazy to think this was me a year ago. A year ago my world fell apart in a matter...'*, *Instagram*. Available at: https://www.instagram.com/p/CfM3qAKpUn7/?utm_source=ig_web_copy_link.

Gonzalez, D. (2022c) *'It's hard to push yourself when you feel the weight of the world on your shoulders. My mind wants to...'*, *Instagram*. Available at: https://www.instagram.com/p/CezkyRpN7qc/?img_index=1.

Governor Ron DeSantis commemorates the anniversary of the Champlain Towers collapse (2021) *Florida Governor Ron DeSantis*. Available at: https://www.flgov.com/2022/06/24/governor-ron-desantis-commemorates-the-anniversary-of-the-champlain-towers-collapse/.

Gross, S.J., Cohen, H. and Goodhue, D. (2021) *Edgar Gonzalez's surviving Surfside family remembers a devoted dad and his hugs Read more at: https://www.miamiherald.com/news/local/community/miami-dade/miami-beach/article252897728.html#storylink=cpy*, *Miami Herald*. Available at: https://www.miamiherald.com/news/local/community/miami-dade/miami-beach/article252897728.html#storylink=cpy.

Gts (2022) *Our Story, The Phoenix Life Project*. Available at: https://phoenixlifeproject.org/our-story/.

Hanna, J. and Santiago, L. (2021) *Search continues into the night with almost 100 people unaccounted for in deadly Florida building collapse, CNN*. Available at: https://www.cnn.com/2021/06/24/us/building-collapse-miami-thursday/index.html.

Henry, M. (no date) *Daniel 3 Commentary—MH Commentary on the whole Bible (complete), biblestudytools.com*. Available at: https://www.biblestudytools.com/commentaries/matthew-henry-complete/daniel/3.html.

History.com Editors (2010) *September 11 attacks: Facts, background & impact, History.com*. Available at: https://www.history.com/topics/21st-century/9-11-attacks.

Hyatt, M. (2011) *Three reasons why you must guard your heart, Full Focus*. Available at: https://fullfocus.co/three-reasons-why-you-must-guard-your-heart/.

Johnny Joey Jones reflects on losing his legs in Afghanistan 10 years ago (2020) *Yahoo! News.* Available at: https://news.yahoo.com/ johnny-joey-jones-reflects-losing-192922548.html.

Jonathan Cluett, M. (2022) *Treatment of open fractures requires these considerations, Verywell Health.* Available at: https://www.verywell-health.com/treatment-of-an-open-fracture-2549329.

Jones, J. (2020) *Johnny 'joey' jones: I marked my 'alive day' this week, 10 years after losing my legs, and want to share this, Fox News.* Available at: https://www.foxnews.com/opinion/ johnny-joey-jones-alive-day-losing-legs.

Judge approves removal of teen's life-support (2021) *Sun Sentinel.* Available at: https://www.sun-sentinel.com/news/fl-xpm-1985-10-04-8502120227-story.html.

Katje, C. (2022) *'my trip to space was supposed to be a cele-bration, instead, it felt like a funeral': William Shatner shares experience in Book—paramount global (NASDAQ:para), Amazon.com (NASDAQ:AMZN), Benzinga.* Available at: https:// www.benzinga.com/general/entertainment/22/10/29207326/ my-trip-to-space-was-supposed-to-be-a-celebration-instead-it-felt-like-a-funeral-william-sh.

Keller, T. (2017) *If your god never disagrees with you, you might be worshiping..., SermonQuotes.* Available at: https://sermonquotes. com/tim-keller-2/13011-if-your-god-never-disagrees-with-you-you-might-be-worshiping-an-idealized-version-of-yourself-tim-keller. html.

Kelly, E. (2021) *Timeline: Signs of trouble before the deadly tower collapse in Surfside, Yahoo Finance.* Available at: https:// finance.yahoo.com/finance/news/timeline-signs-trouble-deadly-tower-012500352.html.

King, N. (2021) *Experienced team from Israel helps search through Florida condo debris, NPR.* Available at: https://www.npr. org/2021/07/01/1012065402/ experienced-team-from-isra-el-helps-search-throughflorida-condo-debris.

Lapin, T. (2021) *Some surfside victims may have been alive for hours after initial collapse, report claims, New York Post.* Available at: https://nypost.com/2021/08/24/some-surfside-victims-may-have-been-alive-for-hours-after-initial-collapse-report/.

Lewis, C.S. (2012) *The Four Loves.* Boston, MA: Mariner Books/ Houghton Mifflin Harcourt.

Lowry, L. (1999) *The Giver.* Niagara Falls, NY: On the Mark Press—S & S Learning Materials.

Mahatma Gandhi Quotes about Christianity: A-Z quotes (no date) *AZ Quotes.* Available at: https://www.azquotes.com/author/5308-Ma-hatma_Gandhi/tag/christianity (Accessed: 17 July 2023).

Miller, R.W., Rhodes, W. and Neale, R. (2021) *Controlled explosions as demolition crews blast what's left of collapsed Florida Condo, USA Today.* Available at: https://www.usatoday.com/story/news/nation/2021/07/04/florida-condo-collapse-demolition-planned-amid-tropical-storm-elsa/7858252002/.

Musgrave, J. (2021) *Teen boy was sitting beside his mom when Surfside Building collapsed...*, The Palm Beach Post. Available at: https://www.palmbeachpost.com/story/news/2021/07/09/teenage-boy-sitting-beside-his-mom-when-building-fell-down/7917198002/.

Noguerra, A.J. (2022) *30 Mighty Oak Tree Facts you never knew, Facts.net.* Available at: https://facts.net/oak-tree-facts/.

Noriega, M. (2021) *'It's not promised that all things that happen to us are good. Rather, all things work for the good of...'*, Instagram {CNN}. Available at: https://www.instagram.com/tv/CQoOu0tDaz5/?utm_source=ig_web_copy_link.

Our Story (2022) *Global Empowerment Mission.* Available at: https://www.globalempowermentmission.org/about/ our-story/.

OVERVIEW (2012) *Vimeo.* Planetary Collective. Available at: https://vimeo.com/55073825?embedded=true&+source=vimeo_logo&owner=1979047.

O'Riley, J. (2019) *Humanly best, Frederick Buechner.* Available at: https://www.frederickbuechner.com/quote-of-the-day/2019/1/15/humanly-best.

Press, A. (2004) *Woman found alive in Iran quake rubble, NBCNews.com.* Available at: https://www.nbcnews.com/id/wbna3866095.

A Quote from Texts and Pretexts (no date) *Goodreads.* Available at: https://www.goodreads.com/quotes/92753-experience-is-not-what-happens-to-a-man-it-is.

Rhodes, W. (2021) *'Treat her gently': How an Israeli military search team helped recover Surfside victims*, The Palm Beach Post. Available at: https://www.palmbeachpost.com/story/news/2021/07/26/surfside-condo-collapse-how-israeli-team-found-majority-victims/8021350002/.

Rozsa, L. (2021) *Survivor describes escape from Florida condo collapse: 'I kept going, screaming... I want to live'*, The Washington Post. Available at: https://www.washingtonpost.com/nation/2021/06/29/florida-condo-collapse-survivor/.

Sanchez, R. and Conlon, K. (2022) *The woman whose voice was heard in rubble of surfside condo collapse has been identified. this is how it happened*, CNN. Available at: https://www.cnn.com/2022/05/22/us/surfside-collapse-voice-theresa-velasquez/index.html.

Schulze-Makuch, D. (2022) *The overview effect is another reason to speed up space exploration, Big Think.* Available at: https://bigthink.com/hard-science/overview-effect-space-exploration/.

Smedes, L.B. (1996) *Forgive & forget: Healing the hurts we don't deserve.* New York, NY: HarperCollins Publishers.

Solomon, M. and Margol, I. (2021) *Surfside collapse: Family reunification center moving from community space to Hotel, WPLG.* Available at: https://www.local10.com/news/local/2021/06/25/surfside-collapse-family-reunification-center-moving-from-community-space-to-hotel/.

South, T. (2010) *A terrible cost: Chattanooga Times Free Press, Times Free Press.* Available at: https://www.timesfreepress.com/news/2010/oct/24/forever-changed/.

Spector, D. (2014) *Here's how many days a person can survive without water, Business Insider.* Available at: https://www.businessinsider.com/how-many-days-can-you-survive-without-water-2014-5.

Spencer, T. (2021) *Recovery workers vow not to let up in Florida condo collapse, AP News.* Available at: https://apnews.com/article/miami-surfside-building-collapse-e1873e009c96af8b-f693b791726f62f0.

Spencer, T. and Bynum, R. (2021) *Families of the missing visit site of Surfside Condo collapse, Tampa Bay Times.* Available at: https://www.tampabay.com/news/florida/2021/06/27/families-of-the-missing-visit-site-of-surfside-condo-collapse/.

Sullivan, M. (2022) *Exclusive: The 'miracle boy' of Surfside shares his story of surviving the condo collapse—and rebuilding his life, Rolling Stone.* Available at: https://www.rollingstone.com/culture/culture-features/surfside-condo-collapse-jonah-handler-survivor-lawsuit-1372434/.

Surfside Tower Collapse (2022) *Global Empowerment Mission.* Available at: https://www.globalempowermentmission.org/mission/surfside-tower-collapse/.

Surviving Surfside: Deven's Story (2022) *YouTube.* CBS Miami. Available at: https://www.youtube.com/watch?v=8sQbDyyV8u0.

Surviving Surfside: Year One (2022) *YouTube.* CBS Miami. Available at: https://www.youtube.com/watch?v=puRjH5NAZCM&t=335s.

Teilhard de Chardin, P. (no date) *A quote by Pierre Teilhard de Chardin, Goodreads.* Available at: https://www.goodreads.com/quotes/21263-we-are-not-human-beings-having-a-spiritual-experience-we.

Thoreau, H.D. (no date) *"Every man is the builder of a temple called his body.", Goodreads.* Available at: https://www.goodreads.com/quotes/31275-every-man-is-the-builder-of-a-temple-called-his.

Today in earthquake history (2021) *U.S. Geological Survey.* Available at: https://earthquake.usgs.gov/learn/today/index. php?month=12&day=26.

Todd, M. (2021) *Crazy faith: It's only crazy until it happens.* Colorado Springs, CO: WaterBrook.

Tolan, C. (2021) *Condo owners in Surfside Building were facing assessments for $15 million worth of repairs, CNN.* Available at: https://www.cnn.com/2021/06/28/us/surfside-condo-owners-as-sessments-invs/index.html.

Torres, A. (2021a) *Timeline: Miami-Dade Police releases identi-ties of 98 surfside building collapse victims, WPLG.* Available at: https://www.local10.com/news/local/2021/07/09/timeline-miami-dade-police-releases-identities-of-surfside-build-ing-collapse-victims-found-dead/.

Torres, A. (2021b) *Timeline: Miami-Dade Police releases identi-ties of 98 surfside building collapse victims, WPLG.* Available at: https://www.local10.com/news/local/2021/07/09/timeline-miami-dade-police-releases-identities-of-surfside-build-ing-collapse-victims-found-dead/.

Vazquez, C. (2022) *Surfside 1 year later: 65-year-old survivor still strug-gling to rebuild her life, WPLG.* Available at: https://www.local10.com/news/local/2022/06/24/surfside-building-collapse-my-es-cape-was-like-mission-impossible/.

Warren, R. (2017) *When we confess, we begin to heal, Pastor Rick's Daily Hope.* Available at: https://pastorrick.com/when-we-confess-we-begin-to-heal/.

Warren, R. (2023) *God's Purpose in your Pain, Plough.* Available at: https://www.plough.com/en/topics/faith/discipleship/gods-purpose-in-your-pain.

Wellspring Definition & Meaning (no date) *Dictionary.com.* Available at: http://www.dictionary.com/browse/wellspring.

Wermus, K. (2022) *Structural supports added to Florida Condo Building Raise Safety Concerns, Newsweek.* Available at: https://www.newsweek.com/structural-supports-addedflorida-con-do-building-raise-safety-concerns-1675581.

What does spirit mean? bible definition and references (no date) *bible-studytools.com.* Available at: https://www.biblestudytools.com/dictionary/spirit/.

What is dialysis? (2021) *National Kidney Foundation.* Available at: https://www.kidney.org/atoz/content/dialysisinfo.

White, F. and Kelly, K.W. (2017) *The Overview Effect, Overview Institute.* Available at: https://www.overviewinstituteaustralia.org/the-overview-effect.

Wilkerson, R. (2022) *Single & Secure: Break up with the lies and fall in love with the truth.* Miami, FL: VOUS Church.

Willard, D. (no date) *A conversation with Dallas willard about renovation of the heart—...*, *Renovaré*. Available at: https://renovare.org/articles/interview-dallas-willard-renovation-of-the-heart.

Zak, D. (2019) *Butterflies were symbols of rebirth. then they started disappearing.*, The Washington Post. Available at: https://www.washingtonpost.com/lifestyle/style/butterflies-were-symbols-of-rebirth-then-they-started-disappearing/2019/03/07/8eb5f784-3b91-11e9-a2cd-307b06d0257b_story.html.

Zeal (no date) *zeal noun—Definition and usage notes | Oxford Advanced Learner's Dictionary at OxfordLearnersDictionaries. com.* Available at: https://www.oxfordlearnersdictionaries.com/us/definition/english/zeal.

'Voice in the Rubble' victim of Surfside Condo collapse identified as music executive Theresa Velasquez by Miami-Dade Fire Rescue (2022) *CBS News.* Available at: https://www.cbsnews.com/news/surfside-condo-collapse-victim-voice-in-rubble-identified-theresa-velasquez/.

* * *

1. https://www.palmbeachpost.com/story/news/2021/07/09/teenage-boy-sitting-beside-his-mom-when-building-fell-down/7917198002/
2. https://www.the-sun.com/news/3159934/first-victim-miami-condo-tower-stacie-fang/
3. https://wsvn.com/news/local/victim-who-died-at-hospital-following-surfside-condo-collapse-identified-as-mother-of-teen-pulled-from-rubble/
4. https://nypost.com/2021/08/24/some-surfside-victims-may-have-been-alive-for-hours-after-initial-collapse-report/
5. https://www.washingtonpost.com/nation/2021/06/29/florida-condo-collapse-survivor/
6. https://www.cnn.com/2021/06/24/us/miami-building-collapse-victims-missing/index.html
7. https://www.mysuncoast.com/2021/06/24/desantis-declares-state-emergency-miami-dade-county/
8. https://www.npr.org/2021/07/01/1012065402/experienced-team-from-israel-helps-search-through-florida-condo-debris
9. https://earthquake.usgs.gov/learn/today/index.php?month=12&day=26
10. https://www.theguardian.com/environment/2003/dec/27/iran.naturaldisasters4

11. https://www.nbcnews.com/id/wbna3866095
12. https://www.washingtonpost.com/lifestyle/style/butterflies-were-symbols-of-rebirth-then-they-started-disappearing/2019/03/07/8eb5f784-3b91-11e9-a2cd-307b06d0257b_story.html
13. Chase The Lion
14. https://www.history.com/topics/21st-century/9-11-attacks
15. https://www.georgewbushlibrary.gov/research/topic-guides/global-war-terror
16. https://www.yahoo.com/video/johnny-joey-jones-reflects-losing-192922548.html
17. https://www.timesfreepress.com/news/news/story/2010/oct/24/forever-changed/32575/
18. https://www.foxnews.com/opinion/johnny-joey-jones-alive-day-losing-legs
19. Proverbs 24:16
20. https://www.cnn.com/2022/05/22/us/surfside-collapse-voice-theresa-velasquez/index.html
21. https://www.cbsnews.com/news/surfside-condo-collapse-victim-voice-in-rubble-identified-theresa-velasquez/
22. COLLAPSE: Disaster in Surfside podcast. Episode 1. 29:20
23. https://finance.yahoo.com/finance/news/timeline-signs-trouble-deadly-tower-012500352.html
24. COLLAPSE: Disaster in Surfside podcast. Episode 2. 33:00
25. https://www.local10.com/news/local/2021/06/25/surfside-collapse-family-reunification-center-moving-from-community-space-to-hotel/
26. http://www.cnn.com/2010/WORLD/americas/01/22/haiti.earthquake/index.html
27. https://www.palmbeachpost.com/story/news/2021/07/26/surfside-condo-collapse-how-israeli-team-found-majority-victims/8021350002/
28. COLLAPSE: Disaster in Surfside podcast. Episode 3. 24:48
29. https://www.nbcmiami.com/news/deeply-emotional-family-members-of-surfside-victims-visit-site-of-collapse/2482065/
30. CBS Miami- Surviving Surfside: Deven's Story 0:45 https://www.youtube.com/watch?v=8sQbDyyV8u0
31. https://www.palmbeachpost.com/story/news/2021/08/24/florida-building-collapse-surfside-victims-life-labor-love/8168803002/
32. https://www.miamiherald.com/news/local/community/miami-dade/miami-beach/article252897728.html
33. Youtube: Edgar Gonzalez - Celebration of Life 1:28:00 https://www.youtube.com/watch?v=i3SMgxbr8rl

34.   Youtube: Edgar Gonzalez - Celebration of Life 1:35:00 https://www.youtube.com/watch?v=i3SMgxbr8rl

35.   COLLAPSE: Disaster in Surfside podcast. Episode 3. 5:56

36.   https://www.fema.gov/fact-sheet/federal-response-surfside-building-collapse-florida

37.   COLLAPSE: Disaster in Surfside podcast. Episode 3. 25:45

38.   https://www.tampabay.com/news/florida/2021/06/27/families-of-the-missing-visit-site-of-surfside-condo-collapse/

39.   https://apnews.com/article/miami-surfside-building-collapse-e1873e009c96af8bf693b791726f62f0

40.   https://www.local10.com/news/local/2021/07/09/timeline-miami-dade-police-releases-identities-of-surfside-building-collapse-victims-found-dead/

41.   https://www.usatoday.com/story/news/nation/2021/07/04/florida-condo-collapse-demolition-planned-amid-tropical-storm-elsa/7858252002/

42.   https://www.ajc.com/news/nation-world/crews-nearly-done-drilling-for-florida-condo-demolition/4CNST74K5FGPNIWHLGD3KXNDHU/

43.   https://www.rollingstone.com/culture/culture-features/surfside-condo-collapse-jonah-handler-survivor-lawsuit-1372434/

44.   https://www.verywellhealth.com/treatment-of-an-open-fracture-2549329

45.   https://my.clevelandclinic.org/health/diseases/21843-compound-fracture

46.   Forgive & Forget: Healing the Hurts We Don't Deserve, by Lewis B Smedes. Harper, 1984

47.   https://www.local10.com/news/local/2022/06/24/surfside-building-collapse-my-escape-was-like-mission-impossible/

48.   https://www.miamiherald.com/news/local/community/miami-dade/miami-beach/article252760408.html

49.   The Giver, novel by Lois Lowry

50.   Surviving Surfside: Year One 3:45-10:23 https://www.youtube.com/watch?v=puRjH5NAZCM&t=335s

51.   2 Corinthians 4:16 NIV

52.   https://www.newsweek.com/structural-supports-added-florida-condo-building-raise-safety-concerns-1675581

53.   https://www.cnn.com/2021/06/28/us/surfside-condo-owners-assessments-invs/index.html

54.   https://www.psychologytoday.com/us/blog/psychoanalysis-unplugged/201808/why-it-s-important-get-the-root-your-emotions

55.   https://www.collinsdictionary.com/us/dictionary/english/faith

56. https://www.local10.com/news/local/2021/07/11/surfside-building-collapse-efforts-ongoing-to-remove-all-victims-from-champlain-towers-south-rubble/

57. https://www.sun-sentinel.com/news/fl-xpm-1985-10-04-8502120227-story.html

58. https://www.instagram.com/tv/CQoOu0tDaz5/?utm_source=ig_web_copy_link

58. https://www.google.com/search?q=grand+definition&o-q=grand+def&aqs=chrome.1.69i57j0i433i512j0i512l2j46i-512j0i512l2j46i175i199i512j0i512l2.3500j1j4&sourceid=chrome&ie=UTF-8#ip=1

59. 1 Cor 13:13 (NLT)

61. https://www.instagram.com/p/CezkyRpN7qc/?utm_source=ig_web_copy_link

62. https://www.instagram.com/tv/Ce_ge8qDlTV/?utm_source=ig_web_copy_link

63. https://www.instagram.com/p/CfM3qAKpUn7/?utm_source=ig_web_copy_link

64. Chase the Lion by Mark Batterson Chapter 15, page 159

65. Chase the Lion by Mark Batterson Chapter 8, page 85

66. Crazy Faith by Michael Todd Chapter 1, pages 8 & 9

67. Ruth 1: 20-21 (NLT)

68. SINGLE & SECURE by Rich Wilkerson Jr. Chapter 3, page 66

69. 1 John 4:18 CSB

70. C.S. Lewis, The Four Loves

71. Kathy Noriega https://apnews.com/article/87b5d4fb64640d3e0d9bd3996290cc75

72. Proverbs 9:10 (CSB)

73. Edgar Gonzalez - Celebration of Life 2:07:00 https://www.youtube.com/watch?v=i3SMgxbr8rl

74. James 5:16 (NLT)

75. Proverbs 18:21 (NIV)

76. Proverbs 4:23 (NIV)

77. Luke 6:45 (CSB)

78. https://www.kidney.org/atoz/content/dialysisinfo

79. Jeremiah 17:9 (ESV)

80. Matthew 15:17-19 (ISV)

81. Ezekiel 36:26–27 (VOICE)

82. www.dictionary.com/browse/wellspring

83. Proverbs 17:22 NIV

84. https://www.businessinsider.com/how-many-days-can-you-survive-without-water-2014-5

85. Matthew 6:21

86. www.fullfocus.co/three-reasons-why-you-must-guard-your-heart/#:~:text=King%20Solomon%20said%20it%20best,(Proverbs%204%3A23).

87. https://www.oxfordlearnersdictionaries.com/us/definition/english/zeal

88. Ephesians 6:12 (ISV)

89. https://pastorrick.com/when-we-confess-we-begin-to-heal/

90. https://facts.net/oak-tree-facts/

91. https://www.enkiquotes.com/quotes-about-oak-trees-and-love.html

92. https://www.youtube.com/watch?v=i3SMgxbr8rI 02:07:00 - 02:10:00

93. https://www.goodreads.com/quotes/312751-nothing-in-the-world-is-worth-having-or-worth-doing

94. https://www.goodreads.com/quotes/6398-if-there-is-no-struggle-there-is-no-progress-those

95. https://www.biblestudytools.com/commentaries/matthew-henry-complete/daniel/3.html

96. https://sermonquotes.com/tim-keller-2/13011-if-your-god-never-disagrees-with-you-you-might-be-worshiping-an-idealized-version-of-yourself-tim-keller.html

97. Daniel 3:13-28 CSB

98. Good News Translation

99. https://vimeo.com/55073825?embedded=true&source=vimeo_logo&owner=1979047 1:12

100. https://vimeo.com/55073825?embedded=true&source=vimeo_logo&owner=1979047 1:35

101. https://vimeo.com/55073825?embedded=true&source=vimeo_logo&owner=1979047

102. https://www.benzinga.com/general/entertainment/22/10/29207326/my-trip-to-space-was-supposed-to-be-a-celebration-instead-it-felt-like-a-funeral-william-sh

103. https://www.overviewinstituteaustralia.org/the-overview-effect

104. https://bigthink.com/hard-science/overview-effect-space-exploration/

105. https://www.globalempowermentmission.org/about/our-story/

106. Psalm 31:1-5 (GNT)

107. Psalm 31:9-10 (GNT)

108. https://www.globalempowermentmission.org/mission/surfside-tower-collapse/

109. https://dictionary.apa.org/self

110. https://books.google.com/books.id=kGVODwAAQBAJ&pg=PT10620&lpg=PT10620&dq=-George+MacDonald+%E2%80%9CThey+ought+to+be+tau

ght+that+they+have+bodies +and+that+their+bodies+die&-source=bl&ots=zYe23SqT7&sig=ACfU3U2RmEJpIm7tDWi-aeqeE039Ahf7K1A&hl=en&sa=X&ved=2ahUKEwim_rKL2v8Ah-W1nWoFHYMYA14Q6AF6BAghEAM#v=onepage&q=George%20MacDonald%20%E2%80%9CThey%20ought%20to%20be%20taught%20that%20they%20have%20bodies%3B%20and%20that%20their%20bodies%20die&f=false

111. https://www.goodreads.com/quotes/21263-we-are-not-human-beings-having-a-spiritual-experience-we
112. https://renovare.org/articles/interview-dallas-willard-renovation-of-the-heart
113. https://www.biblestudytools.com/dictionary/spirit/
114. https://phoenixlifeproject.org/our-story/
115. Genesis 15:20 NLT
116. https://worldbirds.com/phoenix-symbolism/
117. James 1:2–4 CSB
118. https://www.goodreads.com/quotes/92753-experience-is-not-what-happens-to-a-man-it-is#:~:text=Learn%20more)-,%E2%80%9CExperience%20is%20not%20what%20happens%20to%20a%20man%3B%20it%20is,with%20what%20happens%20to%20him.%E2%80%9D
119. https://www.azquotes.com/author/5308-Mahatma_Gandhi/tag/christianity
120. https://www.frederickbuechner.com/quote-of-the-day/2019/1/15/humanly-best
121. https://www.palmbeachpost.com/story/news/2021/07/08/surfside-condo-collapse-4-family-members-cattarossi-family-identified/7889016002/
122. https://www.local10.com/news/local/2021/07/09/timeline-miami-dade-police-releases-identities-of-surfside-building-collapse-victims-found-dead/
123. https://www.flgov.com/2022/06/24/governor-ron-desantis-commemorates-the-anniversary-of-the-champlain-towers-collapse/
124. ESV
125. NHEB
126. NIV
127. https://apnews.com/article/a080cf57761942b3a6837eb87b088bc5
128. https://www.plough.com/en/topics/faith/discipleship/gods-purpose-in-your-pain

About the Author

www.MikeNoriega.com

Mike Noriega is a humanitarian, Christian leader, and spirited public speaker. On June 24, 2021, the Champlain Towers South condo building in a small Miami town, partially collapsed in the middle of the night. His beloved grandmother was one of 98 lives lost in the third-deadliest structural failure in U.S. history, known as the Surfside Condo Collapse. Mike was appointed as the designated spokesperson for his father, the former Miami Beach Chief of Police & current Chief of Police of North Bay Village PD, Carlos Noriega. Mike has been featured in many nationally & internationally broadcasted high-profile interviews with a powerful message of hope, on major media networks such as Fox News, CNN, ABC World News Tonight, NBC, Univision, Yahoo, & CBS.

Mike Noriega is an entrepreneur, financial professional, and Miami-born native. He has a heart for people and has counseled with thousands of individuals.

Meet Mike on Social Media

 @the.real.noriega

@the.real.noriega

@the.real.noriega

@UncollapsableSoul

@realMikeNoriega

www.UncollapsableSoul.com

Printed in the USA
CPSIA information can be obtained
at www.ICGtesting.com
LVHW021636260823
756391LV00012B/422